# The
# Reference Shelf®

# Representative American Speeches 2017-2018

The Reference Shelf
Volume 90 • Number 6
H.W. Wilson
A Division of EBSCO Information Services, Inc.

Published by
**GREY HOUSE PUBLISHING**
Amenia, New York
2018

# The Reference Shelf

Cover image: Sheryl Sandberg, by Paul Marotta for Getty Images.

The books in this series contain reprints of articles, excerpts from books, addresses on current issues, and studies of social trends in the United States and other countries. There are six separately bound numbers in each volume, all of which are usually published in the same calendar year. Numbers one through five are each devoted to a single subject, providing background information and discussion from various points of view and concluding with an index and comprehensive bibliography that lists books, pamphlets, and articles on the subject. The final number of each volume is a collection of recent speeches. Books in the series may be purchased individually or on subscription.

Publisher's Cataloging-In-Publication Data
(Prepared by The Donohue Group, Inc.)

Names: Grey House Publishing, Inc., compiler, publisher.
Title: Representative American speeches, 2017-2018 / [compiled by Grey House Publishing].
Other Titles: Reference shelf ; v. 90, no. 6.
Description: [First edition]. | Amenia, New York : Grey House Publishing, 2018. | Includes index. |
Identifiers: ISBN 9781682178690 (v. 90, no. 6) | ISBN 9781682177471 (volume set)
Subjects: LCSH: Speeches, addresses, etc., American--21st century. | United States--Politics and government--2009---Sources. | Civil rights--United States--Sources. | Social action--United States--History--21st century--Sources.
Classification: LCC PS661 .R46 2018 | DDC 815/.608--dc23

# Contents

# 3

## Political Responses to the Establishment

# 4

## Outsiders and Activists

# Preface

*Representative American Speeches 2017-2018* reflects the many controversies surrounding and inspired by the current administration. Separate yet related ripples of debate, disagreement, and activism that surround and permeate current American popular culture and its oratory reflect dominantly in America's artistic, political, and social environments.

The Trump election and administration has inspired passionate discourse primarily in four broad avenues: gender equality, racial violence, immigration policy, and the role of science in policy. Current trends in American thought are seen by national figures through commencement speeches, by protestors who speak out on school gun violence and the #MeToo movement, and by the presidential administration. All of this, and more, is covered in this issue of *Representative American Speeches*.

In a year characterized by partisanship, political speeches—both by the current presidential administration and its opponents—dominate the year in review—and tell the story of a country divided.

## Commencement Speeches

Businessman and philanthropist Michael Bloomberg starts off the section by reminding graduates that the "Honor Code" that has been such a part of their education at Rice University must continue to be an important part of their lives. Oprah Winfrey encourages students to stand up for truth in the media by being "editorial gatekeepers," speaking to graduates at USC Annenberg. At Brandeis University International Business School, economist Kaushik Basu talks about the need for economic innovation as well as compassion and kindness in the face of growing inequality.

The commencement address at Liberty University by former president Jimmy Carter addresses the increasing disparity in wealth as one of the major issues the world faces today, as well as discrimination against women and girls, much of it taking the form of human trafficking. One of the nation's leading female executives, Facebook CEO Sheryl Sandberg, cautions MIT graduates to carefully consider the consequences of game-changing technology, as it can empower those who seek to do harm, and Harvard University professor Danielle Allen revisits the true nature of democracy and citizenship, holding out to graduates the vision of what it should be as defined in the Declaration of Independence. The last speech in this section is by President Donald Trump, delivered at the U.S. Naval Academy, in which he speaks of the importance of the military and his belief that America has rediscovered its identity as a nation during the first two years of his presidency.

of the importance of the military and his belief that America has rediscovered its identity as a nation during the first two years of his presidency.

## Presidential & Political Speeches

The president's first state-of-the-union address details what he considers the success of his administration's economic and immigration policies. Trump's 2018 speech at the United Nations stresses the idea of American sovereignty, rejecting the idea of globalism and foreign interference, including a global compact on migration. U.S. Attorney General Jeff Sessions' speech on immigration policy discusses the "zero tolerance" policy for illegal entry at the Southwest border, including the controversial policy of separating children from parents. President Trump's midterm campaign speech, delivered at a "Make America Great Again" rally in Charleston, West Virginia, in August 2018 discusses his victories and reiterates his promise to support West Virginia's coal workers. First Lady Melania Trump introduces her Be Best program, designed to help children navigate issues specific to their generation, such as social media use, bullying, and opioid abuse. In a joint press conference, both President Trump and Russian President Vladimir Putin stress the need for continued cooperation. In the last speech of this section, Vice President Mike Pence discusses the development of a military "Space Force" to protect the interests of the United States.

## Speeches That Oppose Trump's Policies

Senator Bernie Sanders responds to the 2018 state-of-the-union address, describing several points of the president's claims of success as inaccurate. Former president Barack Obama delivers an impassioned speech detailing how the current administration, backed by a Republican congressional majority, is threatening democracy itself and fueling the bi-partisanship of the nation. Senator Elizabeth Warren discusses corruption in Washington and the lack of trust that most Americans feel toward their government and its institutions. Finally, Congressman Jeff Flake comments on what he considers President Trump's manipulation of the media to mislead the American public.

## Outsiders & Activists

American high school student and activist Emma Gonzalez, in a press conference following the mass shooting at Marjory Stoneman Douglas high school, talks about governmental failures to address gun violence. Viola Davis stresses the importance of speaking out, at the 2018 Women's March in Los Angeles, using the #MeToo movement. Oprah Winfrey makes a similar point in her speech at the Golden Globe Award show, talking about identity, gender and politics. Twelve-year-old Leah Cayasso, the daughter of an undocumented migrant, at the Washington, D.C., "Families Belong Together" protest event, speaks to her fear of losing her mother to deportation. Discussing yet another national form of protest, Beto O'Rourke weighs in on NFL players kneeling during the national anthem at football games, believing that the right to protest in such a manner is fundamental to what it means to be American. In a related speech, former NFL professional Colin Kaepernick delivers a speech at Anmesty International, discussing violence against African Americans and the anthem protests. This section closes with a speech by Ximena Cid at the Los Angeles March for Science at which she talks about the involvement of minorities in science and the importance of diversity in helping to provide different perspectives.

The speeches collected in this volume represent words of wisdom, caution, and inspiration. Some are about the future as much as the present, signifying the perpetual change in power that occurs with transition or power or student bodies. And other speeches in this work represent the various political and social movements that have been most active in the year.

While it is unlikely that any of the speeches of 2018 will be remembered to the degree as some of the nation's most famous examples of public speaking, they each serve as a historical record of America's ideological evolution. Speeches are not simply a record of the physical march of history, but of the way that ideas shaped and reflected the present as it became history.

Examining the ideas, hopes, fears, and debates reflected in public speaking therefore provides the opportunity to see how the evolution of ideas proceeds surrounding the series of victories, losses, triumphs, and tragedies, that occur in each year and collectively shape America's future.

Micah L. Issitt

# 1
# To the Graduating Class

Former New York City mayor and philanthropist Michael Bloomberg asked students at Rice University to remember the university's honor code as they step out into their careers.

# Living by an Honor Code

## By Mike Bloomberg

*Michael Bloomberg is a businessman and philanthropist and the former mayor of New York City from 2002 to 2013. Born into a modest second-generation immigrant family, Bloomberg graduated from Harvard University and, in 1981, started the financial services company Bloomberg LP, which later launched a business news and then national news outlets. Bloomberg is one of America's wealthiest individuals, with an estimated net worth of over $50 billion, and he became an active political contributor known for his preference for progressive politics and political candidates. Since 2016, Bloomberg has been a recognized leader in global health initiatives, working with Johns Hopkins University and the World Health Organization to initiate disease control efforts in impoverished countries. An accomplished author, in 2017 Bloomberg wrote* Climate of Hope *about the international effort to fight climate change. In this 2018 commencement address at Rice University, Bloomberg discusses the importance of honor and truth in people's professional and personal lives.*

David thank you for those kind words.

Good morning, everyone and Members of the Board, faculty, staff, parents and family—it really is an honor to be with you to celebrate the great Class of 2018. How about a nice round of applause for them again?

Today, you're ready to go "beyond the hedges"—and who knows what the future holds for you.

Rice alumni have been Nobel Prize winners, cabinet members, astronauts, titans of industry, award-winning artists, and everything in between—including the two scientists who discovered Bucky balls.

And I'm glad to say that one member of the Class of 2018 has already begun working for my company, bringing the total number of Owls at Bloomberg LP to 13, so I'm doing my part, and many of you have similar exciting plans lined up I'm sure, and that's great.

But if you don't yet know what you're going to do for the rest of your life, don't spend a lot of time worrying about it. Leave that to your parents! As excited as they are today, they'll be even more excited if you don't move back home into their basement.

So let's give a big round of applause to all the parents and families who supported you and made this day possible!

Now for the serious stuff. When I was deciding what I really wanted to say today, I kept thinking about a Rice tradition that's an incredibly important part of student life here. No, I'm not talking about Willy Week. I'm talking about the honor code.

When you first arrived on campus for O-week, you attended a presentation on the Honor Code. Your very first quiz tested your knowledge of the code, you had to say what it was about, and so today, I thought it would be fitting for you as graduates to end your time here the same way you began it: by hearing a few words about the meaning of honor.

Don't worry: There's no quiz involved. But there will be a test when you leave this campus—one that will last for the rest of your life. And that's what I want to explain today—and it actually starts with the opposite of honor.

As a New Yorker, I was surprised to learn that an act of dishonor in my home-town almost blocked Rice from coming into existence. William Marsh Rice was murdered at his home in Manhattan, just a few blocks from my company's head-quarters, by two schemers who tried to re-write his will.

They were caught, his money went where he wanted it to go, the university was built, and fittingly, an honor code was created that has been central to student life here from the beginning.

And ever since you arrived here on campus, on nearly every test and paper you submitted, you signed a statement that began, "On my honor." But have you ever stopped to think about what that phrase really means?

The concept of honor has taken on different meanings through the ages: chiv-alry, chastity, courage, strength. And when divorced from morality, or attached to prejudice, honor has been used to justify murder, and repression, and deceit. But the essence of honor has always been found in the word itself.

As those of you who majored in Linguistics probably know, the words "honor" and "honest" are two sides of the same coin. In fact, the Latin word "honestus" can mean both "honest" and "honorable."

To be honorable, you must be honest. And that means speaking honestly, and acting honestly, even when it requires you to admit wrongdoing—and suffer the consequences. The commitment to honesty is a responsibility that you accepted as an Owl. It is also, I believe, a patriotic responsibility.

As young children, one of the first things we learn about American history is the story of George Washington and the fallen cherry tree. "I cannot tell a lie, " young George tells his father. "I cut it down." That story is a legend, of course. But legends are passed down from generation to generation because they carry some larger truth.

The cherry tree legend has endured because it's not really about George Wash-ington. It's about us, as a nation. It's about what we want for our children—and what we value in our leaders: honesty.

We've always lionized our two greatest presidents—Washington and Lincoln—not only for their accomplishments, but also for their honesty. We see their integrity and morals as a reflection of our honor as a nation.

However, today when we look at the city that bears Washington's name, it's hard not to wonder: What the hell happened?

In 2016, the Oxford English Dictionary's word of the year was "post-truth." And last year brought us the phrase, "alternative facts." In essence, they both mean: Up can be down. Black can be white. True can be false. Feelings can be facts.

A New York Senator known for working across the aisle, my old friend Pat Moynihan, once said: "People are entitled to their own opinions, but not their own facts." That didn't used to be a controversial statement.

Today, those in politics routinely dismiss any inconvenient information, no matter how factual, as fake—and they routinely say things that are demonstrably false. When authoritarian regimes around the world did this, we scoffed at them. We thought the American people would never stand for that!

For my generation, the plain truth about America—the freedom, opportunity, and prosperity we enjoyed—was our most powerful advantage in the Cold War. The more communists had access to real news, the more they would demand freedom. We believed that—and we were right.

Today, though, many of those at the highest levels of power see the plain truth as a threat. They fear it. They deny it. And they attack it—just as the communists once did. And so here we are, in the midst of an epidemic of dishonesty, and an endless barrage of lies.

The trend toward elected officials propagating alternate realities—or winking at those who do—is one of the most serious dangers facing democracies. Free societies depend on citizens who recognize that deceit in government isn't something to shrug your shoulders at.

When elected officials speak as though they are above the truth, they will act as though they are above the law. And when we tolerate dishonesty, we get criminality.

Sometimes, it's in the form of corruption. Sometimes, it's abuse of power. And sometimes, it's both. If left unchecked, these abuses can erode the institutions that preserve and protect our rights and freedoms—and open the door to tyranny and fascism.

Now, you might say: There's always been deceitful politicians and dishonest politicians—in both parties. And that's true. But there is now more tolerance for dishonesty in politics than I have seen in my lifetime. And I've been alive for one-third of the time the United States has existed! I know, you find that hard to believe. So do I, but if you do the math, that's what it is.

My generation can tell you: The only thing more dangerous than dishonest politicians who have no respect for the law, is a chorus of enablers who defend their every lie.

Remember: The Honor Code here at Rice just doesn't require you to be honest. It requires you to say something if you saw others acting dishonestly. Now that might be the most difficult part of an honor code, but it may also be the most important, because violations affect the whole community.

And the same is true in our country. If we want elected officials to be honest, we have to hold them accountable when they are not—or else suffer the consequences.

Now, don't get me wrong: honest people can disagree. That's what democracy is all about! But productive debate requires an acceptance of basic reality.

Take science for example: If 99 percent of scientists whose research has been peer-reviewed reach the same general conclusion about a theory, then we ought to accept it as the best available information—even if it's not a 100 percent certainty.

Yes, climate change is only a theory—just like gravity is only a theory. And the fact that Newton's theory of motion didn't take into account Maxwell's observations on the speed of electromagnetic waves as a constant and that Einstein's special theory of relativity better described motion when things move very fast—doesn't mean that if I let go of this pen it won't fall to the ground.

That, graduates, is not a Chinese hoax. It's called science—and we should demand that politicians have the honesty to respect it.

Hard though it is to believe, some federal agencies have actually banned their employees from using the phrase "climate change." If censorship solved problems, today we'd all be part of the old USSR, and the Soviets would have us speaking Russian.

Of course, it's always good to be skeptical and ask questions. But we must be willing to place a certain amount of trust in the integrity of scientists. If you aren't willing to do that, don't get on an airplane, don't use a cell phone or microwave, don't get treated in a hospital, and don't even think about binge-watching Netflix.

Scientific discovery permeates practically every aspect of our lives—except, too often, our political debates.

The dishonesty in Washington isn't just about science, of course. We weren't tackling so many of the biggest problems that affect your future—from the lack of good jobs in many communities, to the prevalence of gun violence, to the threats to the economy and threats to the environment—because too many political leaders are being dishonest about facts and data, and too many people are letting them get away with it.

So how did we get here? How did we go from a president who could not tell a lie to politicians who can not tell the truth? From a George Washington who embodied honesty, to a Washington, D.C. defined by deceit?

It's popular to blame social media for spreading false information. I for one am totally convinced that Selena Gomez and Justin Bieber are still dating, but the problem isn't just unreliable stories. It's also the public's willingness—even eagerness—to believe anything that paints the other side in a bad light. That's extreme partisanship—and that is what's fueling and excusing all this dishonesty.

Extreme partisanship is like an infectious disease. But instead of crippling the body, it cripples the mind. It blocks us from understanding the other side. It blinds us from seeing the strengths in their ideas—and the weaknesses of our own. And it leads us to defend or excuse lies and unethical actions when our own side commits them.

or example: In the 1990s, leading Democrats spent the decade defending the occupant of the Oval Office against charges of lying and personal immorality, and attempting to silence and discredit the women who spoke out. At the same time, leading Republicans spent that decade attacking the lack of ethics and honesty in the White House.

Today, the roles are exactly reversed—not because the parties have changed their beliefs—but because the party occupying the Oval Office has changed.

When someone's judgment about an action depends on the party affiliation of the person who committed it, they're being dishonest with themselves and with the public. And yet, those kinds of judgments have become so second nature that many people—in both parties—don't even realize that they are making them.

Now, I know it's natural to root for your own side—especially when the other side is the Houston Cougars. But governing is not a game.

When people see the world as a battle between left and right, they become more loyal to their tribe than to our country. When power—not progress—becomes the object of the battle, truth and honesty become the first casualties.

You learned here at Rice that honesty leads to trust and trust leads to freedom—like the freedom to take tests outside the classroom. In democracy, it's no different. If we aren't honest with one another, we don't trust one another, then we place limits on what we ourselves can do, and what we can do together as a country.

It's a formula for gridlock and national decline—but graduates, here's the thing: It doesn't have to be that way.

When I was in city government, I didn't care which party proposed an idea—and I never once asked someone his or her party affiliation during a job interview, or who they voted for. As a result, we had a dream team of Democrats, Republicans, and independents. That diversity made our debates sharper, our policies smarter, and our government better.

Arguments were won and lost on facts and data—not parties and polls. That was why we had success. And it's been great to see other mayors around the country taking that same kind of approach. But at the national level, in Washington today, partisanship is everything. And I think the dishonesty that it produces is one of the greatest challenges that your generation will have to confront.

Of course, partisanship is not a new problem. George Washington warned against it in his Farewell Address. He referred to the "dangers of parties," and called the passion that people have for our parties, quote, "worst enemy" of democracy—a precursor to tyranny. Washington urged Americans to, quote, "discourage and restrain" partisanship. Sadly, in recent years, the opposite has happened.

There is now unrestrained, rabid partisanship everywhere we look. It's not just on social media and cable news. It's in the communities where we live, which are becoming more deeply red or more deeply blue. It's in the groups and associations and churches we join, which increasingly attract like-minded people. It's even in the people we marry.

Fifty years ago, most parents didn't care whether their children married a member of another political party, but they didn't want them marrying outside their race or religion, or inside their gender.

Today, thankfully, polls show a strong majority support for inter-racial, inter-religious, and same-sex marriage and that is progress. But unfortunately, the percentage of parents who don't want their children marrying outside of their political party has doubled and the more people segregate themselves by party, the harder it becomes to understand the other side, and the more extreme each party grows.

Studies show that people become more extreme in their views when they are grouped together with like-minded people. And that's now happening in both parties. And as a result, I think it's fair to say the country is more divided by party than it has ever been since the Civil War.

Last month, legislators in South Carolina—which was the first state in the Union to secede back in 1860—introduced a resolution that contemplated a debate on secession. Now it's easy to dismiss that as a fringe idea—and let's hope it never happens. But in like-minded groups, fringe ideas can gather momentum with dangerous speed—just remember Germany in the late 1930s.

If that continues to happen here, America will become even more divided, and our national anthem may as well become the Taylor Swift song: "We are never, ever, ever, getting back together."

So why do I bring this up as you finish your time at this great university?

Well, I'm hoping you graduates will draw more inspiration from a song by a different artist: Zedd, Maren Morris, and Grey: "Why don't you just meet me in the middle? I'm losing my mind just a little."

Bringing the country back together I know won't be easy. But I believe it can be done—and if we are to continue as a true democracy, it must be done, and it will be up to your generation to help lead it.

Graduates, you're ready for this challenge. Because bringing the country back together starts with the first lesson you learned here at Rice: Honesty matters. And everyone must be held accountable for being honest. So as you go out into the world, I urge you to do what honesty requires.

Recognize that no one, nor either party, has a monopoly on good ideas. Judge events based on what happened, not who did it. Hold yourself and our leaders to the highest standards of ethics and morality. Respect the knowledge of scientists. Follow the data, wherever it leads. Listen to people you disagree with—without trying to censor them or shout over them. And have the courage to say things that your own side does not want to hear.

I just came yesterday from visiting an old friend in Arizona, who has displayed that kind of courage throughout his life: Senator John McCain, who is currently fighting brain cancer.

Now, John and I often don't see eye to eye on issues. But I have always admired his willingness to reach across the aisle, when others wouldn't dare.

He bucked party leaders when his conscience demanded it. He defended the honor of his opponents, even if it cost him votes. And he owned up to his mistakes—just like that young kid with the cherry tree.

Imagine what our country would be like if more of our elected officials had the courage to serve with the honor that John has always shown on the battlefield, in Washington and in his personal life.

Graduates, after today, you will no longer be bound by the Rice honor code. It will be up to you to decide how to live your life—and to follow your own honor code.

This university has given you a special opportunity to learn the true meaning of honor to base that code on. And now, I believe, you have a special obligation to carry it forward—into your work places, your communities, your political discussions, and yes, into the voting booth because the greatest threat to American democracy isn't communism or jihadism, or any other external force or foreign power. It's our own willingness to tolerate dishonesty in service of party, and in pursuit of power.

So let me leave you with one final thought: We can all recite the inspiring words that begin the Declaration of Independence: We hold these truths to be self-evident—

But remember that the Founding Fathers were able to bring those truths to life only because of the Declaration's final words: "We mutually pledge to each other, our Lives, our Fortunes, and our sacred Honor."

That pledge of honor and that commitment to truth is why we are here today. And in order to preserve those truths, and the rights they guarantee us, every generation must take that same pledge, and it's now your turn.

Earlier today, I told President Leebron that I'd like to make a donation to Rice. His eyes lit up! But I said, "No, not a financial donation." I told him I'd like to donate a cherry tree to be planted here on campus with a plaque that reads: "In Honor of the Class of 2018."

And when you come back to campus as alumni, if you pass by the tree, I hope you'll remember why it's there—and what it represents to our great country. And throughout your life, when you chop down a cherry tree, as we all do from time to time, admit it—and demand nothing less from those who represent us.

Graduates, you have earned this great celebration. So tonight, have one last Honey Butter Chicken Biscuit. And tomorrow, carry the values of this great university with you, wherever you go.

You will never regret it. I make that pledge to you on my honor.

Congratulations—and go Owls!

### Print Citations

**CMS:** Bloomberg, Mike. "Commencement Speech to the Rice University Class of 2018." Speech presented at the Rice University Class of 2018 Commencement, Houston, TX, May 12, 2018. In *The Reference Shelf: Representative American Speeches 2017-2018*, edited by Micah L. Issit, 3-10. Ipswich, MA: H.W. Wilson, 2018.

**MLA:** Bloomberg, Mike. "Commencement Speech to the Rice University Class of 2018." Rice University Class of 2018 Commencement, 12 May 2018, Houston, TX. Presentation. *The Reference Shelf: Representative American Speeches 2017-2018*, edited by Micah L. Issit, H.W. Wilson, 2018, pp. 3-10.

**APA:** Bloomberg, M. (2018, May 12). Commencement speech to the Rice University class of 2018. Rice University class of 2018 commencement, Houston, TX. In M.L. Issit (Ed.), *The reference shelf: Representative American speeches 2017-2018* (pp. 3-10). Ipswich, MA: H.W. Wilson. (Original work published 2018)

# Editorial Gatekeepers

## By Oprah Winfrey

*Oprah Winfrey is an American actor, author, and media personality. Winfrey got her start in talk show television in 1976, hosting the Baltimore, Maryland, series "People are Talking," and she later transitioned into mainstream film. In 1985, she was nominated for an Academy Award for her performance in Steven Spielberg's* The Color Purple. *Winfrey began hosting her own syndicated talk show* The Oprah Winfrey Show *in 1986, eventually gaining full ownership over the program and producing the show under her production company Harpo Productions. Winfrey's television program expanded with the introduction of Oprah's Book Club and the publication of* O *Magazine. As of 2018, Winfrey is one of the world's wealthiest celebrities with a net worth of at least $4 billion and has become known for her political activism in addition to her various media projects. In this 2018 commencement address at USC Annenberg, one of the nation's premier schools for journalism and media studies, Winfrey discusses the importance of truth in media and encourages students to become "editorial gatekeepers" for the media of the future.*

Thank you, Wallis Annenberg and a special thank you to Dean Willow Bay for inviting me here today. And to the parents, again I say, and to the faculty, friends, graduates, good morning.

I want to give a special shout out because I was happy that Dean Bay invited me but I was going to be here anyway because one of my lovely daughter girls attends the Annenberg School of Journalism and is getting her masters today, so I was coming whether I was speaking or not. So a special shoutout to a young woman who I met when she was in the seventh grade and it was the first year that I was looking for smart, bright, giving, resilient, kind, open-hearted girls who had "it"—that factor that means you keep going no matter what. And this was the year that I chose everybody individually. And I remember her walking into the office in a little township where we were doing interviews all over South Africa and she came in and recited a poem about her teacher and when she walked out the door I go, "That's an 'it' girl." Thando Dlomo, I'm here to say I am so proud of you. Long way from the township in South Africa and her Aunt has flown 30 hours to be here for this celebration today. Thank you so much.

Today I come bearing some good news and some bad news for anybody who intends to build their life around your ability to communicate. So, I want to get the bad news out first so you can be clear. I always like to get the bad stuff upfront,

Delivered on May 4, 2018, at the USC Annenberg School for Communication and Journalism, Los Angeles, CA.

so here it is: Everything around us, including—and in particular the internet and social media—is now being used to erode trust in our institutions, interfere in our elections, and wreak havoc on our infrastructure. It hands advertisers a map to our deepest desires, it enables misinformation to run rampant, attention spans to run short and false stories from phony sites to run circles around major news outlets. We have literally walked into traffic while staring at our phones.

Now the good news: Many of your parents are probably taking you somewhere really special for dinner tonight. I heard. I can do a little better than that. Now that I have presented some of the bad news, the good news is that there really is a solution. And the solution is each and every one of you. Because you will become the new editorial gatekeepers, an ambitious army of truth seekers who will arm yourselves with the intelligence, with the insight and the facts necessary to strike down deceit. You're in a position to keep all of those who now disparage real news, you all are the ones that are going to keep those people in check. Why? Because you can push back and you can answer false narratives with real information and you can set the record straight. And you also have the ability and the power to give voice, as Dean Bay was saying, to people who desperately now need to tell their stories and have their stories told.

And this is what I do know for sure because I've been doing it a long time: If you can just capture the humanity of the people of the stories you're telling, you then get that much closer to your own humanity. And you can confront your bias and you can build your credibility and hone your instincts and compound your compassion. You can use your gifts, that's what you're really here to do, to illuminate the darkness in our world.

So this is what I also know: This moment in time, this is your time to rise. It is. Even though you can't go anywhere, you can't stand in line at Starbucks, you can't go to a party, you can't go any place where anywhere you turn people are talking about how bad things are, how terrible it is. And this is what I know: The problem is everybody is meeting hysteria with more hysteria and then we're all becoming hysterical and it's getting worse. What I've learned all these years is that we're not supposed to match it or even get locked into resisting or pushing against it. We're supposed to see this moment in time for what it is. We're supposed to see through it and then transcend it. That is how you overcome hysteria. And that is how you overcome the sniping at one another, the trolling, the mean-spirited partisanship on both sides of the aisle, the divisiveness, the injustices, and the out-and-out hatred. You use it. Use this moment to encourage you, to embolden you, and to literally push you into the rising of your life. And to borrow a phrase from my beloved mentor Maya Angelou: Just like moons and like suns, with the certainty of tides, just like hopes springing high, you will rise.

So your job now, let me tell you, is to take everything you've learned here and use what you learned to challenge the left, to challenge the right, and the center. When you see something, you say something, and you say it with the facts and the reporting to back it up. Here's what you have to do: You make the choice every day, every single day, to exemplify honesty because the truth, let me tell you something about the truth, the truth exonerates and it convicts. It disinfects and it galvanizes. The truth has always been and will always be our shield against corruption, our shield against greed and despair. The truth is our saving grace. And not only are you here, USC Annenberg, to tell it, to write it, to proclaim it, to speak it, but to be it. Be the truth. Be the truth.

So I want to get down to the real reason we're here today. In about an hour and a half, you're going to be catapulted into a world that appears to have gone off its rocker. And I can tell you I've hosted the Oprah show for 25 years, number one show. Never missed a day. Never missed a day. Twenty-five years, 4,561 shows. So I know how to talk, I can tell you that, but I was a little intimidated coming here because graduations, it's tough, it's hard trying to come up with something to share with you that you haven't already heard. Any information or guidance I can offer is nothing that your parents or your deans or professors or Siri haven't already provided. So I'm here to really tell you: I don't have any new lessons. I don't have any new lessons. But I often think that it's not the new lessons so much as it is really learning the old ones again and again.

So here are variations on a few grand themes beginning with this: Pick a problem, any problem, the list is long. Here are just a few that are at the top of my list. There's gun violence and there's climate change, there's systemic racism, economic inequality, media bias. The homeless need opportunity, the addicted need treatment, the Dreamers need protection, the prison system needs reforming, the LGBTQ community needs acceptance, the social safety net needs saving, and the misogyny needs to stop. Needs to stop. But you can't fix everything and you can't save every soul. But what can you do? Here and now I believe you have to declare war on one of our most dangerous enemies, and that is cynicism. Because when that little creature sinks its hooks into you, it'll cloud your clarity, it'll compromise your integrity, it'll lower your standards, it'll choke your empathy. And sooner or later, cynicism shatters your faith. When you hear yourself saying, "Ah, it doesn't matter what one person says, oh well, so what, it doesn't matter what I do, who cares?" When you hear yourself saying that, know that you're on a collision course for our culture. And I understand how it's so easy to become disillusioned, so tempting to allow apathy to set in, because anxiety is being broadcast on 157 channels, 24 hours a day, all night long. And everyone I know is feeling it. But these times, these times, are here to let us know that we need to take a stand for our right to have hope and we need to take a stand with every ounce of wit and courage we can muster.

The question is: What are you willing to stand for? That question is going to follow you throughout your life. And here's how you answer it. You put your honor where your mouth is. Put your honor where your mouth is. When you give your word, keep it. Show up. Do the work. Get your hands dirty. And then you'll begin to draw strength from the understanding that history is still being written. You're writing it every day. The wheels still in spin. And what you do or what you don't do will be a part of it. You build a legacy not from one thing but from everything. I remember when I just opened my school in 2007, I came back and I had the great joy of sitting at Maya Angelou's table. She hadn't been able to attend the opening in South

Africa. And I said to her, "Oh Maya, the Oprah Winfrey Leadership Academy, that's going to be my greatest legacy." I remember she was standing at the counter making biscuits, and she turned, she put the dough down, and she looked at me and she said, "You have no idea what your legacy will be." I said, "Excuse me? I just opened this school and these girls, and it's going to be… " And she said, "You have no idea what your legacy will be, because your legacy is every life you touch. Every life you touch." That changed me.

And it's true, you can't personally stop anybody from walking into a school with an assault rifle, nor can you singlehandedly ensure that the rights that your mothers and grandmothers fought so hard for will be preserved for the daughters you may someday have. And it'll take more than you alone to pull more than 40 million Americans out of poverty, but who will you be if you don't care enough to try? And what mountains could we move, I think, what gridlock could we eradicate if we were to join forces and work together in service of something greater than ourselves? You know my deepest satisfactions and my biggest rewards have come from exactly that. Pick a problem, any problem, and do something about it. Because to somebody who's hurting, something is everything. So, I hesitate to say this, because the rumors from my last big speech have finally died down, but here it is. Vote. Vote. Vote. Pay attention to what the people who claim to represent you are doing and saying in your name and on your behalf. They represent you and if they've not done right by you or if their policies are at odds with your core beliefs, then you have a responsibility to send them packing. If they go low, thank you Michelle Obama, if they go low, we go to the polls. People died for that right, they died for that right. I think about it every time I vote. So don't let their sacrifices be in vain.

A couple other thoughts before I go. Eat a good breakfast. It really pays off. Pay your bills on time. Recycle. Make your bed. Aim high. Say thank you to people and actually really mean it. Ask for help when you need it, and put your phone away at the dinner table. Just sit on it, really. And know that what you tweet and post and Instagram today might be asked about at a job interview tomorrow, or 20 years from tomorrow. Be nice to little kids, be nice to your elders, be nice to animals, and know that it's better to be interested than interesting. Invest in a quality mattress. I'm telling you, your back will thank you later. And don't cheap out on your shoes. And if you're fighting with somebody you really love, for god's sakes find your way back to them because life is short, even on our longest days. And another thing, another thing you already definitely know that definitely bears repeating, don't ever confuse what is legal with what is moral because they are entirely different animals. You see, in a court of law, there are loopholes and technicalities and bargains to be struck, but in life, you're either principled or you're not. So do the right thing, especially when nobody's looking. And while I'm at it, do not equate money and fame with accomplishment and character, because I can assure you based on the thousands of people I've interviewed, one does not automatically follow the other.

Something else, something else. You need to know this. Your job is not always going to fulfill you. There will be some days that you just might be bored. Other days, you may not feel like going to work at all. Go anyway, and remember that your job is not who you are, it's just what you are doing on the way to who you will become. Every remedial chore, every boss who takes credit for your ideas—that is going to happen—look for the lessons, because the lessons are always there. And the number one lesson I could offer you where your work is concerned is this: Become so skilled, so vigilant, so flat-out fantastic at what you do that your talent cannot be dismissed.

And finally, this: This will save you. Stop comparing yourself to other people. You're only on this planet to be you, not someone else's imitation of you. I had to learn that the hard way, on the air, live, anchoring the news. One night in my twenties, when I first started broadcasting, I was 19, moved to an anchor by the time I was 20. I was just pretending to be Barbara Walters. I was trying to talk like Barbara, act like Barbara, hold my legs like Barbara. And I was on the air, I hadn't read the copy fully, and I called Canada, Canahdah. I cracked myself up, because I thought, Barbara would never call Canada Canahdah. And that little breakthrough, that little crack, that little moment that I stopped pretending allowed the real me to come through. Your life journey is about learning to become more of who you are and fulfilling the highest, truest expression of yourself as a human being. That's why you're here. You will do that through your work and your art, through your relationships and love.

And to quote Albert Einstein, "Education is what remains after we forget what we're taught." You've learned a lot here at USC. And when all that you've been taught begins to fade into the fabric of your life, I hope that what remains is your ability to analyze, to make distinctions, to be creative, and to wander down that road less traveled whenever you have the opportunity. And I hope that when you go, you go all in, and that your education helps you to walk that road with an open, discerning mind. Discernment is what we're missing. And a kind heart. You know, there are 7 billion people on the planet right now. And here you are. Your degree from the USC Annenberg School for Communication and Journalism: This degree you're about to get is a privilege. It's a privilege. And that privilege obligates you to use what you've learned to lend a hand to somebody who doesn't get to be here. Somebody who's never had a ceremony like the one you're having this morning.

So I hold you in the light, and I wish you curiosity and confidence. And I wish you ethics and enlightenment. I wish you guts. Every great decision I've ever made I trusted my gut. And goodness. I wish you purpose and the passion that goes along with that purpose. And here's what I really hope: I hope that every one of you contributes to the conversation of our culture and our time. And to some genuine communication, which means, you have to connect to people exactly where they are; not where you are, but where they are. And I hope you shake things up. And when the time comes to bet on yourself, I hope you double down. Bet on yourself. I hope you always know how happy and how incredibly relieved everybody is in this room is that you've made it to this place, at this time, on this gorgeous day. Congratulations USC Annenberg Class of 2018!

**Print Citations**

**CMS:** Winfrey, Oprah. "Address to the USC Annenberg Class of 2018." Speech presented at the USC Annenberg Class of 2018 Commencement, Los Angeles, CA, May 14, 2018, Los Angeles, CA. In *The Reference Shelf: Representative American Speeches 2017-2018*, edited by Micah L. Issit, 11-16. Ipswich, MA: H.W. Wilson, 2018.

**MLA:** Winfrey, Oprah. "Address to the USC Annenberg Class of 2018." USC Annenberg Class of 2018 Commencement, 14 May, 2018, USC Annenberg School for Communication and Journalism, Los Angeles, CA. Presentation. *The Reference Shelf: Representative American Speeches 2017-2018,* edited by Micah L. Issit, H.W. Wilson, 2018, pp. 11-16.

**APA:** Winfrey, O. (2018, May 14). Address to the USC Annenberg. USC Annenberg class of 2018 commencement, USC Annenberg School for Communication and Journalism, Los Angeles, CA. In M.L. Issit (Ed.), *The reference shelf: Representative American speeches 2017-2018* (pp. 11-16). Ipswich, MA: H.W. Wilson. (Original work published 2018)

# Remarks to the Class of 2018 Brandeis University International Business School

## By Kaushik Basu

*Indian economist Kaushik Basu is one of the most respected experts on global economics. Born in India, Basu was professor of economics at the Delhi School of Economics, where he helped to found the Centre for Developing Economics. Basu later became chief economist for the World Bank from 2012 to 2016 and has since worked as professor of International Studies for Cornell University and as the president of the International Economic Association. In the 2018 commencement address for Brandeis University's International Business School, Basu discusses inequality, narrow-mindedness, and the need for economic innovation.*

The Dean of the Brandeis International Business School, Professor Peter Petri, the incoming Dean, Professor Katy Graddy—it feels odd to add the "dean" to Katy's name since it was just the other day that Katy was a student in my Industrial Organization Theory class in Princeton—, graduating students, their parents and friends, and professors and staff of the university, it fills my heart with a sense of warmth and joy as I rise to speak on this important occasion.

The joy comes from partaking in the celebration of a great university and its students. A nation's progress depends more critically on its universities and intellectual nurture than most people realize. There should be no surprise that Greece was the seat of philosophy and mathematics in the 4th and 5th centuries BC and it was also one of the world's most advanced economies. Likewise, the Age of Enlightenment in Europe coincided with Europe's rise as an economy. And I believe there is a close connection between the fact that United States is one of the world's leading economies and that it has absolutely the best universities of the world.

As Louis Brandeis, who provides the eponym for your university, observed, "The greatest danger to liberty lies in the insidious encroachment by men of zeal, well-meaning but without understanding". The university is that critical seat of understanding, which all nations need. Brandeis' observation needs repetition today as the world reels with political leaders who have little understanding, and, to make matters worse, provide no evidence of being well-meaning either.

The second reason for my joy is personal. It feels good to see a university celebrate but I cannot deny that it feels even better when the celebration includes an

Delivered on May 13, 2018, at Brandeis International Business School, Brandeis University, Waltham, MA.

award being given to me. It is an honor to receive the Dean's award and to give this commencement address. Thank you.

I have been lucky in life. As a child growing up in Calcutta, I enjoyed solving puzzles and paradoxes. It was only after I went to the London School of Economics for my master's degree that I realized that solving puzzles and paradoxes could be a full time career—it is called research. And I decided that was what I wanted and so I became a professor. It was a decision made on a whim and in my case it clicked. I have led a life in which the lines between work and leisure are entirely blurred.

I loved the life of research and would have gone on doing so if it was not for that fateful phone call in the year 2009, on 9th August. At the end of my usual summer months in India, as I prepared to return to my job of Chairman of the Economics Department at Cornell, I got a phone call, out of the blue, from the Indian Prime Minister's office, to ask if I would consider becoming the Chief Economic Adviser to his government. I replied this was too big a question for a spot answer. Minimally I would need to talk to the Prime Minister to know what he had in mind. So on the following evening, on my way to the airport, I met with Dr. Manmohan Singh at his residence. At the end of our conversation I knew that this was something I would like to try my hand at.

From December 8th that year I moved to policymaking, and that would be my world for close to 7 years—nearly 3 years as Chief Economic Adviser to the Indian government and then 4 years as Chief Economist of the World Bank, in Washington.

Economics may be the only discipline in which when you refer to the world, you are expected to use the adjective 'real.' In its absence, we assume you are referring to some model. To be suddenly diverted from the modeled world and planted in the real world was a great learning experience. I am glad I did not spend a life-time in policymaking—temperamentally that would not suit me—but I feel blessed that I had the opportunity to take my ideas from books and journals to the real world; and now I am in a position to bring ideas from the real world back to research and analysis.

My early days in the world of policymaking were not easy. The then Prime Minister, Dr. Manmohan Singh, is a remarkable human being—honorable, modest and honest, rare qualities in politics. India was fortunate to have had him at the helm and I was glad for the opportunity to work with him.

But the job was demanding. With inflation raging, the fallout of the US sub-prime crisis palpable in several sectors of India's economy, and fiscal strain building up as a result of repeated expenditure injections that we had to make to protect India against the global recession, it was round-the-clock work.

The only cheer came from my mother's unmitigated faith in me. She had turned 90 and she was certain that I could stop the countrywide inflation and maybe even the US sub-prime crisis. Her only problem was she was beginning to get confused between the words 'economist' and 'communist'. Proud, like mothers are, she told all and sundry that I was "one of the leading communists in India".

I tried to correct her. I gently explained her mistake to her, and then told her about my various engagements as an economist around the world, exaggerating a little, the way one does to make a parent happy. A few days later my wife asked me what I had told my mother because she was now calling up friends and relatives to say that she had made a mistake—that I was "one of the leading communists in the world."

Except for such moments of levity, it was onerous work, made more onerous by my acknowledgment that as a researcher I had led a life of indulgence—reading what I wanted to read, developing ideas primarily for their aesthetic beauty, whereas now, as a policymaker I decided to do what economists ought to do but at least I did not do as a researcher: strive to make the world a better place.

And there is scope for that. The world is going through a difficult phase. There is an explosion of narrow-mindedness, with effort to build walls to exclude 'others', and an alarming rise in xenophobic protectionism. Dear students, as you go out into the big wide world, into diverse careers, there will be good times and bad. You will have your own personal problems to attend to and you must attend to them. At the same time, I must urge you not to forget your global responsibilities, and to have concern for fellow human beings whatever their religion, race, gender or sexual orientation, and wherever they reside.

There are many species that survived thousands of years but eventually perished because they developed traits that were evolutionarily dysfunctional or failed to develop traits that would make their lives viable in a changing world. In a recent paper I call this the "dinosaur risk"—the risk that we human beings may become, like dinosaurs, a species carrying on merrily but on an evolutionary course that is not viable in the long run. If we do not make course correction, we, like the dinosaur, will go extinct.

Fortunately, we humans are probably the first species on earth able to analyze its own evolutionary predicament, and so have the capacity to make corrections and veer off the path to extinction. It is, for instance, now clear that if we continue to destroy the environment and pay no heed to climate change, we will go extinct. This is now known to all human beings—well, almost all. We are therefore trying to create global conventions and have rules and regulations which steer us off the path of this dinosaur risk.

But there are other risks. Global inequality is today reaching a level that is unconscionable and is bound to damage democracy and cause strife and turmoil. A simple calculation shows that the 3 wealthiest persons on earth have greater wealth than all the people of 3 vast nations—Angola, Burkina Faso, and the Democratic Republic of Congo, which together have a population of approximately 130 million.

As an economist I am aware that we need some inequality for the economy to function efficiently, for people to strive and work hard. But the inequality we have today is out of all proportions. Given that extreme relative poverty tends to make people lose their voice, this huge inequality is an assault on democracy. In the words of Louis Brandeis: "We can have democracy in this country, or we can have great wealth concentrated in the hands of a few, but we can't have both."

I think we need to bring the best of mind and morality to take on this challenge of inequality. It is not an easy task as we know from the failures of many a radical movement in the past.

As you go out into the world, let me give one piece of advice to you. This is not an advice on how to further your career, or do better wealth management for yourself. I am assuming you will take care of those without being urged to do so in a commencement speech. The advice concerns morality in personal life.

By morality I do not mean religion nor deontological codes written in some book. Many a religious person adheres to codes of behavior because they expect they will be rewarded by being sent to heaven. But that is not morality; that is profit- maximization.

I use the word morality in the sense in which it was used by the enlightenment philosophers from David Hume to Immanuel Kant. Morality is about compassion and kindness, about treating all human beings as equal, about trying not to do unto others what you do not want others to do unto you. This kind of morality is compatible with both atheism and theism, and with being deeply religious and irreligious.

We need to vote in elections with this moral hat on. When we do business and play the market we must have a self-enforced moral code, which comes from respect for other human beings, including future generations. The power of political leaders ultimately resides in the beliefs of ordinary citizens, in the choices that people make in the course of their daily lives. That is what gives us ordinary human beings a responsibility much bigger than most people realize. That we carry this out with diligence is therefore essential to preserve democracy, create a better world and, ultimately, to avoid the dinosaur risk.

Thank you.

### Print Citations

**CMS:** Basu, Kaushik. "Remarks to the Class of 2018 Brandeis University International Business School." Speech presented at the Brandeis University International Business School Class of 2018 Commencement, Waltham, MA, May 13, 2018. In *The Reference Shelf: Representative American Speeches 2017-2018*, edited by Micah L. Issit, 17-20. Ipswich, MA: H.W. Wilson, 2018.

**MLA:** Basu, Kaushik. "Remarks to the Class of 2018 Brandeis University International Business School." Brandeis University International Business School Class of 2018 Commencement, 13 May, 2018, Waltham, MA. Presentation. *The Reference Shelf: Representative American Speeches 2017-2018*, edited by Micah L. Issit, H.W. Wilson, 2018, pp. 17-20.

**APA:** Basu, K. (2018, May 13). Remarks to the class of 2018 Brandeis University International Business School. Brandeis University International Business School class of 2018 commencement, Waltham, MA. In M.L. Issit (Ed.), *The reference shelf: Representative American speeches 2017-2018* (pp. 17-20). Ipswich, MA: H.W. Wilson. (Original work published 2018)

# Address to the Liberty University Class of 2018

## By Jimmy Carter

*Former president Jimmy Carter is one of the world's most accomplished philanthropists and human rights advocates. Awarded the Nobel Peace Prize in 2002 for his international efforts to promote humanitarian causes, Carter served as an officer in the US Navy before entering local politics in his home town of Plains, Georgia. After serving as governor of Georgia in 1971, Carter made a bid for the presidency, beating Gerald Ford in the 1976 elections. After the presidency, Carter founded the nonprofit Carter Center that organizes and helps to fund charitable operations around the world. In this commencement speech at Liberty University, Carter discusses his life in politics and activism and the state of modern politics in 2018.*

To Dr. Hawkins, who is retiring now as provost of this great university, and to Secretary Carson, who is here, whom I have admired for a long time, to President Falwell and all of his family, to the students who are graduating, to the parents who have supported them, and to all the rest of you: This is a wonderful crowd. Jerry told me before we came here that it's even bigger—I hate to say this—than it was last year. I don't know if President Trump will admit that or not, but to me it means a lot.

I am truly grateful for the invitation to speak to the graduates of this remarkable Christian university. I understand that there are 110,000 students enrolled, and I understand that also this year 20,000 or more are graduating, that 30,000 students who enrolled here are in the military, and that 27 percent of all those online are minority students—African American and others. This is an all-new way to get an education, and I want to thank Liberty University for giving that opportunity to them. Also, I've notice that among the graduates, the youngest one is only 16 years old, and the oldest one is almost 90 years old. (It's a female, and she doesn't want anyone to know who she is, because she doesn't want anyone to know her age, but she's four years younger than I am.) The students contribute almost a million hours a year of service to other people.

I have to admit that I was somewhat surprised to be invited to speak to you, and I want to thank President Falwell for making it possible for me to do so.

I remember receiving a whole lot of letters from Liberty University students and faculty when I was in the White House. Most of them referred to my giving away our Panama Canal, or forming what they considered to be an unnecessary new

Delivered on May 19, 2018, at Liberty University, Lynchburg, VA.

Department of Education, or normalizing diplomatic relations with the communist government of China. But those critical letters pretty well ended when the 1980 election results brought my involuntary retirement from the White House. After that, I didn't get very many letters from Liberty, and I particularly appreciate the opportunity to come here today.

President Falwell wanted me to say a few words about my background. It might duplicate some of the things he just said—and correct a few minor mistakes that he made. I grew up on a peanut farm near Plains, Georgia, in a community named Archery, with about 50 other families, almost all of whom were African American. And so were my playmates. It was during segregation time, but the only ranking among us then was who could run fastest, had just caught the biggest fish, or could pick the most cotton in a day.

I left home when I was 17 years old, and World War II was just beginning; this was in 1941. I went to Georgia Tech, where I joined the Naval ROTC. Then I went on to the Naval Academy at Annapolis, and that's where I began to teach Bible lessons on Sunday. As a matter of fact, I taught the children of the families that were stationed there permanently. I later served as a submarine officer, and my last sea duty, at sea in the Pacific Ocean, was during the Korean War. I served in the Navy for 11 years, and then I came back to Plains, Georgia, and to a life of farming.

One of the most memorable occasions I had then was to volunteer as part of what the Southern Baptist Convention called a "pioneer missionary" program. Every year, I would go somewhere, assigned by the Southern Baptist Convention to bring other people to Christ. One of my most memorable was to go to Massachusetts, and I had a leader there who was from Brooklyn, New York. He was a Cuban American, and his name was Eloy Cruz. I would read a few verses from the Bible in Spanish (using a different Spanish vocabulary than I had used in the Navy) and then Eloy Cruz would give the plan of salvation to prospective followers of Christ. And he was remarkably successful in winning those souls to be Christians.

When we finished our assignment in Massachusetts and got ready to leave to go back home, I asked Eloy Cruz, "What is the secret to your success in winning souls to Christ?" He was a little embarrassed by my question, but then he finally said, "I try to have two loves in my heart: One love is for God, and the other love I have in my heart is for the person who happens to be in front of me at any particular time." That's a very profound statement, and one that I have remembered ever since that time.

Since leaving the White House, I have been a professor at Emory University—I just finished my 36th year as a professor—and I still teach Sunday school at Maranatha Baptist Church in Plains, Georgia. Plains is a town of 700 people—It's grown a lot since I was a child—and we have 11 churches in town. Maranatha is a very small church; we only have about 25 regular members, but when I teach the Bible classes every Sunday we have several hundred visitors. Last Sunday we had 700 visitors; we had to turn away 200 who we couldn't get into the church or in our classrooms.

I have made a living writing—Jerry said 29 books; actually, I've written 32 books, and I gave him a copy of one of them last night so he could remember how many books I've written. And Rosalynn and I have not been married quite as long as he said.

If we stay together for two more months, Rosalynn and I will celebrate our 72nd anniversary as a married couple.

Rosalynn and I founded and still work at The Carter Center, where we try to do two things: One is to promote peace, and the other one is to be a champion of human rights. This is a major operation, and we've had programs in 80 countries of the world, trying to bring peace and democracy and freedom, and a better life for the people who live there. It's a big job. For instance, in Ethiopia, we have trained almost 37,000 nurses— it took us 10 years to do it—and now, when we go to Ethiopia to treat diseases like trachoma and others, we can treat as many as 10 million people in five days with the help of those 37,000 nurses. This is more people than live in the state of Virginia or the state of Georgia.

We try to eradicate some of these neglected diseases—do away with them completely, all over the world. In fact, at The Carter Center we have the only organization on earth that analyzes constantly every human illness, to see which ones might be eliminated completely from one country or one region, or eradicated from the entire earth. One of our programs is against Guinea worm. Guinea worm grows to a length of about 36 inches long in the human body after the human drinks filthy water from a stagnant pond. Then, about a year later, that worm emerges from the body through an excruciatingly painful sore. Farmers can't go to the field and children can't go to school. To start with, we found 3.5 million cases of Guinea worm in 21 different countries. As of the beginning of this month, which is the last report I've had, we only have three cases in the whole world now, in the country of Chad.

For 35 years, Rosalynn and I have volunteered to lead an annual Habitat [for Humanity] work project somewhere, one year overseas and the next in America. This year we're going to be near South Bend, Indiana; last year we were in Canada. Our biggest project was in the Philippines a number of years ago. We had 14,000 other volunteers join me and Rosalynn, and in five days we started and completed 293 homes for people who are desperately poor. The woman who would live in our house had three daughters, and before she got her new home, she and her daughters spent every night in an abandoned septic tank; they pulled a canvas cover over the top of it to keep the rain out. I understand that you resident students at Liberty are building Habitat houses here in Lynchburg. I hope you will keep up your work because Habitat needs you every day.

As a younger person, I lived during two serious crises, much worse than anything we face today. One was the Great Depression when I was a child growing up on a farm, and the second one was the Second World War.

When I face difficult times, I remember the advice that my favorite schoolteacher used to give us. Miss Julia Coleman would tell us students: "We must accommodate changing times, but cling to principles that never change."

All of us Americans now have other crises to face. Let me mention a few: I remember back in 1999, toward the end of that year, I was asked to make two major speeches; one was in Taiwan, and the other was in Oslo, Norway. The subject I was assigned to talk about was, "What is the greatest challenge the world faces or will face in the new millennium." I said it was the great disparity in wealth between the richest people and those who still worked for a living with their families. Since then, this disparity in wealth has gotten much greater, both within nations and between nations. Right now, for instance, eight people (six of them Americans) control more wealth than the poorest 3.5 billion—half of the world's total population.

Recently I've changed my mind about the biggest challenge that the world faces. I think now it's a human rights problem, and it is the discrimination against women and girls in the world. Let me give you a couple of examples. There are about 160 million girls and women who are not living today because their parents, in order to comply with laws or customs, had to have just male babies, sons, and either had to kill their babies by strangling them at birth, or having the modern-day ability to determine before the baby is born what gender it is going to be, if the fetus is female, then they abort the child. Atlanta, where The Carter Center is located, is the greatest center for human trafficking, or slavery, in America. One reason is we have the busiest airport in America for passengers, and a lot of our passengers come from the Southern Hemisphere. A girl who is brown-skinned or black-skinned can be sold, according to the New York Times, to a brothel owner for about $1,000, and a brothel owner makes about $35,000 for these forced brothel prostitutes.

Also, the last time we did a check on our military, it was found that there were about 16,000 cases of sexual abuse every year in the U.S. military, probably one of the finest organizations on earth.

The portion of people in prison has also skyrocketed in recent decades—there are more than seven times as many Americans in prison as there were when I left the White House, more than any other country on Earth. We also know that the partisan and racial divisions in our country are becoming deeper and deeper.

All our major religions are also divided—Protestant, Catholic, Jewish, Islamic, I'm sure Hinduism and Buddhism. On two occasions, you might be interested to know, in 1981 I brought about 40 of the top Southern Baptists together at The Carter Center in Atlanta. I was just out of the White House, and when I asked them to come, they came. Seven of those mostly men who came would become presidents of the Southern Baptist Convention. We tried but failed to resolve the differences between us and keep all of the Baptists together. One of the differences we couldn't resolve was the equal status of women.

I am glad to say that our common faith in worshiping Jesus Christ, though, is slowly bringing us back together, and Jerry and I talked last night about the possibility that he and I—and all of you, I hope—will work as much as we can to unify all Christians in the world. We as Baptists, most of all, ought to be able to come together as friends and not be alienated one from another.

More recently, the threat of nuclear war has become more acute, America has abandoned its leadership as the world's champion of a clean and healthy environment, broad confidence in our public officials has gone down, and we citizens have tended to lose faith in ourselves and in each other. We've also lost our support and our commitment to those "principles that never change," but I'm very glad to say that most of you have chosen the unchangeable principles of Christianity.

Only one time in human history have people tried to adopt these high principles that never change and are worthy of adopting. That was after the death of more than 60 million people in the Second World War, and the Holocaust that was orchestrated by Adolf Hitler. I monitored those proceedings closely from the deck of the first ship where I was assigned after I finished at Annapolis, when the United Nations was established to make sure there was never any more armed conflict between people. The Universal Declaration of Human Rights was adopted to ensure that everybody would be treated equally and would have justice. We know that the United Nations has failed to bring peace, and universal human rights have not been realized.

However, we also know that the modern ability to travel rapidly and instantly communicate, along with the wide use of social media, have brought an enormous step toward a truly global society for the first time. We evangelical Christians—and I consider myself to be one of them, one of you—must use this world coming-together and communicating instantly with each other to promote the word of the gospel about Jesus Christ.

Theologian Reinhold Niebuhr, one of my favorites, used these words: "The sad duty of politics is to establish justice in a sinful world." This in itself would be a great achievement. But we Christians know that there is one step greater than just bringing justice to our society, and that is to promote the use of agape love—self-sacrificial love—among people.

When I became president, before I was inaugurated, I was given a briefing by the military leaders of our country. I learned, really for the first time, that if I permitted a nuclear war, the use of atomic weapons, the arsenals of the Soviet Union and the United States alone might—would—end the ability of all human beings and animals to survive. Because of the direct explosions, the atomic fallout, and the covering of the sky by dark clouds of smoke and debris from the nuclear devices. No human being and no animal could survive a nuclear war. We now still have that great responsibility and threat, and we have to share it with seven or eight other countries: Russia, France, Great Britain, China, Israel, India, Pakistan, and perhaps North Korea.

With this threat to human existence, what then can you and I do about it? For a long time, humans had to contend with animals, and we depended on our speed, our agility, our strength just to survive in our competition with animals. Now, for several generations, human intelligence and the weapons we have developed permit us to prevail over other animals. So what is there to do? How can we prevail as human beings? One of the things we have to learn is how to get along, to do good for one another, and to get along with our potential enemies instead of how we can prevail in combat. In other words, just follow the mandates of the Prince of Peace: just learning how to live with our enemies in peace is what Jesus taught. And that will be our only chance for survival in the future.

We don't need enemies to fight, nor do we need inferior people whom we can dominate. Let me just quote this one verse of scripture, in Galatians 3:28: "There is neither Jew nor Greek, there is neither slave nor master, there is neither male nor female, for ye are all one in Christ Jesus."

So far, we Americans down through history have had a hard time adjusting to this concept of equality: We fought the Civil War, the War Between the States, that finally ended slavery; in the 1920s and then 40 years later we had a struggle in our country with granting white women and then black women 40 years later the right to vote; and more recently we have been struggling to end racial segregation. Even now, some of us are still struggling to accept the fact that all people are equal in the eyes of God.

As when I was in the Navy and when I was president, I want the United States to be strong enough so that we never have to prove we are strong. But there are attributes of a superpower that go beyond military strength; it's the same as those of a person. Our nation should be known as the champion of peace. Our nation should be known as the champion of equality. Our nation should be known as the champion of human rights. We should also be admired for our generosity to other people in need, and other moral values. In other words, for those principles that never change. There is no reason why the United States of America cannot epitomize these high virtues.

Despite all these challenges that I've already outlined, maybe to your discouragement, as a Christian I believe that the ultimate fate of human beings will be good, with God's love prevailing.

As new graduates, you are probably now blessed with the maximum freedom you will ever know. In the past, your parents and others have had a major influence over your lives, and in years ahead you'll also have a major influence from the job that you accept or the career that you choose—and also from the husband or wife that you might choose. So right now, in fact, you now have maximum opportunity to use three gifts that God gives every one of us: life, freedom, and in effect a guarantee that every single one of us will have enough talent and enough opportunity to live a completely successful life be a success—as judged by God.

We may not be rich. We may not live to be an old person. We may not have many loyal friends. And neither did Jesus have any of those things, but he lived a perfect life.

Without any interference from anybody else, all by ourselves, we have complete freedom to make a judgment. Everyone decides: "This is the kind of person I choose to be." We decide whether we tell the truth or benefit from telling lies. We're the ones that decide: "Do I hate? Or am I filled with love?" We're the ones who decide: "Will I think only about myself, or do I care for others?" We ourselves make these decisions, and no one else.

There are no limits to our ambition as a human being, and we have available to us, every one of us, constant contact with God in heaven, the creator of a universe and the creator of each one of us. How many of us decide ahead of time when we're going to be born, or where we will be born, or who our parents will be, or what our native intelligence level will be? You see, through prayer, we can have constant contact, day or night, with our Creator, who knows everything and can do anything. And we have a perfect example to follow if we're in doubt: We just have to remember the perfect life of Jesus Christ.

Thank you very much, and congratulations to all of you.

## Print Citations

**CMS:** Carter, Jimmy. "Address to the Liberty University Class of 2018." Speech presented at the Liberty University Class of 2017 Commencement, May 19, 2018, Lynchburg, VA. In *The Reference Shelf: Representative American Speeches 2017-2018*, edited by Micah L. Issit, 21-27. Ipswich, MA: H.W. Wilson, 2018.

**MLA:** Carter, Jimmy. "Address to the Liberty University Class of 2018." Liberty University Class of 2018 Commencement, 19 May 2018, Lynchburg, VA. Presentation. *The Reference Shelf: Representative American Speeches 2017-2018*, edited by H.W. Wilson, Salem Press, 2018, pp. 21-27.

**APA:** Carter, J. (2018, May 19). Address to the Liberty University class of 2018. Liberty University class of 2018 commencement, Lynchburg, VA. In M.L. Issit (Ed.), *The reference shelf: Representative American speeches 2017-2018* (pp. 21-27). Ipswich, MA: H.W. Wilson. (Original work published 2018)

# It's Not Just About Technology: It's About People

## By Sheryl Sandberg

---

*Sheryl Sandberg is one of the nation's leading female executives, serving as chief operating officer (COO) of the social media company Facebook since 2008. Prior to leading Facebook, Sandberg spent six years as vice president of the media company Google. Sandberg is also known for her writing about gender, politics, and business in her famous book* Lean In, *which led to the start of the Lean In foundation, a nonprofit promoting women in business, and the book* Option B, *which discusses the importance of resilience in overcoming difficulties. In her 2018 commencement address at MIT, Sandberg discusses the importance of emerging technology to addressing some of the world's most pressing challenges and problems.*

Esteemed faculty, proud parents, devoted friends, squirming siblings but especially Class of 2018: Congratulations, you made it!

It wasn't always easy. You plowed through four years of problem sets. You conquered the snow of 2015. You survived way too many Weekly Wednesdays at the Muddy Charles [Pub] and learned this important life lesson: There's no such thing as a free chicken wing.

Today, you are graduates of the most revered technical institution in the world. The Harvard people tried to get me to say "most revered institution within a 2-mile radius." I said no, but you'll soon find out how persistent alumni associations can be. Just ask the class of '68: They've been to more fundraisers than you've eaten chicken wings. One thing I remember from graduation is that feeling of turning one corner and not being able to see clearly around the next.

For someone like me who, yes, very annoyingly started studying for finals the first day of the semester, that was unsettling. Graduation was the first time in my life that the next steps were not clearly laid out. I remember the feeling of excitement and possibility, mixed in with just a teeny bit of crushing uncertainty.

If you know exactly what you're going to do for your career, raise your hand. There are always some. That is impressive.

I did not. I didn't know where I would fit in best or contribute most. These days, when I need advice, I turn to Mark Zuckerberg, but back then, he was in elementary school.

---

Delivered on June 8, 2018, at the Massachusetts Institute of Technology, Cambridge, MA.

I was sure of only one thing: I didn't want to go into business, and it never even occurred to me to go into technology.

I guess that's a warning for those of you who put your hands up: Certainty is one of the great privileges of youth. Things won't always end up as you think, but you will gain valuable lessons along life's uncertain path.

The lesson I want to share with you today is one I learned in my very first job out of college: working on a leprosy treatment program in India. Since biblical times, leprosy patients were ostracized from communities to prevent the disease from spreading.

By the time I graduated from college, the technical challenges had been solved. Doctors could easily diagnose leprosy that showed up in skin patches on your chest and medicine could easily treat the disease. But the stigma remained, so patients hid their disease instead of seeking care.

I will never forget meeting patients for the first time, extending my arm and watching them recoil because they were not used to even being touched.

The real breakthrough didn't come from technicians or doctors but from local community leaders. They knew that they had to erase the stigma before they could erase the disease, so they wrote plays and songs in local languages and went around the local community, encouraging people to come forward without fear.

They understood that the most difficult problems and the greatest opportunities we have are not technical. They are human.

In other words, it's not just about technology. It's about people.

This is a lesson you've learned here at MIT, and not just those of you graduating with technical degrees, but those who studied management or urban planning, or Course 11 or Course 15, in MIT speak. You know it's people who build technology, and people who use it to make their lives better, to get educated, to get health care, to share an infinite number of cat videos that are all unique and totally adorable— unless you're a dog person.

Today, anyone with an internet connection can inspire millions with a single sentence or a single image. This gives extraordinary power to those who use it to do good—to march for equality; to reignite the movement against sexual harassment; to rally around the things they care about and the people they want to be there for be there for.

But it also empowers those who seek to do harm.

When everyone has a voice, some raise them in hatred. When everyone can share, some share lies. When everyone can organize, some organize against the things we value the most.

Journalist Anne O'Hare McCormick wrote about the impact of new technology. She said we had created the ultimate democracy, where anything said by anyone could be heard by everyone, but she worried about whether it provoked partisanship or tolerance, whether it was time wasted or time well spent. She wondered if it explained "all the furious fence-building, the fanned-up nationalisms, and the angers and neuroses of our time."

She wrote this in 1932, about the radio—and by the way, she was the first woman to win the Pulitzer Prize for journalism.

The fact that the challenges we face today are not new does not make them less pressing. Like the generations before us, we have to solve the problems that our technology brings.

I believe there are three ways we can deal with these challenges: We can retreat in fear, we can barrel ahead with a single-minded belief in our technology or we can fight like hell to do all the good we can do with the understanding that what we build will be used by people and people are capable of great beauty and great cruelty.

I encourage you to choose the third option: To be clear-eyed optimists; to see that building technology that supports equality, democracy, truth and kindness means looking around corners—and throwing up every possible roadblock against hate, violence and deception.

You might be thinking, given some of the issues Facebook has had, isn't what I'm saying hitting pretty close to home?

Yes. It is.

I am proud of what Facebook has done around the world— proud of the connections people have created. Proud of how people use Facebook to organize for democracy, the Women's March, Black Lives Matter. Proud of how people use Facebook to start and grow businesses and create jobs all around the world.

But at Facebook, we didn't see all the risks coming, and we didn't do enough to stop them.

It's painful when you miss something, when you make the mistake of believing so much in the good you are seeing that you don't see the bad. It's hard when you know that you let people down.

In the middle of one of my toughest moments, Michael Miller, former Superintendent of the Naval Academy, kindly reached out to remind me that smooth seas never make good sailors.

He's right. The times in my life that I have learned the most have definitely been the hardest. That is when you will learn the most about yourself. You can almost feel yourself growing; you can feel the growing pains. When you own your mistakes, you can work harder to correct them and even harder to prevent the next ones.

That's my job now. It won't be easy and it's not going to be fast. But we will see it through.

Yet the larger challenge is one all of us here must face. The role of technology in our lives is growing and that means our relationship with technology is changing.

We have to change too. We have to recognize the full weight of our responsibilities. It's not enough to be technologists, we have to make sure that technology serves people. It's not enough or even possible to be neutral. Tools are shaped by the minds that make them as well as the hands that use them.

It's not enough to have a good idea, we have to know when to stop a bad one. This is hard because technology changes faster than society. When I was in college, no one had a cell phone. Today there are more cell phones than people on earth.

We are in one of the most remarkable moments in human history and you will not just live through it, you will shape it.

Many of you will work on technologies that will change the world. You will connect the rest of the world, create new jobs and disrupt old ones, give machines new powers to think and give us the means to communicate in ways we haven't even thought of.

We are not passive observers of these changes. We can't be. Trends do not just happen, they are the result of choices people make.

We are not indifferent creators, we have a duty of care and when even with the best of intentions you go astray, as many of us have, you have the responsibility to course correct.

We are accountable to the people who use what we build, to our colleagues, to ourselves

and to our values.

So if you are thinking about joining a team, an NGO, a startup or a company, ask if they are doing good for the world.

Research at that other school down the river shows that we become more creative when we ask "Could we?" And we become more ethical when we ask "Should we?"

So ask both.

Know that you have an obligation to never shy away from doing the right thing, because the fight to ensure tech is used for good is never over; to make sure that technology reflects and upholds the right values, we have to build with awareness, and the best way to be more aware is to have more people in the room with different voices and different views.

There are still skeptics out there when it comes to the value of diversity. They dismiss it as something we do to feel better, not to be better.

They are wrong. We cannot build technology for equality and democracy unless we have and we harness diversity in its creation.

More people with more diverse backgrounds are working in technology than ever before and are graduating in your class today than ever before.

But our industry is still lagging at MIT. Even the newest technology can contain the oldest prejudices and our lack of diversity is at the root of some of the things we fail to see and prevent.

It is up to all of us to fix that, people like me, and people like you; everyone graduating today and all the graduates to come.

So continue the example you have lived at MIT. Continue to engage with people outside your discipline, your gender, your race. Talk with people who grew up in different places, who believe different things, who live and worship differently than you do. Talk with them, listen to them, get their perspectives as you have done here and encourage them to work in and with technology too.

To all the current and future educators here today, let's reform our educational system so we give everyone the opportunity to learn to code. This is a basic language now that needs to be taught in all of our schools so that more people have a choice.

When some kids learn it and some don't, that creates an unequal playing field long before people go into the workforce.

And to all the future leaders in tech, that's you. Know that you have a chance to right wrongs, not reinforce them.

Tech institutions can be some of the strongest voices for progress in the workplace, but we can always do better. Encourage your employers and policymakers to ensure that everyone, including contractors, earns a living wage. Fight for paid family leave with equal time for all genders because equality in the workplace will not happen until we have equality in the home and because no one should be forced to choose between the job they need and the family they love. Give people bereavement leave because when tragedy strikes, we need to be there for each other.

And build workplaces where everyone, everyone, is treated with respect.

We need to stop harassment and hold both perpetrators and enablers accountable and we need to make a personal commitment to stop racism and sexism, including the expressions of bias that become commonplace and accepted instead of rejected and fought.

I want you to know that you can impact the workplace from the very day you enter it.

A few months ago, LeanIn.org surveyed people to understand how the #MeToo movement was influencing work. After so many brave women spoke out, we found evidence of an unintended backlash: Almost half of male managers in the U.S. are now uncomfortable having a work meeting alone with a woman and even more uncomfortable having a work dinner alone with a female colleague.

These are the informal moments where men have long gotten more mentoring than women—and now it looks like it could get worse. For the men here: Someone may pull you aside in your first week at work and say, "never being alone with a woman."

You know they're wrong. You know how to work with all people. So give them advice instead.

Tell them they have the responsibility to make access equal for women and that if they don't feel comfortable having dinner with women, they shouldn't have dinner with men. Group lunches for everyone.

In one of my early jobs, I had a boss who treated me quite differently from the two men on my team and not in a good way. He spoke to them with kindness and respect but belittled me publicly. I tried to talk to him, but that made it worse. My two male teammates right out of school themselves stepped up and it stopped.

Even if you're the most junior person in the room, you have power. Use it, and use it well.

Class of 2018, it's not the technology you build that will define you. It's the teams you build and what people do with your technology. We have to get this right because we need technology to solve our greatest challenges.

When I sat where you are sitting today, I never thought I would work in technology, but somewhere along that uncertain path, I learned new lessons and became a technologist.

And technologists have always been optimists.

We're optimists because we have to be. If you want to do something that has never been done before, so many people will tell you it cannot be done.

Graduates of this amazing university have helped sequence the human genome, paved the way for the treatment of AIDS and made an MIT balloon appear in the middle of the Harvard-Yale football game.

We're optimists because we run the numbers.

Our world can feel polarized and dangerous, but in many critical ways, we are so much better off. A century ago, global life expectancy was 35 for 2 billion people.

Today it is 70, for 7 billion.

When I graduated, 1 in 3 people lived in extreme poverty. Today it is 1 in 10. It is still way too high but we have made more progress in our lifetimes than in all of human history.

Our challenge now is to be clear-eyed optimists, or to paraphrase President Kennedy, optimists without illusions: To build technology that improves lives and gives voice to those who often have none while preventing misuse, to build teams that better reflect the world around us with all its complexity and diversity.

If we succeed—and we'll succeed—we will build technology that better serves not just some of us, but all of us.

MIT graduate and former faculty member David Baltimore won a Nobel Prize for his work on the interaction between viruses and the genetic material of the cell. But before that, he helped bring biologists, lawyers and physicians together to debate new gene editing technology. They were worried that it had the potential to cause more harm than good, but they concluded that the opportunities for progress were too great, so they created voluntary ethical guidelines and continued the research.

That decision led to some of the greatest advances in genetic science and medicine. It also set a standard that we as technologists can follow: Seek advice from people with different perspectives, look deeply at the risks as well as the benefits of new technology and if those risks can be managed, keep going even in the face of uncertainty.

Class of 2018, you are now graduates of one of the most forward-thinking places on earth.

You will have tremendous opportunities and you will be highly sought after. You will use what you learned here to work on some of the most critical questions we face.

I hope you will use your influence to make sure technology is a force for good in the world. Technology needs a human heartbeat; the things that bring us joy and the things that bring us together are the things that matter most.

The future is in your hands. Congratulations!

## Print Citations

**CMS:** Sandberg, Sheryl. "It's Not Just About Technology: It's About People." Speech presented at the Massachusetts Institute of Technology Class of 2018 Commencement, Cambridge, MA, June 8, 2018. In *The Reference Shelf: Representative American Speeches 2017-2018*, edited by Micah L. Issit, 28-34. Ipswich, MA: H.W. Wilson, 2018.

**MLA:** Sandberg, Sheryl. "It's Not Just About Technology: It's About People." Massachusetts Institute of Technology Class of 2018, 4 June 2018, Cambridge, MA. Presentation. *The Reference Shelf: Representative American Speeches 2017-2018*, edited by Micah L. Issit, H.W. Wilson, 2018, pp. 28-34.

**APA:** Sandberg, S. (2018, June 8). It's Not Just About Technology: It's About People. Massachusetts Institute of Technology class of 2018 commencement, Cambridge, MA. In M.L. Issit (Ed.), *The reference shelf: Representative American speeches 2017-2018* (pp. 28-34). Ipswich, MA: H.W. Wilson. (Original work published 2018)

# Remarks to the Pomona College Class of 2018

## By Danielle Allen

*Danielle Allen is a Harvard University professor whose professional research has focused on democratic and political sociology. Allen is the author of a number of books on the history of political theory including* Cuz: The Life and Times of Michael A. *and* Education and Equality. *Allen also leads the Democratic Knowledge Project, a research center at Harvard University that seeks to increase public political knowledge and to foster research into strengthening democracy. In this speech at Pomona College, Allen discusses race, foundational constitutional principles, and the importance of core values to building a strong democracy.*

I know you've come here for many reasons. I believe that many of you, despite what you may say about the life of the mind, have come here for a job. And I am sure you will succeed. This place has equipped you.

And I am sure many of you have also come to enrich yourselves as human beings—to find the connections that your colleagues spoke about so eloquently. I worried, to be honest, before coming, that you had not come here to find your civic purpose. The data that we read about suggests that young people don't much care for democracy anymore.

For instance, only 30 percent of people born in the most recent generation consider democracy essential to our way of life. And 25 percent of 18-to-24-year-olds think that democracy is either a bad or very bad way of running things. I can tell that you are not apathetic, I have learned that this morning. Nonetheless, the work of democracy is hard. And before you leave I want to share a few more thoughts on that subject of preparing yourself for your civic responsibilities.

For the last 20 years, for reasons that are too complicated to explain in this moment, I have been journeying with the Declaration of Independence.

Many of you will be skeptical of the worth of that text. You think that it was written by Thomas Jefferson, a slave owner. Let me just tell you one important lesson: If you want credit for something, put it on your tombstone. Jefferson's tombstone says, "Author, Declaration of Independence."

That's why he gets the credit.

In fact, it was written by a committee. He happened to chair the committee, and it's true that he wrote the first draft. But the other members of the committee,

Delivered on June 4, 2018, at Pomona College, Claremont, CA.

and in particular John Adams, man of Massachusetts who never owned slaves and thought slavery was a bad thing, were just as important as intellectual architects of the document.

Adams is my favorite of that Founding generation.

Let me just ask you to think through with me … about what I take to be the pithiest, most efficient lesson in the conduct of citizenship and civic agency there is. I say citizenship and civic agency because citizenship is not about a formal status, it is about empowerment and taking responsibility for your world. So here is the shortest lesson there is:

> We hold these truths to be self-evident, that all men are created equal, that they are endowed by their Creator with certain unalienable Rights, that among these are Life, Liberty and the pursuit of Happiness. That to secure these rights, Governments are instituted among Men, deriving their just powers from the consent of the governed. That whenever any Form of Government becomes destructive of these ends, it is the Right of the People to alter or to abolish it, and to institute new Government, laying its foundation on such principles and organizing its powers in such form, as to them shall seem most likely to effect their Safety and Happiness.

Tell the truth: Do you remember it was that long?

It's not *just* about individual rights—about life, liberty, and the pursuit of happiness—it moves from those rights to the notion that government is something that we build together to secure our safety and happiness.

Were you listening closely?

We have two jobs: laying the foundation on principle—clarify your values, know what you stand for; and organize the power of government to secure those rights, to effect of safety and happiness. The best we can do is figure out what is most likely to effect our safety and happiness. We make probabilistic judgments. We make mistakes! We have to enter into the business of democratic agency *with humility*.

And this job of laying the foundation of principle and connecting it to how we organize the powers of government entails two important things.

That foundation of principle, what does it amount to?

The sentence gives us some ideas. It says we have these rights, *among which* are life, liberty, and the pursuit of happiness. Among which! It's examples, people!

It's not a complete list! The job of thinking is not done.

*It is your job*. All right?

Clarify your values. Maybe you care about sustainability. Maybe you care about gender equality. Maybe you care about free markets and capitalism.

But connect them to the basic question of what is good for our community together. A shared story. And then, don't forget: Activism is valuable, no question about it, but our job at the end of the day is to build institutions that secure our shared rights. That means understanding the user manual. All right? The institutions. And yes, we can alter them. They're not given in perpetuity. Originalism is about understanding democratic empowerment, which is about recognizing that democratic citizens build and change their world.

All right?

You lay the foundation on principle—and that requires talking to each other and everybody else—and figure out how to organize the powers of government. Understand the user manual well enough to use it and modify it.

All right.

So I'll leave you again with my last lesson for you, for your civic preparation:

We hold these truths to be self-evident.

That all men are created equal.

That they are endowed by their Creator with certain *unalienable* Rights.

That *among these* are Life, Liberty and the pursuit of Happiness.

That to secure these rights, Governments are instituted among people, deriving their just powers from the consent of the governed.

That whenever *any* Form of Government becomes destructive of these ends, it is the Right of the People to alter or to abolish it, and to institute new Government.

Laying its foundation on such *principles* and organizing its powers in such form, as to *US* shall seem most likely to effect *Our* safety and happiness.

Congratulations, class of 2018.

## Print Citations

**CMS:** Allen, Danielle. "Remarks to the Pomona College Class of 2018." Speech presented at the Pomona College Class of 2018 Commencement, Claremont, CA, June 4, 2018. In *The Reference Shelf: Representative American Speeches 2017-2018*, edited by Micah L. Issit, 35-37. Ipswich, MA: H.W. Wilson, 2018.

**MLA:** Allen, Danielle. "Remarks to the Pomona Class of 2018." Pomona College Class of 2018 Commencement, 4 June 2018, Claremont, CA. Presentation. *The Reference Shelf: Representative American Speeches 2017-2018,* edited by Micah L. Issit, H.W. Wilson, 2018, pp. 35-37.

**APA:** Allen, D. (2018, June 4). Remarks to the Pomona class of 2018. In M.L. Issit (Ed.), *The reference shelf: Representative American speeches 2017-2018* (pp. 35-37). Ipswich, MA: H.W. Wilson. (Original work published 2018)

# Commencement Address to the US Naval Academy Class of 2018

## By Donald Trump

---

*President Donald Trump is a celebrity businessman turned politician known for his management of the Trump family real estate business started by his father in the 1960s and for his role in the reality television series* The Apprentice. *In this commencement address at the US Naval Academy, Trump discusses the importance of the military and his accomplishments during the first two years of his presidency.*

Thank you. Thank you. Hello, midshipmen, hello. Let me say to the entire brigade—please be at ease—enjoy yourselves, because we are all here to celebrate the amazing class of 2018. Amazing job. Thank you. Really something. Admiral Carter, thank you for that wonderful introduction and for your leadership, an incredible job you have done at this storied academy. And thank you, Captain Chadwick, for your dedication and service. Thank you to Undersecretary Modly, Admiral Richardson, General Walters, for joining us today. Thanks also to Senator Wicker, Congressman Wittman, Congressman Valadao.

I want to recognize the entire brigade for a tremendous year. This has been a spectacular year for you. I have heard all about your achievements. And a very special recognition for the midshipmen fourth class, you are plebs no more. To all of the distinguished faculty and staff, to the local sponsor families, and most importantly, to the parents and grandparents and family members who have helped our graduates reached this joyous hour, today is your incredible achievement also. They would have never made it without you, know this. I want to thank the midshipmen and your families, and thank you. America thanks you more than anybody. You have done a spectacular job. Thank you very much.

Finally, to the men and women about to be commissioned as ensigns in the Navy and second lieutenants in the Marine Corps, let me say on behalf of the entire nation, we could not be more proud of the United States Naval Academy Class of 2018. Thank you. Great job.

Congratulations to you all. Four years ago, each of you made the most important decision of your lives. You chose the path of hard work, sweat, and sacrifice. You chose the life of honor, courage, and commitment. You chose to serve the nation and defend our great American flag. You chose the Navy, blue and gold, from the

---

Delivered on May 25, 2018, at the US Naval Academy, Annapolis, MD.

first moments of induction day. Through a grueling six weeks of pleb summer, you endured and you persevered.

And then the rest of the brigade returned, and the real test began. You developed morally, mentally, and physically. You poured yourselves into military tactics, seamanship, navigation, ethics, and engineering. And when hard work was not enough, like generations before you, you gathered your pennies and sought favor from the all-powerful Tecumseh. All-powerful. A little bit different. Others worked hard for their demerits at McGarvey's and the Fleet Reserve Club. And so today in keeping with tradition, I declare that all midshipmen on restriction for minor offenses, you are hereby absolved.

That sounds like a lot of people. The Admiral will define exactly what that means, so Admiral, please go easy. This is a great group of people here, Admiral. I am told this class led Navy athletics to the highest win percentage in your 172-year history. Think about that. That includes taking the Army–Navy Star Series for the fourth straight year, a remarkable achievement in sport and athletics. And because you care about every contest against Army, for the record, this year, Navy beat Army 19 times. And I will not mention, I promised, who won the football game. I will not mention it. I refuse to say it. But that is a great achievement.

And let me take a guess, you are still not tired of winning. Winning is such a great feeling, isn't it? Winning is such a great feeling. Nothing like winning, you got to win. In every endeavor, the class of 2018 has shown its metal and it's proved its might. You have earned your place in the ancient league of sailors and shipmates, captains and commanders, warriors and mariners, and Marines. You crave adventure. Hello, folks, back there. You chase discovery, and you never flinch in the eye of a raging storm. America is in your heart. The ocean is in your soul. The saltwater runs through your veins. You live your life according to the final law of the Navy. The word impossible does not exist, because Navy never quits.

You don't give up. You don't give in. You don't back down. And you never surrender. Wherever you go, wherever you serve, wherever your mission takes you, you only have one word in mind, and that's victory. That is why you are here. Victory. A very important word. You are now leaders in the most powerful and righteous force on the face of the planet. The United States military. And we are respected again, I can tell you that. We are respected again.

A lot of things have happened. We are respected again. For the last four years, you have walked the same paths as Navy's greatest legends, the giants of Midway and Coral Sea and Manila Bay. Here in Annapolis, the glorious past is all around you, and so are the stories of your great heroes.

One such hero who appears in the pages of your old yearbooks is Bruce Voorhees. Well-known all over. Bruce hailed from Nevada and was a member of the Naval Academy class of 1929. Beneath his picture in the 1929 Lucky Bag, Bruce's classmates wrote that he spent most of his time teaching the city slickers from the east the correct pronunciation of Nevada. And I had to learn that, too, to win the state. Great place.

He saw studying as an unnecessary evil, and they remembered in three cruises and four years in blue-serge brass buttons, he left a trail of broken hearts extending the full length of both coasts and radiating for miles around Crabtown. In other words, he was just like you in many ways. Just like you. Not a lot of difference. Just over a decade after his graduation, Lieutenant Commander Voorhees found himself at war.

Seventy-five years ago this summer, he was in the South Pacific commanding Bombing Squadron 102 during the battle of the Solomon Islands. That was a rough battle. His only brother had been killed and the Bataan Death March. On July 6, Bruce volunteered for a mission to destroy a crucial enemy base. It was a rough time. It was a rough, tough situation. He knew full-well that he would likely never return. He knew he was going to die. But he also knew his daring action could prevent a surprise attack on large-scale American forces.

So, his plane took off alone on a 700-mile flight. Bruce flew through the darkness to his target, a tiny speck on the vast open sea. He braved unrelenting antiaircraft fire, like nobody had ever seen at that time, and a trail of enemy planes to single-handedly destroy this large enemy base, including multiple fortifications, and a critical communications link. And in this final act of valor, Bruce was caught in the blast of one of his own bombs and perished in a remote lagoon very far from here. His life was lost, but his legacy will live forever.

Many of you have seen his old room at Bancroft Hall, commemorating his Congressional Medal of Honor, our highest honor. Some here today will trace his path to Pensacola to earn your wings. You may even make it all the way out to the legendary combat-training school known as Top Gun in Bruce's beloved hometown in Nevada. There, you will have the honor to take flight from the Voorhees Field, and remember a hero who fought for his country, and died for his homeland, and saved so many lives with his bravery.

Each of you inherits the legacy of the heroes who came before you. It's a living history passed down from officer to officer and generation to generation. Each of you will make your own mark on the Navy, the Marine Corps, the military, and the history of our great nation. Seize today and you will shape tomorrow.

In a few moments, you will be commissioned into the mightiest fighting forces of the air, the land, and the sea. Together, you will blast off carriers of which we are just now finishing, the largest aircraft carrier in the world, and launch off submarines of which we have many under construction, and ward off evil.

You will bring comfort to our friends and strike fear into the hearts of our enemies. Among our graduates today will be 283 naval aviators, 134 submariners, 256 surface-warfare officers, 70 restricted-line officers, and 15 explosive-ordnance-disposal officers. Two-hundred-and-thirty-six United States Marines, and 35 very tough, very well-conditioned Navy SEALs.

Together, you are the tip of the spear, the edge of the blade, and the front of the shield defending and protecting our great country. You know, there is no mission our pilots can't handle. There is no hill our Marines can't take, and there is no stronghold the SEALs can't reach. There is no sea the Navy can't brave, and there is no storm the American sailor can't conquer. Because you know that together, there is nothing Americans can't do. Absolutely nothing.

In recent years and even decades, too many people have forgotten that truth. They have forgotten that our ancestors trounced an empire, tamed a continent, and triumphed over the worst evils in history. In every generation, there have been cynics and critics that try to tear down America. But in recent years, the problem grew worse. A growing number used their platforms to denigrate America's incredible heritage, challenge America's sovereignty, and weaken America's pride.

We know the truth, will speak the truth, and defend that truth. America is the greatest fighting force for peace, justice, and freedom in the history of the world. And in case you have not noticed, we have become a lot stronger lately. A lot. We are not going to apologize for America. We are going to stand up for America. No more apologies. We are going to stand up for our citizens. We are going to stand up for our values. And we are going to stand up for our men and women in uniform.

Because we know that a nation must have pride in its history to have confidence in its future. We are the nation that built the highways, the railroads, the Empire State Building in one year, the Golden Gate Bridge, and we are the nation that built the Panama Canal.

We trekked the mountains, explored the oceans, and settled the vast frontier. We won two world wars, defeated communism and fascism, and put a man on the face of the moon. We cured disease, pioneered science, and produced timeless works of art that inspire the human soul. And on distant islands, far-away battlefields, above the skies and beneath the sea, the entire world has borne witness to the unstoppable strength, skill, and courage of the United States Navy and the American Marines.

Each of you enters service at a truly exciting time for our country. For we are witnessing the great reawakening of the American spirit and of American might. We have rediscovered our identity, regained our stride, and we are proud again. Prosperity is booming at home. Our economy is the strongest it has ever been. And our country has regained the respect that we used to have long ago abroad. Yes, they are respecting us again. Yes, America is back.

We have begun the great rebuilding of the United States military. We have ended the disastrous defense sequester. No money for the military? Those days are over. And we have just secured, you have read all about it, a $700 billion, largest-ever amount of money to support our great war fighters. And I might add that next year— the $700 billion, not million. They're liking the sound of million, but billion is better—the $700 billion goes to $716 billion, and we are going to be stronger than ever before. We will have the strongest military that we have ever had, and it won't even be close. And when did we need it more than now?

That means new ships. You like that. We have now the lowest number of ships we have had since World War I. And very soon, we are going to get to 355 beautiful ships. That is almost a couple of hundred more ships. So you will be around for a long time. We are not running out of equipment. We're not running out of ships. And that has been approved. And we are honored by it.

You are going to have new equipment, and well-deserved pay raises. We just got to a big pay raise for the first time in 10 years. We got to a big pay increase, first time in over 10 years. I fought for you. That was the hardest one to get. But you never had a chance of losing. I represented you well. I represented you well.

And this week, we passed new landmark legislation to give more choice and better care to our great veterans. We are going to take care of our veterans. We are doing a great job with it. We are taking care, finally, after decades, we are taking care of our veterans. We passed VA accountability. Everybody said it could not be done. If you didn't do a good job, you could not get fired. Now, you don't do a good job and take care of our veterans, they will look you in the eye and they say, "Jim, you're fired! You're out! Out!" Get him out of here. They all said you could not get it. They tried to get it for 35 years. We will say, "Get him out of here, he doesn't take care of our vets."

Next year, we are committing even more to our defenses, and we are committing even more to our veterans. Because we know that the best way to prevent war is to be fully prepared for war. And hopefully, we never have to use all of this beautiful, new, powerful equipment. But you know, you are less likely to have to use it if you have it and know how to work it. And nobody knows how to work it like you.

And if a fight must come, there is no other alternative. Victory, winning, beautiful words, but that is what it is all about. We are reestablishing the second fleet in the Atlantic: bigger, better, stronger than it has ever been before. We are rebuilding our defense industrial base to forge American iron, aluminum, and steel, which, by the way, we just put tariffs on when it comes in from other countries. Okay? We are taking in a lot of money now, our country. They pay that big, beautiful tariff and it goes right into building new ships.

We have been taken advantage of by the world. That is not going to be happening anymore. You see what is going on. So, we are building a modern fleet manned by the greatest sailors. We're sharpening the fighting edge from Marines infantry squads to combat ships to deliver maximum, lethal force. The enemy has to know we have that. We are recommitting to this fundamental truth: We are a maritime nation.

Being a maritime nation, we are surrounded by sea. We must always dominate that sea. We will always dominate the oceans. We are showing what we can achieve when natural American confidence is backed by unrivaled American power and un-questioned American resolve.

Also, there is another word that's never used, and I will use it today. It's called talent. We have talent and a lot of other people don't, and a lot of other countries don't. We have great talent and I have seen it. In other words, we are showing what is possible when America starts acting like its sailors and Marines. Our nation can-not be strong without the heroes whose hearts stir the words: Don't give up the ship. Famous phrase. We even use it in business. Things are going bad, you say, "Don't give up the ship." Keep fighting. Don't give up the ship. But it's really—you guys started it.

Our country cannot prevail without those who rally to the famous cry, to Admiral Farragut's cry, you know it well, "Damn the torpedoes. Full speed ahead." Damn the torpedoes, full speed ahead. You hail from every background and you come from every walk of life. But each of you is formed by the same defining choice, to answer the call. You all share the same heart, the same blood, and swear by the same motto: Not for self but country. It's a great motto.

With us today are living symbols of that long and unbroken chain of American patriots, members of the Naval Academy class of 1968. That's great. Stand up, please. Exactly 50 years ago, they were in your shoes. They embarked into service and they made America very proud. To everyone in the class of 1968, we thank you and we salute you.

Like those who came before them, today's graduates will serve America through times of triumph and some hours of peril. There will be hours of peril. You will face new challenges, even challenges that you can't envision, but you'll find new solutions that nobody can even imagine. Among your ranks is the next Chester Nimitz, the next Grace Hopper, the next John Lejeune. Future generations will talk about you. They will tell your stories, speak of your courage, and someone many years from now will be standing right here, in my position, paying tribute to your great service. It will happen. Because you already know the keys to success. You know that as long as we are proud of who we are, and what we are fighting for, we will not fail. We will not fail. We cannot fail. We will always succeed, always.

As long as we are united with the same mission, the same purpose, the same patriotic heart, we will win, because we are one people, one family, and one glorious nation under God.

Together we struggle. Together we strive. Together we pray. And together we triumph as citizens, as patriots, as Americans. We stand on the shoulders of heroes who gave their sweat, their blood, their tears, and their very lives for this great country of ours. This is our heritage. This is our home. And this is our pledge. We are all in for America, like never before. We are all in for our great country.

So to the Naval Academy of the class of 2018, I say a number of things. Number one, I say that I was given an option. I could make this commencement address, which is a great honor for me, and immediately leave and wave goodbye, or I could stay and shake hands with just the top 100, or I could stay for hours and shake hands with 1,100 and something. What should I do? What should I do? I'll stay. I'll stay. I will stay.

But to the class of 2018, I do say strive for excellence. Live for adventure. Think big. Dream bigger. Push further. Sail faster. Fly higher. And never, ever stop reaching for greatness. Never stop reaching for the stars. You know you're up to the task. You're among the finest people anywhere in the world, the smartest, the strongest. You know you will make us proud. We know that glory will be yours because you are winners. You are warriors. You are fighters. You are champions, and you will lead us only to victory. Good luck. May god be with you. God bless America, and anchors away.

## Print Citations

**CMS:** Trump, Donald. "Commencement Address to the US Naval Academy Class of 2018." Speech presented at the US Naval Academy Class of 2018 Commencement, Annapolis, MD, May 25, 2018. In *The Reference Shelf: Representative American Speeches 2017-2018*, edited by Micah L. Issit, 38-44. Ipswich, MA: H.W. Wilson, 2018.

**MLA:** Trump, Donald. "Commencement Address to the US Naval Academy Class of 2018." US Naval Academy Class of 2018 Commencement, 25 May 2018, Annapolis, MD. Presentation. *The Reference Shelf: Representative American Speeches 2017-2018,* edited by Micah L. Issit, H.W. Wilson, 2018, pp. 38-44.

**APA:** Trump, D. (2018, May 25). Commencement address to the US Naval Academy class of 2018. In M.L. Issit (Ed.), *The reference shelf: Representative American speeches 2017-2018* (pp. 38-44). Ipswich, MA: H.W. Wilson. (Original work published 2018)

# 2
# Politics and Policies

Donald Trump by Michael Vadon, via Wikimedia

President Donald Trump delivered several speeches during the past year detailing what he considers the successes of his first two years in office, including strengthening the US economy, as well as his continued support for immigration control, clean coal, and a strong US military.

# State of the Union Address, 2018

## By Donald Trump

*President Donald Trump is a businessman known for his leadership of the Trump Cor-poration, an international real estate conglomerate started by his father in the 1960s, and for his role in the reality television series* The Apprentice. *Elected president in the 2016 presidential elections, Trump has become a divisive political figure. In this speech from January 30, 2018, Donald Trump delivers his first State of the Union address as president of the United States.*

Mr. Speaker, Mr. Vice President, Members of Congress, the First Lady of the Unit-ed States, and my fellow Americans:

Less than one year has passed since I first stood at this podium, in this ma-jestic chamber, to speak on behalf of the American People—and to address their concerns, their hopes, and their dreams. That night, our new Administration had already taken very swift action. A new tide of optimism was already sweeping across our land. Each day since, we have gone forward with a clear vision and a righteous mission—to make America great again for all Americans.

Over the last year, we have made incredible progress and achieved extraordi-nary success. We have faced challenges we expected, and others we could never have imagined. We have shared in the heights of victory and the pains of hardship. We have endured floods and fires and storms. But through it all, we have seen the beauty of America's soul, and the steel in America's spine.

Each test has forged new American heroes to remind us who we are, and show us what we can be.

We saw the volunteers of the "Cajun Navy," racing to the rescue with their fish-ing boats to save people in the aftermath of a totally devastating hurricane.

We saw strangers shielding strangers from a hail of gunfire on the Las Vegas strip.

We heard tales of Americans like Coast Guard Petty Officer Ashlee Leppert, who is here tonight in the gallery with Melania. Ashlee was aboard one of the first helicopters on the scene in Houston during the Hurricane Harvey. Through 18 hours of wind and rain, Ashlee braved live power lines and deep water to help save more than 40 lives. Ashlee, we all thank you. Thank you very much.

We heard about Americans like firefighter David Dahlberg. He's here with us also. David faced down walls of flame to rescue almost 60 children trapped at a California summer camp threatened by those devastating wildfires.

Delivered on January 30, 2018, U.S. Capitol, Washington, DC.

To everyone still recovering in Texas, Florida, Louisiana, Puerto Rico, and the Virgin Islands—everywhere—we are with you, we love you, and we always will pull through together, always.

Thank you to David and the brave people of California. Thank you very much, David. Great job.

Some trials over the past year touched this chamber very personally. With us tonight is one of the toughest people ever to serve in this House—a guy who took a bullet, almost died, and was back to work three and a half months later: the legend from Louisiana, Congressman Steve Scalise. I think they like you, Steve.

We're incredibly grateful for the heroic efforts of the Capitol Police officers, the Alexandria Police, and the doctors, nurses, and paramedics who saved his life and the lives of many others; some in this room.

In the aftermath—yes, yes—In the aftermath of that terrible shooting, we came together, not as Republicans or Democrats, but as representatives of the people. But it is not enough to come together only in times of tragedy. Tonight, I call upon all of us to set aside our differences, to seek out common ground, and to summon the unity we need to deliver for the people. This is really the key. These are the people we were elected to serve.

(Thank you.) [off mic]

Over the last year, the world has seen what we always knew: that no people on Earth are so fearless or daring or determined as Americans. If there is a mountain, we climb it. If there's a frontier, we cross it. If there's a challenge, we tame it. If there's an opportunity, we seize it. So let's begin tonight by recognizing that the state of our Union is strong because our people are strong. And together, we are building a safe, strong, and proud America.

Since the election, we have created 2.4 million new jobs, including—including 200,000 new jobs in manufacturing alone. Tremendous numbers. After years and years of wage stagnation, we are finally seeing rising wages.

Unemployment claims have hit a 45-year low. It's something I'm very proud of. African American unemployment stands at the lowest rate ever recorded. And Hispanic American unemployment has also reached the lowest levels in history.

Small-business confidence is at an all-time high. The stock market has smashed one record after another, gaining 8 trillion dollars, and more, in value in just this short period of time. The great news—The great news for Americans' 401(k), retirement, pension, and college savings accounts have gone through the roof.

And just as I promised the American people from this podium 11 months ago, we enacted the biggest tax cuts and reforms in American history.

Our massive tax cuts provide tremendous relief for the middle class and small business. To lower tax rates for hardworking Americans, we nearly doubled the standard deduction for everyone. Now, the first 24,000 dollars earned by a married couple is completely tax-free. We also doubled the child tax credit. A typical family of four making 75,000 dollars will see their tax bill reduced by 2,000 dollars, slashing their tax bill in half.

In April, this will be the last time you will ever file under the old and very broken system, and millions of Americans will have more take-home pay starting next month—a lot more.

We eliminated an especially cruel tax that fell mostly on Americans making less than 50,000 dollars a year, forcing them to pay tremendous penalties simply because they couldn't afford government-ordered health plans. We repealed the core of the disastrous Obamacare. The individual mandate is now gone. Thank heaven.

We slashed the business tax rate from 35 percent all the way down to 21 percent, so American companies can compete and win against anyone else anywhere in the world. These changes alone are estimated to increase average family income by more than 4,000 dollars—a lot of money. Small businesses have also received a massive tax cut, and can now deduct 20 percent of their business income.

Here tonight are Steve Staub and Sandy Keplinger of Staub Manufacturing, a small, beautiful business in Ohio. They've just finished the best year in their 20-year history. Because of tax reform, they are handing out raises, hiring an additional 14 people, and expanding into the building next door. Good feeling.

One of Staub's employees, Corey Adams, is also with us tonight. Corey is an all-American worker. He supported himself through high school, lost his job during the 2008 recession, and was later hired by Staub, where he trained to become a welder. Like many hardworking Americans, Corey plans to invest his tax cut raise into his new home and his two daughters' education.

Corey, please stand. And he's a great welder. I was told that by the man that owns that company that's doing so well. So congratulations, Corey.

Since we passed tax cuts, roughly three million workers have already gotten tax cut bonuses—many of them thousands and thousands of dollars per worker. And it's getting more every month, every week. Apple has just announced it plans to invest a total of 350 billion dollars in America, and hire another 20,000 workers. And just a little while ago, ExxonMobil announced a 50 billion dollar investment in the United States, just a little while ago.

This, in fact, is our new American moment. There has never been a better time to start living the American Dream.

So to every citizen watching at home tonight, no matter where you've been, or where you've come from, this is your time. If you work hard, if you believe in yourself, if you believe in America, then you can dream anything; you can be anything; and together, we can achieve absolutely anything.

Tonight, I want to talk about what kind of future we're going to have, and what kind of a nation we're going to be. All of us, together, as one team, one people, and one American family can do anything.

We all share the same home, the same heart, the same destiny, and the same great American flag.

Together, we are rediscovering the American way. In America, we know that faith and family—not government and bureaucracy—are the center of American life. The motto is, "In God We Trust."

And we celebrate our police, our military, and our amazing veterans as heroes who deserve our total and unwavering support.

Here tonight is Preston Sharp, a 12-year-old boy from Redding, California, who noticed that veterans' graves were not marked with flags on Veterans Day. He decided all by himself to change that, and started a movement that has now placed 40,000 flags at the graves of our great heroes. Preston, a job well done.

Young patriots, like Preston, teach all of us about our civic duty as Americans. And I met Preston a little while ago, and he is something very special—that I can tell you. Great future. Thank you very much for all you've done, Preston. Thank you very much.

Preston's reverence for those who have served our nation reminds us of why we salute our flag, why we put our hands on our hearts for the Pledge of Allegiance—and why we proudly stand for the National Anthem.

Americans love their country, and they deserve a government that shows them the same love and loyalty in return. For the last year, we have sought to restore the bonds of trust between our citizens and their government.

Working with the Senate, we are appointing judges who will interpret the Constitution as written, including a great new Supreme Court justice, and more circuit court judges than any new Administration in the history of our country.

We are totally defending our Second Amendment, and have taken historic actions to protect religious liberty.

And we are serving our brave veterans, including giving our veterans choice in their healthcare decisions. Last year, Congress also passed, and I signed, the landmark VA Accountability Act. Since its passage, my Administration has already removed more than 1,500 VA employees who failed to give our veterans the care they deserve. And we are hiring talented people who love our VETS as much as we do.

And I will not stop until our veterans are properly taken care of, which has been my promise to them from the very beginning of this great journey.

All Americans deserve accountability and respect, and that's what we are giving to our wonderful heroes, our veterans. Thank you.

So, tonight, I call on Congress to empower every Cabinet Secretary with the authority to reward good workers and to remove federal employees who undermine the public trust or fail the American people.

In our drive to make Washington accountable, we have eliminated more regulations in our first year than any Administration in the history of our country.

We have ended the war on American energy, and we have ended the war on beautiful clean coal. We are now very proudly an exporter of energy to the world.

In Detroit, I halted government mandates that crippled America's great, beautiful autoworkers so that we can get Motor City revving its engines again. And that's what's happening. Many car companies are now building and expanding plants in the United States—something we haven't seen for decades. Chrysler is moving a major plant from Mexico to Michigan. Toyota and Mazda are opening up a plant in Alabama—a big one. And we haven't seen this in a long time. It's all coming back.

Very soon, auto plants and other plants will be opening up all over our country. This is all news Americans are totally unaccustomed to hearing. For many years, companies and jobs were only leaving us, but now they are roaring back. They're coming back. They want to be where the action is. They want to be in the United States of America. That's where they want to be.

Exciting progress is happening every single day. To speed access to breakthrough cures and affordable generic drugs, last year the FDA approved more new and generic drugs and medical devices than ever before in our country's history.

We also believe that patients with terminal conditions, and terminal illness, should have access to experimental treatment immediately that could potentially save their lives. People who are terminally ill should not have to go from country to country to seek a cure. I want to give them a chance right here at home. It's time for Congress to give these wonderful, incredible Americans the right to try.

One of my greatest priorities is to reduce the price of prescription drugs. In many other countries, these drugs cost far less than what we pay in the United States. And it's very, very unfair. That is why I have directed my Administration to make fixing the injustice of high drug prices one of my top priorities for the year. And prices will come down substantially. Watch.

America has also finally turned the page on decades of unfair trade deals that sacrificed our prosperity and shipped away our companies, our jobs, and our wealth. Our nation has lost its wealth, but we're getting it back so fast. The era of economic surrender is totally over. From now on, we expect trading relationships to be fair and, very importantly, reciprocal.

We will work to fix bad trade deals and negotiate new ones. And they'll be good ones, but they'll be fair. And we will protect American workers and American intellectual property through strong enforcement of our trade rules.

As we rebuild our industries, it is also time to rebuild our crumbling infrastructure.

America is a nation of builders. We built the Empire State Building in just one year. Isn't it a disgrace that it can now take 10 years just to get a minor permit approved for the building of a simple road? I am asking both parties to come together to give us safe, fast, reliable, and modern infrastructure that our economy needs and our people deserve.

Tonight, I'm calling on Congress to produce a bill that generates at least 1.5 trillion dollars for the new infrastructure investment that our country so desperately needs. Every federal dollar should be leveraged by partnering with state and local governments and, where appropriate, tapping into private sector investment to permanently fix the infrastructure deficit. And we can do it.

Any bill must also streamline the permitting and approval process, getting it down to no more than two years, and perhaps even one. Together, we can reclaim our great building heritage.

We will build gleaming new roads, bridges, highways, railways, and waterways all across our land. And we will do it with American heart, and American hands, and American grit.

We want every American to know the dignity of a hard day's work. We want every child to be safe in their home at night. And we want every citizen to be proud of this land that we all love so much. We can lift our citizens from welfare to work, from dependence to independence, and from poverty to prosperity.

As—As tax cuts create new jobs, let's invest in workforce development and let's invest in job training, which we need so badly. Let's open great vocational schools so our future workers can learn a craft and realize their full potential. And let's support working families by supporting paid family leave.

As America regains its strength, opportunity must be extended to all citizens. That is why this year we will embark on reforming our prisons to help former inmates who have served their time get a second chance at life.

Struggling communities, especially immigrant communities, will also be helped by immigration policies that focus on the best interests of American workers and American families.

For decades, open borders have allowed drugs and gangs to pour into our most vulnerable communities. They've allowed millions of low-wage workers to compete for jobs and wages against the poorest Americans. Most tragically, they have caused the loss of many innocent lives.

Here tonight are two fathers and two mothers: Evelyn Rodriguez, Freddy Cuevas, Elizabeth Alvarado, and Robert Mickens. Their two teenage daughters—Kayla Cuevas and Nisa Mickens—were close friends on Long Island. But in September 2016, on the eve of Nisa's 16th Birthday—such a happy time it should have been— neither of them came home. These two precious girls were brutally murdered while walking together in their hometown.

Six members of the savage MS-13 gang have been charged with Kayla and Nisa's murders. Many of these gang members took advantage of glaring loopholes in our laws to enter the country as illegal, unaccompanied alien minors, and wound up in Kayla and Nisa's high school.

Evelyn, Elizabeth, Freddy, and Robert: Tonight, everyone in this chamber is praying for you. Everyone in America is grieving for you. Please stand. Thank you very much. I want you to know that 320 million hearts are right now breaking for you. We love you. Thank you.

While we cannot imagine the depths of that kind of sorrow, we can make sure that other families never have to endure this kind of pain.

Tonight, I am calling on Congress to finally close the deadly loopholes that have allowed MS-13, and other criminal gangs, to break into our country. We have proposed new legislation that will fix our immigration laws and support our ICE and Border Patrol agents—these are great people; these are great, great people—that work so hard in the midst of such danger so that this can never happen again.

The United States is a compassionate nation. We are proud that we do more than any other country anywhere in the world to help the needy, the struggling, and the underprivileged all over the world. But as President of the United States, my highest loyalty, my greatest compassion, my constant concern is for America's children, America's struggling workers, and America's forgotten communities. I want our youth to grow up to achieve great things. I want our poor to have their chance to rise.

So, tonight, I am extending an open hand to work with members of both parties, Democrats and Republicans, to protect our citizens of every background, color, religion, and creed. My duty, and the sacred duty of every elected official in this chamber, is to defend Americans, to protect their safety, their families, their communities, and their right to the American Dream. Because Americans are dreamers too.

Here tonight is one leader in the effort to defend our country, Homeland Security Investigations Special Agent Celestino Martinez. He goes by "DJ" and "CJ." He said, "Call me either one." So we'll call you "CJ." Served 15 years in the Air Force before becoming an ICE agent and spending the last 15 years fighting gang violence and getting dangerous criminals off of our streets. Tough job.

At one point, MS-13 leaders ordered CJ's murder. And they wanted it to happen quickly. But he did not cave to threats or to fear. Last May, he commanded an operation to track down gang members on Long Island. His team has arrested nearly 400, including more than 220 MS-13 gang members.

And I have to tell you, what the Border Patrol and ICE have done—we have sent thousands and thousands and thousands of MS-13 horrible people out of this country or into our prisons.

So I just want to congratulate you, CJ. You're a brave guy. Thank you very much.

And I asked CJ, "What's the secret?" He said, "We're just tougher than they are." And I like that answer. Now let's get Congress to send you—and all of the people in this great chamber have to do it; we have no choice. CJ, we're going to send you reinforcements, and we're going to send them to you quickly. It's what you need.

Over the next few weeks, the House and Senate will be voting on an immigration reform package. In recent months, my Administration has met extensively with both Democrats and Republicans to craft a bipartisan approach to immigration reform. Based on these discussions, we presented Congress with a detailed proposal that should be supported by both parties as a fair compromise, one where nobody gets everything they want, but where our country gets the critical reforms it needs and must have.

Here are the four pillars of our plan: The first pillar of our framework generously offers a path to citizenship for 1.8 million illegal immigrants who were brought here by their parents at a young age. That covers almost three times more people than the previous Administration covered. Under our plan, those who meet education and work requirements, and show good moral character, will be able to become full citizens of the United States over a 12-year period.

The second pillar fully secures the border. That means building a great wall on the southern border, and it means hiring more heroes, like CJ, to keep our communities safe. Crucially, our plan closes the terrible loopholes exploited by criminals and terrorists to enter our country, and it finally ends the horrible and dangerous practice of catch and release.

The third pillar ends the visa lottery, a program that randomly hands out green cards without any regard for skill, merit, or the safety of American people. It's time to begin moving towards a merit-based immigration system, one that admits people who are skilled, who want to work, who will contribute to our society, and who will love and respect our country.

The fourth and final pillar protects the nuclear family by ending chain migration. Under the current broken system, a single immigrant can bring in virtually unlimited numbers of distant relatives. Under our plan, we focus on the immediate family by limiting sponsorships to spouses and minor children. This vital reform is necessary, not just for our economy, but for our security and for the future of America.

In recent weeks, two terrorist attacks in New York were made possible by the visa lottery and chain migration. In the age of terrorism, these programs present risks we can just no longer afford.

It's time to reform these outdated immigration rules, and finally bring our immigration system into the 21st century.

These four pillars represent a down-the-middle compromise, and one that will create a safe, modern, and lawful immigration system.

For over 30 years, Washington has tried and failed to solve this problem. This Congress can be the one that finally makes it happen.

Most importantly, these four pillars will produce legislation that fulfills my iron-clad pledge to sign a bill that puts America first. So let's come together, set politics aside, and finally get the job done.

These reforms will also support our response to the terrible crisis of opioid and drug addiction. Never before has it been like it is now. It is terrible. We have to do something about it. In 2016, we lost 64,000 Americans to drug overdoses—174 deaths per day; 7 per hour. We must get much tougher on drug dealers and pushers if we are going to succeed in stopping this scourge.

My Administration is committed to fighting the drug epidemic and helping get treatment for those in need, for those who have been so terribly hurt. The struggle will be long and it will be difficult, but as Americans always do—in the end, we will succeed. We will prevail.

As we have seen tonight, the most difficult challenges bring out the best in America. We see a vivid expression of this truth in the story of the Holets family of New Mexico. Ryan Holets is 27 years old, an officer with the Albuquerque Police Department. He's here tonight with his wife Rebecca. Thank you, Ryan.

Last year, Ryan was on duty when he saw a pregnant, homeless woman preparing to inject heroin. When Ryan told her she was going to harm her unborn child, she began to weep. She told him she didn't know where to turn, but badly wanted a safe home for her baby.

In that moment, Ryan said he felt God speak to him: "You will do it, because you can." He heard those words. He took out a picture of his wife and their four kids. Then, he went home to tell his wife Rebecca. In an instant, she agreed to adopt. The Holets named their new daughter Hope. Ryan and Rebecca, you embody the goodness of our nation. Thank you. Thank you, Ryan and Rebecca.

As we rebuild America's strength and confidence at home, we are also restoring our strength and standing abroad.

Around the world, we face rogue regimes, terrorist groups, and rivals like China and Russia that challenge our interests, our economy, and our values. In confronting these horrible dangers, we know that weakness is the surest path to conflict, and unmatched power is the surest means to our true and great defense.

For this reason, I am asking Congress to end the dangerous defense sequester and fully fund our great military.

As part of our defense, we must modernize and rebuild our nuclear arsenal, hopefully never having to use it, but making it so strong and so powerful that it will deter any acts of aggression by any other nation or anyone else.

Perhaps someday in the future, there will be a magical moment when the countries of the world will get together to eliminate their nuclear weapons. Unfortunately, we are not there yet, sadly.

Last year, I also pledged that we would work with our allies to extinguish ISIS from the face of the Earth. One year later, I am proud to report that the coalition to defeat ISIS has liberated very close to 100 percent of the territory just recently held by these killers in Iraq and in Syria and in other locations, as well. But there is much more work to be done. We will continue our fight until ISIS is defeated.

Army Staff Sergeant Justin Peck is here tonight. Near Raqqa, last November, Justin and his comrade, Chief Petty Officer Kenton Stacy, were on a mission to clear buildings that ISIS had rigged with explosive so that civilians could return to that city hopefully soon, and hopefully safely.

Clearing the second floor of a vital hospital, Kenton Stacy was severely wounded by an explosion. Immediately, Justin bounded into the booby-trapped and unbelievably dangerous and unsafe building, and found Kenton, but in very, very bad shape. He applied pressure to the wound and inserted a tube to reopen an airway. He then performed CPR for 20 straight minutes during the ground transport, and maintained artificial respiration through two and a half hours and through emergency surgery.

Kenton Stacy would have died if it were not for Justin's selfless love for his fellow warrior. Tonight, Kenton is recovering in Texas. Raqqa is liberated. And Justin is wearing his new Bronze Star, with a "V" for "valor." Staff Sergeant Peck, all of America salutes you.

Terrorists who do things like place bombs in civilian hospitals are evil. When possible, we have no choice but to annihilate them. When necessary, we must be able to detain and question them. But we must be clear: Terrorists are not merely criminals. They are unlawful enemy combatants. And when captured overseas, they should be treated like the terrorists they are.

In the past, we have foolishly released hundreds and hundreds of dangerous terrorists, only to meet them again on the battlefield—including the ISIS leader, al-Baghdadi, who we captured, who we had, who we released.

So today, I'm keeping another promise. I just signed, prior to walking in, an order directing Secretary Mattis, who is doing a great job, thank you—to reexamine our military detention policy and to keep open the detention facilities in Guantanamo Bay.

I am asking Congress to ensure that, in the fight against ISIS and al Qaeda, we continue to have all necessary power to detain terrorists, wherever we chase them down, wherever we find them. And in many cases, for them, it will now be Guantanamo Bay.

At the same time, as of a few months ago, our warriors in Afghanistan have new rules of engagement.

Along with their heroic Afghan partners, our military is no longer undermined by artificial timelines, and we no longer tell our enemies our plans.

Last month, I also took an action endorsed unanimously by the U.S. Senate just months before. I recognized Jerusalem as the capital of Israel.

Shortly afterwards, dozens of countries voted in the United Nations General Assembly against America's sovereign right to make this decision. In 2016, American taxpayers generously sent those same countries more than $20 billion in aid.

That is why, tonight, I am asking Congress to pass legislation to help ensure American foreign-assistance dollars always serve American interests, and only go to friends of America, not enemies of America.

As we strengthen friendships all around the world, we are also restoring clarity about our adversaries.

When the people of Iran rose up against the crimes of their corrupt dictatorship, I did not stay silent. America stands with the people of Iran in their courageous struggle for freedom.

I am asking Congress to address the fundamental flaws in the terrible Iran nuclear deal.

My Administration has also imposed tough sanctions on the communist and socialist dictatorships in Cuba and Venezuela.

But no regime has oppressed its own citizens more totally or brutally than the cruel dictatorship in North Korea. North Korea's reckless pursuit of nuclear missiles could very soon threaten our homeland. We are waging a campaign of maximum pressure to prevent that from ever happening.

Past experience has taught us that complacency and concessions only invite aggression and provocation. I will not repeat the mistakes of past Administrations that got us into this very dangerous position.

We need only look at the depraved character of the North Korean regime to understand the nature of the nuclear threat it could pose to America and to our allies.

Otto Warmbier was a hardworking student at the University of Virginia—and a great student he was. On his way to study abroad in Asia, Otto joined a tour to North Korea. At its conclusion, this wonderful young man was arrested and charged with crimes against the state. After a shameful trial, the dictatorship sentenced Otto to 15 years of hard labor, before returning him to America last June, horribly injured and on the verge of death. He passed away just days after his return.

Otto's wonderful parents, Fred and Cindy Warmbier, are here with us tonight, along with Otto's brother and sister, Austin and Greta. Please. Incredible people. You are powerful witnesses to a menace that threatens our world, and your strength truly inspires us all. Thank you very much. Thank you.

Tonight, we pledge to honor Otto's memory with total American resolve. Thank you.

Finally, we are joined by one more witness to the ominous nature of this regime. His name is Mr. Ji Seong-ho.

In 1996, Seong-ho was a starving boy in North Korea. One day, he tried to steal coal from a railroad car to barter for a few scraps of food, which were very hard to get. In the process, he passed out on the train tracks, exhausted from hunger. He woke up as a train ran over his limbs. He then endured multiple amputations without anything to dull the pain or the hurt. His brother and sister gave what little food they had to help him recover and ate dirt themselves, permanently stunting their own growth.

Later, he was tortured by North Korean authorities after returning from a brief visit to China. His tormentors wanted to know if he'd met any Christians. He had—and he resolved, after that, to be free.

Seong-ho traveled thousands of miles on crutches all across China and Southeast Asia to freedom. Most of his family followed. His father was caught trying to escape and was tortured to death.

Today he lives in Seoul, where he rescues other defectors, and broadcasts into North Korea what the regime fears most: the truth.

Today, he has a new leg. But, Seong-ho, I understand you still keep those old crutches as a reminder of how far you've come. Your great sacrifice is an inspiration to us all. Please. Thank you. Seong-ho's story is a testament to the yearning of every human soul to live in freedom.

It was that same yearning for freedom that nearly 250 years ago gave birth to a special place called America. It was a small cluster of colonies caught between a great ocean and a vast wilderness. It was home to an incredible people with a revolutionary idea: that they could rule themselves; that they could chart their own destiny; and that, together, they could light up the entire world.

That is what our country has always been about. That is what Americans have always stood for, always strived for, and always done.

Atop the dome of this Capitol stands the Statue of Freedom. She stands tall and dignified among the monuments to our ancestors who fought, and lived, and died to protect her. Monuments to Washington, and Jefferson, and Lincoln, and King. Memorials to the heroes of Yorktown and Saratoga; to young Americans who shed their blood on the shores of Normandy and the fields beyond; and others, who went down in the waters of the Pacific and the skies all over Asia.

And freedom stands tall over one more monument: this one. This Capitol—this living monument—this is the moment to the American people.

**Audience: USA! USA! USA!**

**President Trump:** We're a people whose heroes live not only in the past, but all around us, defending hope, pride, and defending the American way.

They work in every trade. They sacrifice to raise a family. They care for our children at home. They defend our flag abroad. And they are strong moms and brave kids. They are firefighters, and police officers, and border agents, medics, and

Marines. But above all else, they are Americans. And this Capitol, this city, this nation, belongs entirely to them.

Our task is to respect them, to listen to them, to serve them, to protect them, and to always be worthy of them.

Americans fill the world with art and music. They push the bounds of science and discovery. And they forever remind us of what we should never, ever forget: The people dreamed this country. The people built this country. And it's the people who are making America great again.

As long as we are proud of who we are and what we are fighting for, there is nothing we cannot achieve. As long as we have confidence in our values, faith in our citizens, and trust in our God, we will never fail.

Our families will thrive. Our people will prosper. And our nation will forever be safe and strong and proud and mighty and free.

Thank you. And God bless America. Goodnight.


## Print Citations

**CMS:** Trump, Donald. "State of the Union Speech." Speech presented at the US Capitol, Washington, DC, January 30, 2018. In *The Reference Shelf: Representative American Speeches 2017-2018*, edited by Micah L. Issit, 47-58. Ipswich, MA: H.W. Wilson, 2018.

**MLA:** Trump, Donald. "State of the Union Speech." US Capitol, 30 January 2018, Washington, DC. Presentation. *The Reference Shelf: Representative American Speeches 2017-2018,* edited by Micah L. Issit, H.W. Wilson, 2018, pp. 47-58.

**APA:** Trump, D. (2018, January 30). State of the Union speech. US Capitol, Washington, DC. In M.L. Issit (Ed.), *The reference shelf: Representative American speeches 2017-2018* (pp. 47-58). Ipswich, MA: H.W. Wilson. (Original work published 2018)

# Remarks to the United Nations General Assembly

## By Donald Trump

*President Donald Trump is the 45th president of the United States and a business and television personality known for his management of the Trump family real estate business and for his role in the popular television series* The Apprentice. *In this speech from the 2018 meeting of the United Nations, Trump discusses the "America First" strategy and the benefits of political isolationism.*

Madam President, Mr. Secretary-General, world leaders, ambassadors, and distinguished delegates:

One year ago, I stood before you for the first time in this grand hall. I addressed the threats facing our world, and I presented a vision to achieve a brighter future for all of humanity.

Today, I stand before the United Nations General Assembly to share the extraordinary progress we've made.

In less than two years, my administration has accomplished more than almost any administration in the history of our country.

America's—so true. [Laughter] Didn't expect that reaction, but that's okay. [Laughter and applause.]

America's economy is booming like never before. Since my election, we've added $10 trillion in wealth. The stock market is at an all-time high in history, and jobless claims are at a 50-year low. African American, Hispanic American, and Asian American unemployment have all achieved their lowest levels ever recorded. We've added more than 4 million new jobs, including half a million manufacturing jobs.

We have passed the biggest tax cuts and reforms in American history. We've started the construction of a major border wall, and we have greatly strengthened border security.

We have secured record funding for our military—700 billion this year, and $716 billion next year. Our military will soon be more powerful than it has ever been before.

In other words, the United States is stronger, safer, and a richer country than it was when I assumed office less than two years ago.

We are standing up for America and for the American people. And we are also standing up for the world.

---

Delivered on September 25, 2018, at the United Nations, New York, NY.

This is great news for our citizens and for peace-loving people everywhere. We believe that when nations respect the rights of their neighbors, and defend the interests of their people, they can better work together to secure the blessings of safety, prosperity, and peace.

Each of us here today is the emissary of a distinct culture, a rich history, and a people bound together by ties of memory, tradition, and the values that make our homelands like nowhere else on Earth.

That is why America will always choose independence and cooperation over global governance, control, and domination.

I honor the right of every nation in this room to pursue its own customs, beliefs, and traditions. The United States will not tell you how to live or work or worship. We only ask that you honor our sovereignty in return.

From Warsaw to Brussels, to Tokyo to Singapore, it has been my highest honor to represent the United States abroad. I have forged close relationships and friendships and strong partnerships with the leaders of many nations in this room, and our approach has already yielded incredible change.

With support from many countries here today, we have engaged with North Korea to replace the specter of conflict with a bold and new push for peace.

In June, I traveled to Singapore to meet face to face with North Korea's leader, Chairman Kim Jong Un. We had highly productive conversations and meetings, and we agreed that it was in both countries' interest to pursue the denuclearization of the Korean Peninsula. Since that meeting, we have already seen a number of encouraging measures that few could have imagined only a short time ago.

The missiles and rockets are no longer flying in every direction. Nuclear testing has stopped. Some military facilities are already being dismantled. Our hostages have been released. And as promised, the remains of our fallen heroes are being returned home to lay at rest in American soil.

I would like to thank Chairman Kim for his courage and for the steps he has taken, though much work remains to be done. The sanctions will stay in place until denuclearization occurs.

I also want to thank the many member states who helped us reach this moment—a moment that is actually far greater than people would understand; far greater—but for also their support and the critical support that we will all need going forward.

A special thanks to President Moon of South Korea, Prime Minister Abe of Japan, and President Xi of China.

In the Middle East, our new approach is also yielding great strides and very historic change.

Following my trip to Saudi Arabia last year, the Gulf countries opened a new center to target terrorist financing. They are enforcing new sanctions, working with us to identify and track terrorist networks, and taking more responsibility for fighting terrorism and extremism in their own region.

The UAE, Saudi Arabia, and Qatar have pledged billions of dollars to aid the people of Syria and Yemen. And they are pursuing multiple avenues to ending Yemen's horrible, horrific civil war.

Ultimately, it is up to the nations of the region to decide what kind of future they want for themselves and their children.

For that reason, the United States is working with the Gulf Cooperation Council, Jordan, and Egypt to establish a regional strategic alliance so that Middle Eastern nations can advance prosperity, stability, and security across their home region.

Thanks to the United States military and our partnership with many of your nations, I am pleased to report that the bloodthirsty killers known as ISIS have been driven out from the territory they once held in Iraq and Syria. We will continue to work with friends and allies to deny radical Islamic terrorists any funding, territory or support, or any means of infiltrating our borders.

The ongoing tragedy in Syria is heartbreaking. Our shared goals must be the de-escalation of military conflict, along with a political solution that honors the will of the Syrian people. In this vein, we urge the United Nations-led peace process be reinvigorated. But, rest assured, the United States will respond if chemical weapons are deployed by the Assad regime.

I commend the people of Jordan and other neighboring countries for hosting refugees from this very brutal civil war.

As we see in Jordan, the most compassionate policy is to place refugees as close to their homes as possible to ease their eventual return to be part of the rebuilding process. This approach also stretches finite resources to help far more people, increasing the impact of every dollar spent.

Every solution to the humanitarian crisis in Syria must also include a strategy to address the brutal regime that has fueled and financed it: the corrupt dictatorship in Iran.

Iran's leaders sow chaos, death, and destruction. They do not respect their neighbors or borders, or the sovereign rights of nations. Instead, Iran's leaders plunder the nation's resources to enrich themselves and to spread mayhem across the Middle East and far beyond.

The Iranian people are rightly outraged that their leaders have embezzled billions of dollars from Iran's treasury, seized valuable portions of the economy, and looted the people's religious endowments, all to line their own pockets and send their proxies to wage war. Not good.

Iran's neighbors have paid a heavy toll for the region's [regime's] agenda of aggression and expansion. That is why so many countries in the Middle East strongly supported my decision to withdraw the United States from the horrible 2015 Iran Nuclear Deal and re-impose nuclear sanctions.

The Iran deal was a windfall for Iran's leaders. In the years since the deal was reached, Iran's military budget grew nearly 40 percent. The dictatorship used the funds to build nuclear-capable missiles, increase internal repression, finance terrorism, and fund havoc and slaughter in Syria and Yemen.

The United States has launched a campaign of economic pressure to deny the regime the funds it needs to advance its bloody agenda. Last month, we began re-imposing hard-hitting nuclear sanctions that had been lifted under the Iran deal. Additional sanctions will resume November 5th, and more will follow. And we're working with countries that import Iranian crude oil to cut their purchases substantially.

We cannot allow the world's leading sponsor of terrorism to possess the planet's most dangerous weapons. We cannot allow a regime that chants "Death to America," and that threatens Israel with annihilation, to possess the means to deliver a nuclear warhead to any city on Earth. Just can't do it.

We ask all nations to isolate Iran's regime as long as its aggression continues. And we ask all nations to support Iran's people as they struggle to reclaim their religious and righteous destiny.

This year, we also took another significant step forward in the Middle East. In recognition of every sovereign state to determine its own capital, I moved the U.S. Embassy in Israel to Jerusalem.

The United States is committed to a future of peace and stability in the region, including peace between the Israelis and the Palestinians. That aim is advanced, not harmed, by acknowledging the obvious facts.

America's policy of principled realism means we will not be held hostage to old dogmas, discredited ideologies, and so-called experts who have been proven wrong over the years, time and time again. This is true not only in matters of peace, but in matters of prosperity.

We believe that trade must be fair and reciprocal. The United States will not be taken advantage of any longer.

For decades, the United States opened its economy—the largest, by far, on Earth—with few conditions. We allowed foreign goods from all over the world to flow freely across our borders.

Yet, other countries did not grant us fair and reciprocal access to their markets in return. Even worse, some countries abused their openness to dump their products, subsidize their goods, target our industries, and manipulate their currencies to gain unfair advantage over our country. As a result, our trade deficit ballooned to nearly $800 billion a year.

For this reason, we are systematically renegotiating broken and bad trade deals.

Last month, we announced a groundbreaking U.S.-Mexico trade agreement. And just yesterday, I stood with President Moon to announce the successful completion of the brand new U.S.-Korea trade deal. And this is just the beginning.

Many nations in this hall will agree that the world trading system is in dire need of change. For example, countries were admitted to the World Trade Organization that violate every single principle on which the organization is based. While the United States and many other nations play by the rules, these countries use government-run industrial planning and state-owned enterprises to rig the system in their favor. They engage in relentless product dumping, forced technology transfer, and the theft of intellectual property.

The United States lost over 3 million manufacturing jobs, nearly a quarter of all steel jobs, and 60,000 factories after China joined the WTO. And we have racked up $13 trillion in trade deficits over the last two decades.

But those days are over. We will no longer tolerate such abuse. We will not allow our workers to be victimized, our companies to be cheated, and our wealth to be plundered and transferred. America will never apologize for protecting its citizens.

The United States has just announced tariffs on another $200 billion in Chinese-made goods for a total, so far, of $250 billion. I have great respect and affection for my friend, President Xi, but I have made clear our trade imbalance is just not acceptable. China's market distortions and the way they deal cannot be tolerated.

As my administration has demonstrated, America will always act in our national interest.

I spoke before this body last year and warned that the U.N. Human Rights Council had become a grave embarrassment to this institution, shielding egregious human rights abusers while bashing America and its many friends.

Our Ambassador to the United Nations, Nikki Haley, laid out a clear agenda for reform, but despite reported and repeated warnings, no action at all was taken. So the United States took the only responsible course: We withdrew from the Human Rights Council, and we will not return until real reform is enacted.

For similar reasons, the United States will provide no support in recognition to the International Criminal Court. As far as America is concerned, the ICC has no jurisdiction, no legitimacy, and no authority. The ICC claims near-universal jurisdiction over the citizens of every country, violating all principles of justice, fairness, and due process. We will never surrender America's sovereignty to an unelected, unaccountable, global bureaucracy.

America is governed by Americans. We reject the ideology of globalism, and we embrace the doctrine of patriotism.

Around the world, responsible nations must defend against threats to sovereignty not just from global governance, but also from other, new forms of coercion and domination.

In America, we believe strongly in energy security for ourselves and for our allies. We have become the largest energy producer anywhere on the face of the Earth. The United States stands ready to export our abundant, affordable supply of oil, clean coal, and natural gas.

OPEC and OPEC nations, are, as usual, ripping off the rest of the world, and I don't like it. Nobody should like it. We defend many of these nations for nothing, and then they take advantage of us by giving us high oil prices. Not good.

We want them to stop raising prices, we want them to start lowering prices, and they must contribute substantially to military protection from now on. We are not going to put up with it—these horrible prices—much longer.

Reliance on a single foreign supplier can leave a nation vulnerable to extortion and intimidation. That is why we congratulate European states, such as Poland, for leading the construction of a Baltic pipeline so that nations are not dependent on

Russia to meet their energy needs. Germany will become totally dependent on Russian energy if it does not immediately change course.

Here in the Western Hemisphere, we are committed to maintaining our independence from the encroachment of expansionist foreign powers.

It has been the formal policy of our country since President Monroe that we reject the interference of foreign nations in this hemisphere and in our own affairs. The United States has recently strengthened our laws to better screen foreign investments in our country for national security threats, and we welcome cooperation with countries in this region and around the world that wish to do the same. You need to do it for your own protection.

The United States is also working with partners in Latin America to confront threats to sovereignty from uncontrolled migration. Tolerance for human struggling and human smuggling and trafficking is not humane. It's a horrible thing that's going on, at levels that nobody has ever seen before. It's very, very cruel.

Illegal immigration funds criminal networks, ruthless gangs, and the flow of deadly drugs. Illegal immigration exploits vulnerable populations, hurts hardworking citizens, and has produced a vicious cycle of crime, violence, and poverty. Only by upholding national borders, destroying criminal gangs, can we break this cycle and establish a real foundation for prosperity.

We recognize the right of every nation in this room to set its own immigration policy in accordance with its national interests, just as we ask other countries to respect our own right to do the same—which we are doing. That is one reason the United States will not participate in the new Global Compact on Migration. Migration should not be governed by an international body unaccountable to our own citizens.

Ultimately, the only long-term solution to the migration crisis is to help people build more hopeful futures in their home countries. Make their countries great again.

Currently, we are witnessing a human tragedy, as an example, in Venezuela. More than 2 million people have fled the anguish inflicted by the socialist Maduro regime and its Cuban sponsors.

Not long ago, Venezuela was one of the richest countries on Earth. Today, socialism has bankrupted the oil-rich nation and driven its people into abject poverty.

Virtually everywhere socialism or communism has been tried, it has produced suffering, corruption, and decay. Socialism's thirst for power leads to expansion, incursion, and oppression. All nations of the world should resist socialism and the misery that it brings to everyone.

In that spirit, we ask the nations gathered here to join us in calling for the restoration of democracy in Venezuela. Today, we are announcing additional sanctions against the repressive regime, targeting Maduro's inner circle and close advisors.

We are grateful for all the work the United Nations does around the world to help people build better lives for themselves and their families.

The United States is the world's largest giver in the world, by far, of foreign aid. But few give anything to us. That is why we are taking a hard look at U.S. foreign assistance. That will be headed up by Secretary of State Mike Pompeo. We will examine what is working, what is not working, and whether the countries who receive our dollars and our protection also have our interests at heart.

Moving forward, we are only going to give foreign aid to those who respect us and, frankly, are our friends. And we expect other countries to pay their fair share for the cost of their defense.

The United States is committed to making the United Nations more effective and accountable. I have said many times that the United Nations has unlimited potential. As part of our reform effort, I have told our negotiators that the United States will not pay more than 25 percent of the U.N. peacekeeping budget. This will encourage other countries to step up, get involved, and also share in this very large burden.

And we are working to shift more of our funding from assessed contributions to voluntary so that we can target American resources to the programs with the best record of success.

Only when each of us does our part and contributes our share can we realize the U.N.'s highest aspirations. We must pursue peace without fear, hope without despair, and security without apology.

Looking around this hall where so much history has transpired, we think of the many before us who have come here to address the challenges of their nations and of their times. And our thoughts turn to the same question that ran through all their speeches and resolutions, through every word and every hope. It is the question of what kind of world will we leave for our children and what kind of nations they will inherit.

The dreams that fill this hall today are as diverse as the people who have stood at this podium, and as varied as the countries represented right here in this body are. It really is something. It really is great, great history.

There is India, a free society over a billion people, successfully lifting countless millions out of poverty and into the middle class.

There is Saudi Arabia, where King Salman and the Crown Prince are pursuing bold new reforms.

There is Israel, proudly celebrating its 70th anniversary as a thriving democracy in the Holy Land.

In Poland, a great people are standing up for their independence, their security, and their sovereignty.

Many countries are pursuing their own unique visions, building their own hopeful futures, and chasing their own wonderful dreams of destiny, of legacy, and of a home.

The whole world is richer, humanity is better, because of this beautiful constellation of nations, each very special, each very unique, and each shining brightly in its part of the world.

In each one, we see awesome promise of a people bound together by a shared past and working toward a common future.

As for Americans, we know what kind of future we want for ourselves. We know what kind of a nation America must always be.

In America, we believe in the majesty of freedom and the dignity of the individual. We believe in self-government and the rule of law. And we prize the culture that sustains our liberty—a culture built on strong families, deep faith, and fierce independence. We celebrate our heroes, we treasure our traditions, and above all, we love our country.

Inside everyone in this great chamber today, and everyone listening all around the globe, there is the heart of a patriot that feels the same powerful love for your nation, the same intense loyalty to your homeland.

The passion that burns in the hearts of patriots and the souls of nations has inspired reform and revolution, sacrifice and selflessness, scientific breakthroughs, and magnificent works of art.

Our task is not to erase it, but to embrace it. To build with it. To draw on its ancient wisdom. And to find within it the will to make our nations greater, our regions safer, and the world better.

To unleash this incredible potential in our people, we must defend the foundations that make it all possible. Sovereign and independent nations are the only vehicle where freedom has ever survived, democracy has ever endured, or peace has ever prospered. And so we must protect our sovereignty and our cherished independence above all.

When we do, we will find new avenues for cooperation unfolding before us. We will find new passion for peacemaking rising within us. We will find new purpose, new resolve, and new spirit flourishing all around us, and making this a more beautiful world in which to live.

So together, let us choose a future of patriotism, prosperity, and pride. Let us choose peace and freedom over domination and defeat. And let us come here to this place to stand for our people and their nations, forever strong, forever sovereign, forever just, and forever thankful for the grace and the goodness and the glory of God.

Thank you. God bless you. And God bless the nations of the world.

Thank you very much. Thank you.

## Print Citations

**CMS:** Trump, Donald. "Speech to the United Nations General Assembly." Speech presented at the United Nations, New York, NY, September 25, 2018. In *The Reference Shelf: Representative American Speeches 2017-2018*, edited by Micah L. Issit, 59-67. Ipswich, MA: H.W. Wilson, 2018.

**MLA:** Trump, Donald. "Speech to the United Nations General Assembly." United Nations, 25 September 2018, New York, NY. Presentation. *The Reference Shelf: Representative American Speeches 2017-2018,* edited by Micah L. Issit, H.W. Wilson, 2018, pp. 59-67.

**APA:** Trump, D. (2018, September 25). Speech to the United Nations General Assembly. United Nations, New York, NY. In M.L. Issit (Ed.), *The reference shelf: Representative American speeches 2017-2018* (pp. 59-67). Ipswich, MA: H.W. Wilson. (Original work published 2018)

# Immigration Enforcement Actions of the Trump Administration

## By Jeff Sessions

*Jeff Sessions, attorney general under President Donald Trump, is a former senator for the State of Alabama and a former lawyer. Prior to becoming attorney general, Sessions served under the Reagan administration as US attorney for the Southern District of Alabama and then as Alabama attorney general. In this speech delivered in May of 2018 to members of the justice department, Sessions discusses controversial Trump administration policies that resulted in the separation of illegal immigrant families and the detention of immigrant children in government facilities.*

Thank you all for being here.

Thank you to Tom Homan. Tom, you have done outstanding work leading ICE. Thank you for your more than 30 years of service in law enforcement. We are going to miss you.

Today we are here to send a message to the world: we are not going to let this country be overwhelmed.

People are not going to caravan or otherwise stampede our border.

We need legality and integrity in the system.

That's why the Department of Homeland Security is now referring 100 percent of illegal Southwest Border crossings to the Department of Justice for prosecution. And the Department of Justice will take up those cases.

I have put in place a "zero tolerance" policy for illegal entry on our Southwest border. If you cross this border unlawfully, then we will prosecute you. It's that simple.

If you smuggle illegal aliens across our border, then we will prosecute you.

If you are smuggling a child, then we will prosecute you and that child will be separated from you as required by law.

If you make false statements to an immigration officer or file a fraudulent asylum claim, that's a felony.

If you help others to do so, that's a felony, too. You're going to jail.

So if you're going to come to this country, come here legally. Don't come here illegally.

In order to carry out these important new enforcement policies, I have sent 35 prosecutors to the Southwest and moved 18 immigration judges to the border.

Delivered on May 7, 2018, at Border Field State Park, San Diego, CA.

These are supervisory judges that don't have existing caseloads and will be able to function full time on moving these cases. That will be about a 50 percent increase in the number of immigration judges who will be handling the asylum claims.

These actions are necessary. And they are made even more necessary by the massive increases in illegal crossings in recent months. This February saw 55 percent more border apprehensions than last February. This March saw triple the number from last March. April saw triple the number last April.

The trends are clear: this must end.

Eleven million people are already here illegally. That's more than the population of Portugal or the state of Georgia.

The Congressional Budget Office estimates that those 11 million have 4.5 million children who are American citizens. Combined, that group would be our fifth-most populous state.

This situation has been many years in the making.

For decades, the American people have been pleading with our elected representatives for a lawful system of immigration that serves the national interest—a system we can be proud of.

That is not too much to ask. The American people are right and just and decent to ask for this. They are right to want a safe, secure border and a government that knows who is here and who isn't.

Donald Trump ran for office on that idea. I believe that is a big reason why he won. He is on fire about this. This entire government knows it.

The American people have a right to expect that the laws that their representatives voted for are going to be carried out. Failure to enforce our duly-enacted laws would be an affront to the American people and a threat to our very system of self-government.

And these laws are the most generous immigration laws in the world. We accept 1.1 million lawful permanent residents every year—that's more than the population of Montana, every single year. These are the highest numbers in the world.

I have no doubt that many of those crossing our border illegally are leaving difficult situations. But we cannot take everyone on Earth who is in a difficult situation.

According to a Gallup poll from a few years ago, 150 million people around the world want to immigrate to the United States. Gallup says that 37 percent of Liberians want to immigrate to the United States. One fifth of Cambodians want to move here. One-in-six Salvadorans are already in the United States—and another 19 percent tell Gallup they want to come here.

It's obvious that we cannot take everyone who wants to come here without also hurting the interests of the citizens we are sworn to serve and protect.

We have to have limits. And Congress has already set them.

And if you want to change our laws, then pass a bill in Congress. Persuade your fellow citizens to your point of view.

Immigrants should ask to apply lawfully before they enter our country. Citizens of other countries don't get to violate our laws or rewrite them for us. People around the world have no right to demand entry in violation of our sovereignty.

This is a great nation—the greatest in the history of the world. It is no surprise that people want to come here. But they must do so properly. They must follow our laws—or not come here at all. Make no mistake, the objections, the lawsuits, the sanctuary jurisdictions are often the product of a radical open border philosophy. They oppose all enforcement.

And so this Department, under President Trump's leadership, is enforcing the law without exception. We will finally secure this border so that we can give the American people safety and peace of mind. That's what the people deserve.

Thank you.

## Print Citations

**CMS:** Sessions, Jeff. "Immigration Enforcement Actions of the Trump Administration." Speech presented at the Border Field State Park, San Diego, CA, May 7, 2018. In *The Reference Shelf: Representative American Speeches 2017-2018*, edited by Micah L. Issit, 68-70. Ipswich, MA: H.W. Wilson, 2018.

**MLA:** Sessions, Jeff. "Immigration Enforcement Actions of the Trump Administration." Border Field State Park, 7 May 2018, San Diego, CA. Presentation. *The Reference Shelf: Representative American Speeches 2017-2018*, edited by Micah L. Issit, H.W. Wilson, 2018, pp. 68-70.

**APA:** Sessions, J. (2018, May 7). Immigration enforcement actions of the Trump administration. Border Field State Park, San Diego, CA. In M.L. Issit (Ed.), *The reference shelf: Representative American speeches 2017-2018* (pp. 68-70). Ipswich, MA: H.W. Wilson. (Original work published 2018)

# Midterm Campaign Speech

## By Donald Trump

*President Donald Trump is the 45th president of the United States and a businessman and television personality known for his leadership of the Trump family real estate business and for his role in the popular reality television series* The Apprentice. *In this speech, Donald Trump discusses the progress of his administration's first two years and the priorities for the remainder of his presidency.*

**TRUMP:** Thank you very much. Wow. Wow.

(APPLAUSE)

That is so beautiful. Thank you. What a great song, too, by the way.

**TRUMP:** Do we like that song? I think so. I think so.

(APPLAUSE)

I'd like to use it all the time, but it only seems to work well in West Virginia, right?

(APPLAUSE)

I am thrilled to be back with all of my friends in the great state of West Virginia. Thank you.

(APPLAUSE)

This is a big victory. We won by 42 points. That's pretty big, right? Forty-two points.

(APPLAUSE)

Over a Democrat, right? Over a Democrat. They didn't do too well. And the people of West Virginia, they're loyal, they're hard-working, and they're true American patriots, remember that.

(APPLAUSE)

They are great. They are great people. And my friends—thank you very much, I love you, too. It is a guy. It's a guy, but I love you, too.

You're proud of our country, you're proud of our history, and unlike the NFL, you always honor and cherish our great American flag.

(APPLAUSE)

It was just announced by ESPN that rather than defending our anthem, our beautiful, beautiful national anthem, and defending our flag, they've decided they just won't broadcast when they play the National Anthem.

(BOOS)

Delivered on August 21, 2018, at the Charleston Civic Center, Charleston, WV.

And we don't like that. So while the players are kneeling—some of them, not all of them at all—you're all proudly standing for our national anthem. Thank you.

(APPLAUSE)

The ESPN thing was terrible. It just came out. Under our administration, America is winning again, and America is being respected again. All over the world, it's America first.

(APPLAUSE)

This is the greatest economy that we've had in our history, the best.

Our steel mills are back. They're roaring back. We're making steel again. United States steel announced a massive infusion of cash. They're opening of seven different plants. Other steel companies all over the country, they're opening up plants.

People said steel will never be back. Steel is back. It's one of the hottest industries in our country, because of what we've done with our tariffs. They were dumping steel all over our country. They were destroying our business. They're not dumping so much anymore. And if they do, they're paying a lot.

(APPLAUSE)

Our military will soon be stronger than it's ever been before.

(APPLAUSE)

We're taking care of our amazing veterans. And I know this doesn't matter to you, but we are putting our great coal miners back to work.

(APPLAUSE)

**AUDIENCE:** Trump! Trump! Trump!

**TRUMP:** Great people. Great people. Brave people. I don't know how the hell you do that. You guys have a lot of courage.

But we love clean, beautiful West Virginia coal. We love it. It's great.

(APPLAUSE)

And you know, that's indestructible stuff. In times of war, in times of conflict, you can blow up those windmills, they fall down real quick.

(LAUGHTER)

You can blow up those pipelines. They go like this, and you're not going to fix them too fast. You could do a lot of things to those solar panels, but you know what you can't hurt? Coal. You can do whatever you want to coal.

(APPLAUSE)

Very important. And we're working now on a military plan that's going to be something very special. So I'm honored tonight to have a friend of mine—he was a Democrat, and I don't want to say because of me, let's say it's because of policy, he decided to become a Republican. And he's a great Republican.

(APPLAUSE)

And I want to bring him up if I could. Can I bring up your governor? He is the largest, most beautiful man, Governor Big Jim Justice.

(APPLAUSE)

JUSTICE

OK, I deputized you, did I not?

(APPLAUSE)

The other thing I know, you as West Virginians are appreciative people. Now just think, we know—we know what this great man right beside me has done for us.

(APPLAUSE)

Now, let me say this: it's time for us to show that appreciation and deliver back. We have to reelect our House members, and we can not, whatever we do, to God above, we can not put Ojeda on this man.

(APPLAUSE)

But it goes further than that—than that. Patrick Morrisey's a little behind right now. He needs you. He needs all of you. He needs you to go out and be warriors and deputies for him. He can win this, and this man needs him. So I would say God bless this great man, God bless this great country, and thank you for having me.

(APPLAUSE)

**TRUMP:** He's a big man. He's all man. Six-foot 11—I won't talk about the weight. I don't know.

(LAUGHTER)

I don't know what the weight is. I won't go there. But he is a big man, and he's a great man. He's a wonderful friend of mine, and it's really what he just said about the man that you want to be your next senator. That's really nice. Thank you very much, Jim.

(APPLAUSE)

Also, we have your senator, who is a special friend of mine. Been so helpful to me and so helpful to you, she loves your state. Shelley Moore Capito.

(APPLAUSE)

Congressman David McKinley, Alex Mooney, and Evan Jenkins—and Evan, you put up one hell of a fight, thank you, Evan. Boy, you were something. And your state GOP Chairwoman, Melody Potter. Melody.

(APPLAUSE)

Thank you, Melody.

**TRUMP:** Also with us is a tremendous senator, somebody that's helped us do our agenda, which is make America great again, pretty much.

(APPLAUSE)

And we have a lot of different names (ph). Did you see "promises made, promises kept"? They—they're copying it now, the Democrats. They're copying it now. Promises made, promises kept, they're copying it. But what are you going to do. But this is a man that really—he makes a promise, and it's 100 percent good. He's tremendous and done so much.

He's from a place called Colorado, and he's helping to lead our campaign to elect more Senate republicans, like the man we're going to elect in West Virginia, Corey Gardner. Thank you, Corey. Thank you, Corey. Great job. You're doing a great job. Thank you.

(APPLAUSE)

And we're thrilled to be joined by the next House members from West Virginia's third congressional district, a woman that works very hard for you, Carol Miller. Carol.

(APPLAUSE)

Thanks, Carol.

Finally, it's my great honor to introduce the person that we are here to support tonight, a tremendous gentleman. I got to know him during the campaign. He has got an energy. It took me a little while to figure it out. I have to be honest.

And once I got to see what was happening, and Evan would be the first to tell you, too, he was so tough, he was so smart. He didn't stop. He does not stop, and he's going to fight for you like nobody's ever fought for the people of West Virginia.

(APPLAUSE)

Your next senator, Patrick Morrisey. Patrick, come up here. Come up here, Patrick. Come up here, Patrick.

**MORRISEY:** Joe does have to go.

(APPLAUSE)

Let me just be clear. Hey, guys. I want to start out by thanking the president for coming back to wild and wonderful West Virginia for the sixth time.

(APPLAUSE)

**TRUMP:** Thank you.

**MORRISEY:** Hey, how about this guy. West Virginia's never seen anything like this. We love you, Mr. President.

(APPLAUSE)

And I'll tell you this. We know that President Trump is making America great again, but even more importantly, President Trump is making West Virginia great again.

Look, tonight, we're joined by some of the Mountain State's finest coal miners. Can you stand up? A round of applause for our hardworking coal miners.

(APPLAUSE)

Donald Trump and I are fighting everyday for our coal miners and the hardworking men and women of our state. He's trying to get the man off your back, and I'm working everyday to help him do it. Amen.

(APPLAUSE)

But I'll tell you what. One of the best ways I can help President Trump is to have you to send me to the U.S. Senate, where I'll be a big ally of this president.

(APPLAUSE)

West Virginia needs to send a conservative fighter to the U.S. Senate to drain that swamp.

(CHANTING)

**MORRISEY:** That's pretty good.

(CHANTING)

**MORRISEY:** Now let me tell you a little bit. I have an opponent in this race. His name is dishonest liberal Joe Manchin.

(BOOING)

And let me be clear, liberal Joe is no supporter of this president. Manchin strongly supported and voted for Hillary Clinton after—ready—all right, hang on, hang on, after she said, we're going to put a lot of coal miners in coal companies out of work.

(BOOING)

Yes, that's pretty bad. Manchin even called Hillary warm, compassionate, engaging, tough. Can you actually believe that?

Let—Joe's got to go. Joe has to go.

CROWD

Lock her up. Lock her up.

**MORRISEY:** Liberal Joe no longer has West Virginia values. Let's go through the record. Manchin was for Obama. Manchin was Hillary. Manchin is for radical gun control, Planned Parenthood. He shills for EpiPen and he opposed the Trump tax cuts. Let me be clear ...

(BOOING)

... Pretty bad, right? Remember, this is West Virginia, we benefit as much or more than anyone from the Trump tax cuts.

(APPLAUSE)

Joe Manchin no longer has West Virginia values, period. When I get to the U.S. Senate, I'm going to be a strong ally of President Trump.

I'm going to be the conservative fighter that you can rely on. We're going to stand up for coal and our energy resources. And we're going to tackle this opiate epidemic more aggressively than anyone.

(APPLAUSE)

It's my honor to be here tonight and be on the same stage with the president. Mr. President, thank you for your leadership, your work and for standing up for West Virginia.

(APPLAUSE)

Amen.

(APPLAUSE)

Together, we're all going to help this guy make sure, not only that we make West Virginia great again, we continue to make West Virginia great again. Best way to do that, liberal Joe's got to go.

(APPLAUSE)

Guys (ph), Joe's got to go. And now, I will turn this back over to the big man who you're here to see. Amen, brother.

(APPLAUSE)

**TRUMP:** (OFF-MIC) Thank you. He's got energy. He's got a lot of talent. And he loves his place, he loves the people and he's going to be fighting for you; he doesn't sleep. He's out campaigning.

I said how many days are you campaigning? Because I said the last 60 days of my campaign, every single day, we'd go out every single day as many stops as you could make humanly. Humanly, you can't get tired. He's got that same thing. He's every single day.

And he's got a very special spark. You see it and you know him. Look, you know him. He's done a hell of a job as your A.G. and you've got to get him with us.

(APPLAUSE)

You've got to get him with us. He's going to bring it back home for the people of West Virginia. So this November, voters in West Virginia will face a very simple choice. A vote for Patrick Morrisey is truly a vote to make America great again. He's going to vote.

(APPLAUSE)

And I like Joe, but Joe doesn't vote. He just doesn't vote for us. It's a vote for Schumer, Nancy Pelosi, their new leader Maxine Waters.

(BOOING)

But between Waters and Pelosi, you have two people that are in charge of Congress. They're not in favor of West Virginia. They don't know that West Virginia exists. They don't like coal. They don't like energy.

**UNKNOWN:** And we don't like them!

**TRUMP:** And they don't like her. So, when you cast your ballot for Congress in November, you aren't just voting for a candidate. You're voting for which party controls the House and which party controls the Senate, so all these Congress people. And I'll tell you, we have to get there; we really have to get there.

So I'm going to be going now, as many days as I can and I'm allowed to. You know, I have sort of a little—with all the Secret Service and all their fantastic people, but it sort of holds you back. Maybe sometimes I'll just make a few trips without them. We'll do them quietly.

(LAUGHTER)

But we're going to be out a lot. We're going to do a lot of different states. And I'm coming back here before the election.

(APPLAUSE)

And it's a very close election. You know, a lot of people don't realize there's a six point spread. Six points could be ended by—this evening he could be up by 12. You've seen what's been happening.

We've had a good record of endorsements. In Georgia a man was down 10. I endorsed him a short while before the election, good man, for governor. And he won 70 to 30.

(APPLAUSE)

So I guess he picked up 45 or 50 points. In Ohio recently there was—he was up and he went down a little bit. We went there and he won, Balderson, good man. Congressman Balderson now, he won. You know, we won eight out of nine special elections, nobody talks about it. They don't talk about it. Eight out of nine special elections and they don't want to talk about it.

(BOOING)

And my record, look, I don't want to brag about it but man, do I have a good record of endorsement. I—in Florida we have a great candidate, his name is Ron DeSantis. And he called me, and asked whether or not I could endorse him? And I said, let me check it out. And he was at three. This was a few months ago. He was at three. And I gave him a nice shot, a nice little tweak—bing, bing. And he went from 3 to like 20-something.

(APPLAUSE)

And then I gave him my full, and total endorsement, and he's now leading by like, 19 points. And that election is next week, leading in the primary. Good man.

And so many others, Staten Island, a Congressman Dan Donovan, he was down before the election. We endorsed him, I think he won by 24 points.

So if we can do just—you know, all my life I've heard endorsements don't mean anything. They said, if you get an endorsement from Ronald Reagan—we like Ronald Reagan. It was a wonderful thing to have, but it didn't move the needle. And if you get an endorsement from a lot of people it never really—is that a correct statement?

If you look Corey (ph), Shelley (ph)—if you get an endorsement it was nice to have but it didn't mean anything. These endorsements, and I'm not saying (ph) it from my standpoint—they're going 20, 30, 40, 50 points. 50 points, it's crazy.

(APPLAUSE)

And then you watch the news, "Will this endorsement mean anything?" Let me tell you, it's going to mean a lot. It's going to mean a lot.

And I don't care, I just want—we have to get senators in. We've got really no majority. We have, if you really look at it probably we could say 49-49, 51-49. We have some people that aren't able to vote. We have some people that are a little unreliable. They don't exactly like what I've done to their career. They don't love what I've done, and that's OK. And I don't like what they've done either, but we need to elect five, six or even seven more senators. And I think we can do it, I think we can do it. And we have to start with Patrick Morrisey, he's going to be fantastic.

(APPLAUSE)

If you vote for Joe Manchin, or any other democrat in November you're voting for the party that wants to really destroy the coal industry. Patrick said it, Joe endorsed Hillary 100 percent. And he got along with her even better after she came out with the statement that she wants to destroy coal and coal companies. That's a bad thing.

(BOOING)

The Democrats want to turn America in to one big, fat sanctuary city for criminal aliens.

**TRUMP:** And honestly, honestly—they're more protective of aliens—the criminal aliens than they are of the people. They want to take away your Second Amendment, you see what's going on. I don't think you want your Second Amendment played with. They want to take over American health care and abuse our courts to rewrite our Constitution.

And how do you like the judges that I've been appointing?

(APPLAUSE)

Justice Kavanaugh, Justice Gorsuch, Supreme Court. There's no worse night-mare for West Virginia this November than Chuck Schumer running the Senate and Nancy Pelosi with Maxine Waters running the House.

(BOOING)

And that is why you must vote Republican. You've got to get out and vote. You know, they keep talking about a blue wave. I don't see it. We have the greatest economy we've ever had. Joe Manchin always voted for Obama, and he voted to keep the disaster known as Obamacare—and I will tell you, it is being chipped away—you know, we had it beaten, but one man—I'm sure nobody knows who I'm talking about—voted no, shockingly.

To—really surprising to a lot of people, because he campaigned on repeal and replace, but we've really knocked it out, including the individual mandate. We got rid—the most unpopular part of Obamacare.

(APPLAUSE)

Where you have the privilege of paying a fortune but not having to pay a fortune for really bad health care, OK? That's not too good. We got rid of it. A lot of people are very happy about that. That came along with the biggest tax cuts in our history.

(APPLAUSE)

And Joe Manchin voted no on the tax cuts. You know, the last time I was here, I saw signs along the highway. Joe, you voted no on tax cuts. And, Joe, you voted no for our president. You voted no. And he's going to vote no. I'm not knocking him, but Schumer's the boss and he may give us a vote on Justice Kavanaugh—he should. Everybody should. I mean, here's the guy, is this central casting? This is what we want. This is a great, brilliant man, but Joe's just not voting with us.

He's voting against your tax cuts, he voted against repeal and replace, he votes against the things that we want, and he votes against the people of West Virginia. You can't do that.

You know, Joe opposed the wall and he opposed the travel ban. And by the way, the wall—right now, that wall is coming along. We're over $3 billion, it's moving along very nicely. Very nicely.

(APPLAUSE)

And if you think it's easy with these people, it's not easy. It's not easy. We're getting the wall built. It's going up, we're getting it built. And we have a big number in it right now (ph)...

(OFF MIC)

So Shelley and Cory (ph), you hear that, right? So we have $3.2 billion. We're looking for $5 billion this year, and all of a sudden it's going to be finished and it's going to be very, very effective.

(APPLAUSE)

You heard about today with the illegal alien coming in very sadly from Mexico and you saw what happened to that incredible beautiful young woman. Should have never happened. Illegally in our country. We've had a huge impact, but the laws are so bad, the immigration laws are such a disgrace. We're getting them changed, but we have to get more Republicans. We have to get.

(APPLAUSE)

This election is bigger than any one race, it's about whether we want to continue the amazing progress we've made for America, or whether we want to surrender that progress to the forces of extremism and obstruction. You know, their—their little phrase that they like, resist? That's all they're good at. They have no policy, they're not good politicians, but they're good at sticking together and resisting.

I have almost 400 people that haven't been approved by the—they're slow-walking. You know what slow walking—they're slow walking them. We have almost 400 people in our administration, people that gave up their careers, that have been waiting over a year to get approved, and they're being slow-walked by the Democrats. It's never happened that way in the history of our country, and it is a disgrace. It's a disgrace.

(BOOING)

The Democrat Party is held hostage by the so-called resistance, left-wing haters and angry mobs. They're trying to tear down our institutions, disrespect our flag, demean our law enforcement, denigrate our history, and disparage our great country. And we're not going to let it happen.

(APPLAUSE)

New York's Democrat Governor Andrew Cuomo even declared that America was never great. Oh, I see. OK. Tell that to our great soldiers at World War I and World War II. Korean War, so many others.

(APPLAUSE)

Tell them to the folks that sent a rocket up to the moon and our great astronauts. Tell them to all of the great medical research we've done in this country. And he says that America was never great.

(BOOING)

I would imagine that's career threatening, right? I would imagine. How did he get away with that one? Did you hear? He was speaking to a room loaded up with socialist, and probably others. Probably others. No, not communist, but there could have been a couple of them too.

And he made the statement, that America was never great. And they go—did you hear? They go whoa, whoa, whoa, they couldn't even believe it. No, that's job threatening. His comments are an insult to the generations of brave Americans whose blood and sweat and tears built our magnificent country.

So this November you can either vote for the party that says, America was never great. That's going to be their theme now. America was never great. Hey, let's do that. You know they copied mine, promises made, promises kept. Let's give them a new theme, quote "America was never great." That's the Democrat's new theme. Can we do that? Yes. We'll re-theme—we'll re-theme their—or you can vote proudly for everything that we stand for. We're the greatest country in the world and we are now—we are now the greatest economy that we have ever had. We're the greatest economy in the world. We've gone up $10 trillion in value since my election.

CROWD
USA! USA! USA!

**TRUMP:** We've gone up $10 trillion. Think of it, since the election, wasn't that a great election? Boy.

(APPLAUSE)

Remember I was here just before the election and I brought a couple of guys into a room and I said fellas, supposing we teach you a new skill, supposing we teach you like how to make little widgets or gidgets or gadgets or (inaudible). These are big strong coal miners. They say, sir, we want to dig coal. I said, I agree with you. I agree. Right? Remember that? Their grandfathers did it. Their fathers did it. It's incredible and it's really happening. We are back. The coal industry is back.

(APPLAUSE)

So when I came here originally, West Virginia, frankly, was down and out. It was not doing exactly well. One of the last. You know that a few months ago it hit where West Virginia on a per capita basis is one of the most successful GDP states in our union.

(APPLAUSE)

So we went from being down and out, you're one of the most successful in the union. Very close to the top. That is some big change. And I've had so many people—I was backstage, and people are coming up to me, Mr. President, thank you sir for saving our nation. Because you understand what that means. We couldn't do anything.

TRUMP: Had the other side won, they have poured on more regulations, raised your taxes. They would have done things that were so bad—you had a very low GDP. It was 1.2 percent. You know 1.2. It was going down. It was going to be a negative.

Last quarter, we just hit, as you all know, 4.1. Nobody thought that was possible.

(APPLAUSE)

If—I always say, and if I would've ever said that, shortly after winning, we're going to 4.1, those people back there would've said, this guy, no good. Fake news. Fake news. How fake are they.

(BOOING)

Fake news and the Russian witch hunt. We got a whole big combination. Where is the collusion? You know, they're still looking for collusion. Where is the collusion? Find some collusion. We want to find the collusion.

At the beating heart of this election is border security. We have to have it, right. We have to have it.

(APPLAUSE)

(Inaudible) officials (ph) and so many other countries have been reporting numbers where they're having a lot of problems with people coming in. People are coming in, but we're getting them out.

We have MS-13 on the run. They poured in here with Obama. We have them on the run, because we love the men and women of ICE.

(APPLAUSE)

A blue wave in November means open borders, which means massive crime. A red wave means safety and strength. That's what it is.

(APPLAUSE)

The new platform of the Democratic Party is abolish ICE. A vote for any Democrat in November is a vote to eliminate immigration enforcement, throw open our borders, and set loose vicious predators and violent criminals. They'll be all over our communities. They will be praying on our communities.

Yet, while many Democrats are calling to abolish ICE, today, our brave ICE officers successfully cared a 14-year-old deportation order against a Nazi criminal who was living in New York, the last known Nazi officer living in the United States.

(APPLAUSE)

They've been trying to get him out for decades. President Obama tried. They all tried. We got them out. Gone. He's gone. He's back in Germany.

ICE officers are hero's who uphold our laws, and they really do. They uphold our laws, and they defend our communities, like nobody you've ever seen.

And yes, they're tough, they're strong, they're smart, they have great heart, but they go into these communities loaded up with the kind of criminals you don't want to be dealing with. They walk in like it's another day in the office.

They're tougher. They're stronger. It's what these other people fear. And by the way, our ICE folks and our border patrol folks, they have no fear. The job they do is incredible.

And by the way, while we're at it, law enforcement, these are great, great people, and they're doing an incredible job.

(APPLAUSE)

Every single day, ICE is tracking down gang members, drug dealers, predators and killers, and we're either throwing in jail or throwing them the hell out of our country.

(APPLAUSE)

If you want to save ICE, if you want to protect our border and our Border Patrol, if you want to stop this craziness of sanctuary cities, were criminals are protected— take a look at Chicago. How about the mayor of Chicago?

(BOOING)

It's like a warzone. That's a great city. That's like a warzone. This is what those policies do. Last week, 62 people were shot; 12 died. This is, like, our country. There's no reason for this.

The Republican Party stands proudly with our courageous ICE officers and Border Patrol agents.

(APPLAUSE)

And by the way, you know who wants the wall more than any of us? ICE and Border Patrol because they know that's going to be a big, big factor in stopping the drugs from coming in, the human traffickers—which is worse all over the world than at any time in the history of our world. Human traffickers, who would believe? And it's because of the Internet.

This election is about security. And this election is also about jobs we have produced; we have produced. Thanks to Republicans, our economy is booming like it has never boomed before. We've created another number that nobody would have believed if I said it during the campaign, 4 million new jobs since the election. Nobody would have believed it.

(APPLAUSE)

Almost 3.9 million Americans have been lifted off food stamps, think of that. They don't need them because they have a job. They're eating better now. They don't need food stamps, almost 4 million think of it.

Last year in West Virginia, per capita income grew 40 percent faster than the national average; 40 percent, congratulations. Congratulations.

(APPLAUSE)

I told you last time I was here, you weren't so happy like you are now. We've added over 400,000 new manufacturing jobs nationwide. That number is soon going to exceed 600,000. And our opponents said there's no such thing as manufacturing jobs anymore, right?

And I'd say, oh, I see. We're not going to make things anymore? Think of it, we'll be close to 600,000 very soon. We have companies pouring in to our country. They're coming back. These are companies that left, they're coming back to Michigan, they're coming back to West Virginia, they're coming back to Pennsylvania and Ohio—they're coming to Florida.

They're coming back, not just opening, they're coming back. They left and now they're coming back because they want to be where the action is. And the action is in the United States of America.

(APPLAUSE)

So the economic growth, as I said when it hit 4.1 percent—everybody was like, that's amazing except me, because it's going to go much higher than that. When I finish these trade deals—and the tariffs are very important—these companies come in.

And I say to the European Union—very nice people—I say, Jean-Claude, we'd like to negotiate a new trade agreement with the European Union. We lost $151 billion over the last number of years, per year. Does anyone know what $151 billion per year is?

And he very respectfully said, Mr. President, but we are very happy with the deal. I said, I'd be happy if I were you, too.

(LAUGHTER)

I'd be very happy. I said a second time, and a third time, and a fourth time, but they were happy with the deal. But we weren't happy because they have barriers up and because they have tariffs, all the things we don't have.

You want to build a car and send it to Europe? How many Chevrolets are there in the middle of Berlin? Not too many, maybe one. I doubt it; I don't think you could find the one.

So they have barriers. So I said, come on, let's go. And then, he said no. I said listen—and I said this to numerous countries. I mean, in all fairness, I don't want to single out anybody, but I said it to them.

And he says, listen, here's what we're going to—it's all about the cars. It's all about the cars; tremendously big industry. We're going to put a 25 percent tax on every car that comes from the European Union into the United States.

(APPLAUSE)

And that'll take our loss and trade deficit of $151 billion, and it'll give us a surplus of $151 billion.

(APPLAUSE)

That's a fairly dramatic swing. And that'll take one little signature, Donald J. Trump.

(APPLAUSE)

And I got a call. Mr. President, when can we meet? We'd like to see you.

TRUMP: And they came in very respectfully; we're working on a deal. But this is happening all over with China. I have great respect for President Xi, great respect, tremendous respect for China. But they have taken advantage of our country for decades. We have rebuilt China. We have rebuilt China. I used to talk about this.

I didn't press it initially because I wanted them to help us with North Korea and they have, and they have. And we're doing well with North Korea. You know these guys it's been what, three months since I left? These guys saying, "What's happening with North Korea?" Hey folks, they've been doing this stuff for 75 years—3 months.

What happened?

(APPLAUSE)

I can tell you, and I got along very well with Kim Jong-un, really well. Good chemistry. But I can tell you there's been no missile launches, there's been no rocket launches, we got the hostages back.

(APPLAUSE)

And we didn't pay $1.8 billion in cash for the hostages.

There's been no nuclear tests, and they say, "What's taking so long?" I say for 40, 50, 60 years—but during the nuclear age for 25 years you've been working and nobody complained about the fact that President Obama was unable to do anything with North Korea. And he considered it like, just read the papers you'll see what he considered it.

So I've been three months, I have a very good relationship with Chairman Kim. We'll see what happens, who knows? Can I be honest, who knows? But I haven't taken off the sanctions. We have massive sanctions. I want to take them off quickly but they've got to get rid of the nukes. We've got to get rid of the nukes. Got to get rid of them.

(APPLAUSE)

But who knows what's going to happen, I mean maybe it will work out—but I think we've done a good job, you know, in a short period of time.

You remember, it started off extremely hostile. Remember they said, "he's going to get us in to a war." They thought my rhetoric was too strong, you remember. I won't say it because I don't want to insult Chairman Kim. You remember, you remember. Elton John.

(LAUGHTER)

I don't want to insult, so I'm not going to mention it. But the fake news back there said, he is going to get us in to a war; he's crazy. This guy is crazy, our president is crazy.

And then I went to meet the leaders and the folks that run NATO, all the leaders of NATO. And they weren't paying their bills. They were delinquent, you know, in real estate. I love real estate. When somebody doesn't pay their rent you say, Shelley you say, They're delinquent; you got to pay your rent.

And I met them last year, and Stoltenberg, Secretary General—great guy of NATO. He's my single biggest fan, bigger than any fan I have in the room, you know why? Because nobody was paying their bills. He was in charge of NATO and he couldn't get any money. But last year I went—a year ago, I said, "you're not paying your bills, you've got to pay your bills," he picked up $44 billion. He told that to the press; they didn't report—$44 billion.

(LAUGHTER)

And then I just left recently, and we're going to pick up at least another close to $100 billion extra. I said to him, you've got to pay your bills. The United States is paying close to 90 percent of the cost of protecting Europe, and I think that's wonderful. I said to Europe, I said, folks, NATO's better for you than it is for us, believe me. And what happened is they asked a question. They have small countries, big countries—all these countries were—we're supposed to protect them. I said, look it's very simple, you've got to pay up. You got to pay your bill.

And somebody said, "Sir"—it's the president of a country calling me sir, that shows respect. I say, "Yes, Mr. President?" He said, "Would you leave us if we don't pay our bills?" Now they hated my answer. I said, "Yeah, I would have to consider it. You've got to pay your bills." They hated the answer.

(APPLAUSE)

What if I said no, I won't leave you, you don't have to pay your bills, I won't leave—I promise we'll always protect you, you will always be protected, don't pay your bills. Then they're never going to pay their bills.

So I said yes, I will leave you if you don't pay your bills, and you could see those checkbooks coming out for billions of dollars.

(APPLAUSE)

They paid their bills. And I think we'll pick up over the next short while over $100 billion. And then they said, the fake news, they said President Trump treated the NATO nation leaders—in brackets, they put brackets—who have been ripping us off. In brackets (ph). Treated the NATO leaders with tremendous contempt and disrespect.

And I said, no, no, no, they disrespected our country because they weren't paying (ph).

(APPLAUSE)

Now they're paying (ph).

(APPLAUSE)

How about if we got into a conflict because a country was attacked, and now we're in World War III and we're protecting a country that was attacked and didn't pay its bills. I'd feel so stupid. We're protecting a country that wasn't paying its bills. So I got them to pay $100 billion—no, it's going to be (ph) much more than that, but tremendous amounts of money, tremendous. They've got to pay up. They're paying up.

And then they made the statement that I showed great disrespect. But actually, I have a great relationship with all of those people, 28 people, all of them. We have a great relationship. Because now they respect us. They respect our country again. They didn't respect our country. They didn't respect our country.

(APPLAUSE)

They respect us again. And you see it with China. China was walking us way down (ph). I don't want them to go down, but they're down close to 30 percent in three months. I don't want them—I want them to do well. I want to be their friend. But we had to do things that we had to do.

When I came, we were heading in a certain direction that was going to allow China to be bigger than us in a very short period of time. That's not going to happen anymore. It's not going to happen anymore.

(APPLAUSE)

Can't let that happen (ph). It's a long winding road. You know, the long winding road, and I have tremendous respect for China. I mean, the energy, the genius, it's incredible what they're done, and hopefully we're going to have a great relationship.

But we can't do it—it's got to be a two-way street. We have only one-way streets. Not only China, with everybody, it's a one-way street. Our enemies, our friends, our allies. I mean, our allies treat us worse than our enemies. Believe it.

So it's all changing, and when we get those trade deals done properly—and you know what bothers me? I have people coming to me, some people in Congress, "Sir, can you get this deal done immediately?" I said it doesn't work that way, I don't want to go too fast, the deals not going to be any good if we do that. We've got to take time—it's got to gestate, right? The word gestate. It's like when you're cooking a chicken.

(LAUGHTER)

Time, time (ph), turkey for Thanksgiving. My mother would say, oh, eight hours. I said, eight hours? She made the greatest turkey I've ever had. It takes time.

(APPLAUSE)

It takes time. So when they run and they say, oh, can you do NATO right now, could we sign it the next week, I said, wait a minute, look. I like Mexico, I like the new leader. I think he's going to be terrific. A little different than us. I think I'm doing better with him than with the capitalists.

But he knows that Mexico needs the United States. They need the United States. Canada charges us close to 300 percent tariffs for dairy products going into Canada, which is essentially saying, "We don't want your dairy products, this is a wall." They have a wall in a different way, it's called an economic wall.

**TRUMP:** I don't want that. I said, Justin, I mean, I don't want to have too much fun with you, Justin. You can't do that. Justin Trudeau. Nice guy. But they've taking advantage of us for so many years that we have to take our time. But with that being said, we're doing very well, we're on our way with a good deal, a fair deal. I don't want a good deal, I want a fair deal for both of us. Fair. With Mexico.

(APPLAUSE)

And you've heard me say it. As an example, when China makes a car, they sell it into the United States. There's 2.5 percent tariff on which they don't pay, so they pay nothing. That is a wonderful deal.

When we make a car, we sell it in to China, and there's a 25 percent tariff, and that's just the beginning. There's others. A man was driving down a street in China, and he looked over, and it was Chevrolet-like Camaro—does that make sense. Is it a Camaro? I think it costs $39,000 or $40,000. He's in China. He's in Beijing. And he shouts across—They're stuck—he shouts across, "Tell me, how much did that car cost in China?" Guy looks, "$119,000."

Now you understand that, right? It's all taxes and taxes and taxes. We can't do that anymore. We can't do it. We are a country with a unbelievable potential. We are a country that has been ripped by everybody. And we're not going to be ripped off anymore.

(APPLAUSE)

And if it takes me a little angst to tell senators and congressmen and all of the people that really do have your—your heart in their hands, in many cases. Sometimes I wonder where they're coming from with these suggestions. But it's going to have to take that little period of time.

With that being said, we're moving so fast nobody could even believe it. And every country wants to make a deal, because we're like a big, fat, piggybank that everybody wants to rob, and we're not going to let them rob us anymore. Is that OK, West Virginia?

(APPLAUSE)

We're not going to let them rob us anymore. Everyday, we're keeping our promises. We're canceling Obama's illegal anti-coal destroying regulations, their so-called "Clean Power Plan."

(APPLAUSE)

Doesn't that sound nice, "clean power." You know, when I ended the Paris Accord—what's a more beautiful name than the Paris Accord. Let's call it the West Virginia accord, maybe I would've signed it.

(APPLAUSE)

But when I entered it, that was going to cost us hundreds of billions of dollars—hundreds of billions. And other countries—as an example, China, didn't kick in until many years in the future. We kicked in immediately. Russia went back many years, which was not a clean time, in terms of the environment. Because you know what, we all agree. We want a clean environment. We want a strong, beautiful, clean environment. I want clean air. I want crystal clean water. And we've got it. We've got the cleanest country in the planet right now. There's nobody cleaner than us, and it's getting better and better, but I'm getting rid of some these ridiculous rules and regulations, which are killing our companies, our states, and our jobs.

(APPLAUSE)

Just today, we announced our new affordable clean energy proposal that will help our coal-fired power plants and save consumers—you, me, everybody—billions and billions of dollars.

(APPLAUSE)

We've eliminated a record number of job killing regulations, and Republicans have passed the biggest tax cuts and reform. The reform's very important, but you know what I've said, I don't want to talk about reform because nobody knows what it means. That could be a tax increase. I said, "How come it's been Ronald Reagan since you got the last big tax cut?" And they looked at me and said, "We don't know." And a lot of the great senators and the congressmen came up to see me, and they had the 2018 tax reform. I said, "What the hell does that mean? Are you going to raise taxes?" Then I found out this is what they've done for 40 years. "Tax Reform," I said, "Nobody knows what it means." And we do have reform in there, great reform, but they said nobody knows—I said, "Nobody knows what it means." Here is—I want to put it down, tax cuts. They said, "What would be your favorite name, Mr. President?" I said, "The Tax Cut, Cut, Cut, Cut bill."

(APPLAUSE)

And we almost did it. We almost did it, but in all fairness, and in this case, Congressman—a couple of them thought it was a little bit tacky. So we call it the "Tax Cut and Jobs Bill."

But you know what? We have done great reform, but the biggest tax in the history of our country. And you people are benefitting by it. You're benefitting by it.

(APPLAUSE)

You're benefiting.

(APPLAUSE)

And companies are betting—benefitting. And those companies are the ones that are providing all of the jobs. We're setting records on jobs.

We're protecting, also—it's so important for West Virginia and a lot of states—we are protecting, again, religious liberty.

(APPLAUSE)

And we're also standing up to social media censorship, that's the new thing. That's the new thing. You know, I'd rather have fake news like CNN. I would rather have fake news—it's true …

(BOOING)

… than have anybody, including liberals, socialists, anything, than have anybody stop and censor it. You've got to live—we got to live with it. We've got to get used to it. We've got to live with fake news, there's too many sources.

Every one of us is sort of like a newspaper. You have Twitter, you have—whatever you have—Facebook. But everyone, you can't have censorship. You can't pick one person and say, well, we don't like what he's been saying. He's out.

So we'll live with fake news. I mean, I hate to say it, but we have no choice because that's by far the better alternative. You can't have people saying censorship because you know what? It can turn around. It could be them next. It could be them next. We believe in the right of Americans to speak their minds.

We repealed the core of Obamacare. I told you, individual mandate, because we want to give critically ill patients—we have to give them access. We have to give health care to people.

We want the right to try. Do you know what the right to try is? They've been trying to get this for 40 years. They couldn't get it.

A person is terminally ill—they're terminally ill, they're really sick. And I know people, if they have money, they travel all over the world to try and find a cure. If they don't have money, they die; they die.

We have the greatest scientists in the world. That's why China and so many other people, they're trying to—countries, they're trying to steal our technology. We can't let them happen (ph).

But we have so many people that want to be able to give. It's like hope. Right to try, I love the name. It's a right to try, they never had it before.

So a person's terminally ill, and we have a great new drug but it's going to take another two, three years to have it approved. OK? Maybe longer. But the tests are really looking good and this person is very sick. And this person is going to be dead in 90 days and we couldn't get that drug for that person, no matter who you were.

And I said wait a minute, what's the story with this? Now, there were a lot of complications because the insurance companies had problems, the medical companies—everybody. A lot of people didn't want them in the stats; horrible things. But I said, well, what's going on?

We're going to take the right to try, and we went through with the help of Cory (ph) with the help of your great, wonderful—you are a coal lover aren't you, Shelley (ph)—but with the help of Shelley (ph)—soon to be with the help of Patrick. Patrick's—oh, he's going to get a lot of things—he's going to get it. We got it approved.

So now, if we have a great drug that hasn't been approved and somebody has a certain illness, they're going to be able to be—to try. And you know what? Some of the drugs we have in the pipeline are amazing. It's going to work for a lot of people and it's going to give them hope. It's going to give them hope; big hope.

(APPLAUSE)

We've just secured $6 billion to fight the opioid epidemic. And I know, in West Virginia that's a big deal, right? That's a big deal.

(APPLAUSE)

We confirmed a record number of circuit court judges, it's a record, and it's going bigger and bigger. We have a lot of them in the line if Schumer would ever get them approved. He's not exactly thrilled about approving them, that I can tell you.

We confirmed the great Neil Gorsuch to the Supreme Court of the United States. And as I just said, Justice Kavanaugh is doing great. He looks like—I don't know, very tough. Central casting, how do you vote against him? But the Democrats may find a way.

We've secured a record $700 billion for our military this year and $716 billion for next (ph).

(APPLAUSE)

Billion with a B. Our military will be stronger, and bigger, and better and more sophisticated than it's ever been. Ever.

(APPLAUSE)

And hopefully we'll never have to use it. You know we've got a lot of good fighters out here. I see some of them. I know some of them. And the one thing about a fighter or a nation or whatever you want, the stronger your military the better chance you have of never having to use it.

(APPLAUSE)

We don't want to use it. We don't want to use it.

And all of that equipment is being built right here in the USA. We make the greatest fighter jets in the world. We make the greatest ships in the world. We make the greatest missiles and rockets.

Nobody does it like us. And on my direction the Pentagon is working hard to create the sixth branch of the American Armed forces the Space Force.

(APPLAUSE)

That's very exciting. We need it. That's the new frontier. And I'm not just talking about sending rockets to the moon. I'm talking about militarily that's where it's at.

Thanks to the leadership of U.N. Ambassador Nikki Haley, we've reduced the United Nation spending by $1.3 billion, saving U.S. taxpayers $350 million. It just came out, but nobody wants to write it.

(APPLAUSE)

We just planned a landmark V.A. accountability law. That's where people that don't treat our vets properly. We look at them and we say you're fired, get the hell out.

(APPLAUSE)

Forty-five years they've been trying to pass it, 45 years they've tried to pass it. We also passed Veterans Choice so that if our veterans can't get the care they need, they have the right to see a private doctor. They don't have to wait in line for three weeks, four weeks, eight weeks, two months.

(APPLAUSE)

I withdrew the United States from the horrible Iran nuclear deal. And this month reimposed some sanctions on Iran's nuclear program, and on Iran.

I also recognized the capital of Israel and opened the American embassy in Jerusalem.

(APPLAUSE)

And I understand now what happened. Because every president—many, many presidents, they said we're going to do it. We're going to move our embassy to Jerusalem. It's going to be in the capital of Israel. And we're going to do it. We're going to do it. And then they don't do it. Politicians, they don't do it. So I said I'm going to do it during the campaign. I said it right here in West Virginia.

(APPLAUSE)

And I now understand why many, many presidents before me said they were going to do it and didn't do it, because I was inundated with calls from foreign lands. Every country. Don't do it. Don't do it. Don't do it. Please don't do it. Don't do it.

And so actually what I did, I was about five days off, I stopped taking calls. I said, I'll call you back next week. Because I knew what they were going to ask me. It's much easier than saying (ph), oh gee, I didn't know you were always calling for that reason.

(LAUGHTER)

So I approved it. And it should have been done years ago.

(APPLAUSE)

And if there's ever going to be peace—remember I said it—with the Palestinians, it was a good thing to have done because we took it off the table.

Because every time there were peace talks, they never got past Jerusalem becoming the capital. So I said let's take it off the table. And you know what? In the negotiation Israel will have to pay a higher price because they won a very big thing.

**TRUMP:** But I took it off the table. They could never get by. You understand that Cory (ph) you both understand that, Shelly (ph). They could never get past the fact of Jerusalem becoming the capital.

Now it's off the table. There's nothing to negotiate. But they'll get something very good because it's their turn next. Let's see what happens. It's very (inaudible). I've always heard that's the toughest deal of all deals. That's called peace between Israel and the Palestinians. They say that's the toughest of all deals. Let's see what happens. Instead of apologize that's what we're doing is we're winning.

(APPLAUSE)

Instead of apologizing for America, we're standing up for America and we're standing up for the heroes who defend our country.

(APPLAUSE)

But to continue this incredible success, we must elect more Republicans. We must elect Patrick Morrisey. We need him.

We need Patrick, so get your friends, your neighbors, your coworkers, your family members, get the people that love our country, and get out to vote. We need his vote so badly. We need his energy. You're going to see, this guy has energy. Loyal citizens like you help to build this country. Together we're taking back our country, returning power to where it belongs, to the American people.

From Morgantown to Madison, to Charleston, this great state was settled by tough pioneer men and strong pioneer women, who tamed the wilderness to build a better life for themselves and for their incredible American families. They didn't have a lot of money, they didn't have a lot of luxury, but they had grit and they had faith, and they loved each other. And I'll tell you why—they were smart. They are smart. We're the smart ones, remember. I say it all the time. You hear the elite—they're not elite; we're elite. You're smarter than they are.

(APPLAUSE)

You have more money than they are. You have better jobs than they do. You're the elite. So let them have the word "elite." You're the super elite—that's what it is.

I always hate—I always hate when they say, "well the elite decided not to go to something I'm doing"—like the elite. I say, well, I have a lot more money than they do. I have a much better education than they have, I'm smarter than they are. I have many much more beautiful homes than they do. I have a better apartment at the top of 5th Avenue. Why the hell are they the elite? Tell me.

Because you're the elite, just remember that. You're the elite; they're not the elite. That's just a name. Aren't you insulted when they say, "the elite?" To me I'm insulted—always insulted. They're the elite—they're not the elite.

Your people and the people that proceeded you in West Virginia were the carpenters and the coal miners, the ministers, the metalworkers, the farmers, the factory workers—but they all had one thing in common: They loved their families, they loved their country and they loved their God.

(APPLAUSE)

We stand on the shoulders of generations of American patriots who knew how to fight, and they knew how to win. We're winning again. We're winning again. Just like them we're going to keep on fighting and we're going to keep on winning, and we're going to win for our nation, our children, our families, and we're going to win for our continued freedom.

(APPLAUSE)

I joke that I'll have Patrick Morrisey coming to me soon, he'll be your Senator, and he'll say, "Mr. President, the people of West Virginia can't stand winning so much. They haven't won in decades and now you're winning with coal; you're winning with everything."

He's going to say—Patrick he's going to say, "Mr. President, please. They don't want to win so much, they can't stand it. Please, you're winning too much for West Virginia, please stop winning." And I'm going to say, "Patrick, I'm sorry."

(LAUGHTER)

I don't care what the hell the people of West Virginia want, we're going to keep on winning anyways, because I believe that's what they want, right? That's what they want. Because the people of West Virginia never give up, they never give in and they never back down.

(APPLAUSE)

Because we are Americans and our hearts bleed red, white, and blue.

(APPLAUSE)

We are one people, one family, and one glorious nation under God.

(APPLAUSE)

And together, we will make America wealthy again. That's happening. That's happening a lot faster than the fake news ever said it could happen.

(APPLAUSE)

We will make America strong again. We will make America safe again. And we will make America great again. Thank you, West Virginia, thank you.

**Print Citations**

**CMS:** Trump, Donald. "Midterm Campaign Stump Speech." Speech presented at the Charleston Civic Center, Charleston, WV, August 21, 2018. In *The Reference Shelf: Representative American Speeches 2017-2018*, edited by Micah L. Issit, 71-92. Ipswich, MA: H.W. Wilson, 2018.

**MLA:** Trump, Donald. "Midterm Campaign Stump Speech." Charleston Civic Center, 21 August 2018, Charleston, WV. Presentation. *The Reference Shelf: Representative American Speeches 2017-2018*, edited by Micah L. Issit, H.W. Wilson, 2018, pp. 71-92.

**APA:** Trump, D. (2018, August 21). Midterm campaign stump speech. Charleston Civic Center, Charleston, WV. In M.L. Issit (Ed.), *The reference shelf: Representative American speeches 2017-2018* (pp. 71-92). Ipswich, MA: H.W. Wilson. (Original work published 2018)

# The Be Best Program

## By Melania Trump

*Slovenian immigrant Melania Trump is a former model and the wife of President Donald Trump. Settling into the role of First Lady, Melania Trump has made anti-bullying the focus of her traditional First Lady public welfare campaign. At this 2018 speech, Melania Trump introduces the program, named "Be Best."*

**M. TRUMP:** Thank you. Good afternoon. Welcome to the White House.

As a mother and as first lady, it concerns me that, in today's fast- paced and ever-connected world, children can be less prepared to express or manage their emotions, and oftentimes turn to forms of destructive or addictive behavior, such as bullying, drug addiction, or even suicide.

I feel strongly that, as adults, we can and should be best at educating our children about the importance of a healthy and balanced life.

So, today, I'm very excited to announce Be Best, an awareness campaign dedicated to the most valuable and fragile among us, our children.

(APPLAUSE)

**M. TRUMP:** There is one goal to Be Best. And that is to educate children about the many issues they are facing today.

If we truly listen to what our kids have to say, whether it is be their concerns or ideas, adults can provide them the support and tools they need to grow up to be happy and productive adults who contribute positively to society and their global communities.

At the same time, children deserve every opportunity to enjoy their innocence. Every child should know it is safe to make mistakes and that there are supportive adults and friends nearby to catch them if they fell.

We also need to be mindful that they should learn to trust in themselves and their own emotions. I believe our responsibility lies in the critical time before a child reaches adulthood.

Let us teach children the importance of all aspects of their well-being, which includes social, emotional and physical health. There are too many critical issues facing children today.

So, the three main pillars of Be Best will include well-being, social media use, and opioid abuse.

Together, I believe we should strive to provide kids with the tools they need to

Delivered on May 7, 2018, at the White House, Washington, DC.

cultivate their social and emotional health. We can and should teach children the importance of social and self-awareness, positive relationship skills, and responsible decision-making.

Once a child understands these vital skills, they will be able to communicate openly with one another and instill positive feelings of mutual respect, compassion, and self-esteem.

Let us teach our children the difference between right and wrong and encourage them to be best in their individual paths in life.

Take, for example, Christian Bucks, a young man from York, Pennsylvania, who is here with us today. When he was in second grade, Christian introduced the buddy bench at his elementary school to address loneliness and help other kids build new friendships.

The buddy bench allows classmates to connect during recess and helps ensure that no student feels lonely. If a child sits on the bench, it signals other students to come over and ask them to play.

Christian's school and community embraced the buddy bench. And, today, at least one can be found in all 50 states.

Thank you, Christian, for your commitment to kindness. You should be very proud of your work, which has, I know, helped our country's children.

Please stand up. (APPLAUSE)

**M. TRUMP:** I would also like to talk about Orchard Lake Middle School in West Bloomfield Township, Michigan.

I visited the school in October as part of National Bullying Prevention Month to speak to its students about the importance of being kind.

While I was there, I visited their Viking Huddle class, which focuses on social-emotional learning and teaches lessons about respecting others, inclusion, and being kind.

As part of Be Best, I plan to highlight ideas and programs such as buddy bench and Viking Huddle class, with the hope that other schools or community groups will be inspired to replace their efforts and take steps to improve the well-being of our children.

We have invited some of the Viking Huddle class here today. Thank you all for being and taking time here with us in the White House.

(APPLAUSE)

**M. TRUMP:** As we all know, social media can be both positively and negatively effect on our children, but too often it's used in negative ways.

When children learn positive online behaviors early on, social media can be used in productive ways and can effect positive change.

I do believe that children should be both seen and heard. And it is our responsibility as adults to educate and remind them that, when they are using their voices, either verbally or online, they must choose their words wisely and speak with respect and compassion.

As an example, Kalani Goldberg, an eighth grade student from Arizona, posted a video to her social media account to share the challenges she faced from bullies.

In the video, she said: "Every day, you are hurting me. Every day, you are hurting each other. So, please stop. Stop hurting me."

Kalani and her family have joined us here today. And I'm happy to report that, since posting her video, many have watched it and, most importantly, people have reached out to offer support and kindness.

Thank you, Kalani, for being brave enough to share your story, and also for using your experience to bring positive change.

Please stand up, Kalani.

(APPLAUSE)

**M. TRUMP:** I first learned about the real consequences of our nation's opioid epidemic during my husband's campaign. Since then, I have met with and learned from many people who have been

affected by this true crisis. In October, I traveled to West Virginia to tour Lily's Place, the nation's first nonprofit infant recovery center.

Lily's Place puts a priority on the whole family, so that infants born dependent on drugs are given the best opportunity to thrive. They have been successful in this endeavor because parents are also given the support and tools needed to recover and succeed.

Lily's Place is a testament to the extraordinary work that everyday people can do when they put their mind to it.

I will use Be Best to bring attention to programs such as this in order to encourage conversation and application.

In February, I went to Cincinnati Children's Hospital in Ohio. And the panel of doctors briefed me on the devastating effects that opioids have—are having, but also their important reference on neonatal abstinence syndrome.

I'm pleased to say that representatives from both Lily's Place and Cincinnati Children's Hospital are here today.

Thank you.

(APPLAUSE)

**M. TRUMP:** Thank you for being here, and thank you for your heroic work on behalf of children.

I want to thank the many people I have met with and learned from over the past year while researching these vital topics on behalf of children.

This includes the Cabinet secretaries who have joined us here today, as well as representative from Microsoft, Google, Facebook, Twitter, Snap, Amazon, National Safety Council, and so many more.

I would like to thank the president, the vice president, Karen Pence, and other members of the administration, as well as the members of Congress who are here today.

I'm honored to have you all with me, and I look forward to working together on the behalf of children in the coming years.

In my time as first lady of the United States, I will make every effort to be best by championing the many successful well-being programs in existence today and teach the tools and skills for emotional, social, and physical well-being.

I will also work to shine a spotlight on the people, organizations, and programs across the country that are helping children overcome the many issues they are facing as they grow up. I will continue speaking with leaders in the technology industry about children's online habits and raising awareness around the importance of positive behaviors.

I will continue to work with those who are fighting drug addiction. And, most importantly, I will continue to travel and speak to children directly about both their victories and difficult realities they face.

My hope is that, together, we can be best at helping children and families find effective ways to educate themselves and support each other.

I'm asking you all to join me in providing support and guidance to our children, so that we can make a real difference.

How we raise and educate our children on a variety of topics will provide the blueprint for the next generation.

Together, let's encourage children to dream big, think big, and do all they can to be best in everything that they do.

Thank you all for being here today. God bless you, your families, our children, and God bless the United States of America.

## Print Citations

**CMS:** Trump, Melania. "The Be Best Program." Speech presented at the White House, Washington, DC, May 7, 2018. In *The Reference Shelf: Representative American Speeches 2017-2018*, edited by Micah L. Issit, 93-96. Ipswich, MA: H.W. Wilson, 2018.

**MLA:** Trump, Melania. "The Be Best Program." White House, 7 May 2018, Washington, DC. Presentation. *The Reference Shelf: Representative American Speeches 2017-2018,* edited by Micah L. Issit, H.W. Wilson, 2018, pp. 93-96.

**APA:** Trump, M. (2018, May 7). The be best program. White House, Washington, DC. In M.L. Issit (Ed.), *The reference shelf: Representative American speeches 2017-2018* (pp. 93-96). Ipswich, MA: H.W. Wilson. (Original work published 2018)

# Joint Press Conference at the Helsinki Summit

## By Donald Trump and Vladimir Putin

*President Donald Trump is the 45th president of the United States and a business leader known for his role in managing the Trump family real estate business and as a television personality through his reality television competition* The Apprentice. *Vladimir Putin has served as president of Russia from 2000 to 2008 and again from 2012 to 2018. A controversial political figure, Putin has been linked to a Russian campaign during the 2016 elections to discredit Hillary Clinton and support Donald Trump's election. This speech drew rebukes from a number of politicians from both political parties as well as current and former members of the intelligence community.*

**PUTIN:** Thank you so much. Shall we start working, I guess? Distinguished Mr. President, ladies and gentlemen. Negotiations with the President of the United States Donald Trump took place in a frank and businesslike atmosphere. I think we can call it a success and a very fruitful round of negotiations. We carefully analyzed the current status—the present and the future of the Russia/United States' relationship—key issues of the global agenda.

It's quite clear to everyone that the bilateral relationship are going through a complicated stage and yet those impediments—the current tension, the tense atmosphere—essentially have no solid reason behind it. The Cold War is a thing of past. The era of acute ideological confrontation of the two countries is a thing of remote past, is a vestige of the past.

The situation in the world changed dramatically.

Today both Russia and the United States face a whole new set of challenges. Those include a dangerous maladjustment of mechanisms for maintaining international security and stability, regional crises, the creeping threats of terrorism and transnational crime, the snowballing problems in the economy, environmental risks and other sets of challenges.

We can only cope with these challenges if we join the ranks and work together, hopefully we will reach this understanding with our American partners.

Today's negotiations reflected our joint wish, our joint wish with President Trump to redress this negative situation and bilateral relationship, outline the first steps for improving this relationship to restore the acceptable level of trust and going back to the previous level of interaction on all mutual interests issues.

---

Delivered on July 16, 2018, at the Presidential Palace, Helsinki, Finland.

As major nuclear powers, we bear special responsibility for maintaining international security.

And it made vital and we mentioned this during the negotiations. It's crucial that we fine-tune the dialogue on strategic stability and global security and nonproliferation of weapons of mass destruction.

We submitted our American colleagues a note with a number of specific suggestions.

We believe it necessary to work together further to interact on the disarmament agenda, military and technical cooperation. This includes the extension of the Strategic Offensive Arms Limitation Treaty.

It's a dangerous situation with the global American anti-missile defense system. It's the implementation issues with the INF treaty. And, of course, the agenda of non-placement of weapons in space.

We favor the continued cooperation in counter-terrorism and maintaining cyber security. And I'd like to point out specifically that our special services are cooperating quite successfully together.

The most recent example is their operational cooperation within the recently concluded World Football Cup.

In general, the contacts among the special services should be put to a system-wide basis should be brought to a systemic framework. I recall—I reminded President Trump about the suggestion to re-establish the working group on anti-terrorism.

We also mentioned a plethora of regional crises. It's not always that our postures dovetail exactly, and yet the overlapping and mutual interests abound.

We have to look for points of contact and interact closer in a variety of international fora. Clearly, we mentioned the regional crisis, for instance Syria. As far as Syria is concerned, the task of establishing peace and reconciliation in this country could be the first showcase example of this successful joint work.

Russia and the United States apparently can act proactively and take—assume the leadership on this issue and organize the interaction to overcome humanitarian crisis and help Syrian refugees to go back to their homes. In order to accomplish this level of successful cooperation in Syria, we have all the required components.

Let me remind you that both Russian and American military acquired a useful experience of coordination of their actions, established the operational channels of communication, which permit it to avoid dangerous incidents and unintentional collisions in the air and in the ground.

Also crushing terrorists in the south west of Syria—the south of Syria—should be brought to the full compliance with the Treaty of 1974 about the separation of forces, about separation of forces of Israel and Syria.

This will bring peace to Golan Heights and bring a more peaceful relationship between Syria and Israel and also to provide security of the state of Israel.

Mr. President paid special attention to the issue during today's negotiations.

And I would like to confirm that Russia is interested in this development and this will act accordingly.

Thus far, we will make a step toward creating a lasting peace in compliance with the respective resolutions of the Security Council, for instance the Resolution 338.

We're glad that the Korean Peninsula issue is starting to resolve. To a great extent it was possible thanks to the personal engagement of President Trump, who opted for dialogue instead of confrontation.

We also mentioned our concern about the withdrawal of the United States from the JCPOA. Well, the U.S., our U.S. counterparts are aware of our posture.

Let me remind you that thanks to the Iranian nuclear deal, Iran became the most controlled country in the world. It submitted to the control of IAEA. It effectively ensures the exclusively peaceful nature of the Iranian nuclear program and strengthens the nonproliferation regime.

While we discussed the internal Ukrainian crisis, we paid special attention to the bona fide implementation of Minsk Agreements by Kiev.

At the same time, the United States could be more decisive and nudging the Ukrainian leadership and encourage it to work actively on this. We paid more attention to economic ties and economic cooperation. It's clear that both countries, the businesses of both countries, are interested in this.

The American delegation was one of the largest delegations in the St. Petersburg Economic Forum. It featured over 500 representatives from American businesses.

We agreed, me and President Trump, we agreed to create the high level working group that would bring together captains of Russian and American business. After all, entrepreneurs and businessmen know better how to articulate this successful business cooperation. We'll let them think and make their proposals and their suggestions in this regard.

Once again, President Trump mentioned the issue of the so-called interference of Russia when the American elections and I had to reiterate things I said several times, including during our personal contacts that the Russian state has never interfered and is not going to interfere into internal American affairs, including the election process.

Any specific material, if such things arise, we are ready to analyze together. For instance, we can analyze them through the joint working group on cyber security, the establishment of which we discussed during our previous contacts.

And clearly, it's past time we restore our cooperation in the cultural area, in the humanitarian area.

As far as...I think you know that recently we hosted the American congressmen delegation and now it's perceived and portrayed almost as a historic event, although it should have been just a current affairs, just business as usual. And in this regard, we mentioned this proposal to the president. But we have to think about the practicalities of our cooperation but also about the rationale, the underlying logic of it.

And we have to engage experts on bilateral relationship, who know history and the background of our relationship. The idea is to create an expert council that would include political scientists, prominent diplomats and former military experts from both countries, who would look for points of contact between the two countries, that would look for ways on putting the relationship on the trajectory of growth.

In general, we are glad with the outcome of our first full-scale meeting because previously we only had a chance to talk briefly on international fora.

We had a good conversation with President Trump and I hope that we start to understand each other better and I'm grateful to Donald for it.

Clearly, there are some challenges left when we were not able to clear all the backlog but I think that we made a first important step in this direction.

And in conclusion, I want to point out that this atmosphere of cooperation is something that we are especially grateful for to our Finnish hosts. We are grateful for Finnish people and Finnish leadership for what they've done. I know that we have caused some inconvenience to Finland and we apologize for it.

Thank you for your attention.

**TRUMP:** Thank you. Thank you very much. I have just concluded a meeting with President Putin on a wide range of critical issues for both of our countries.

We had direct, open, deeply productive dialogue. Went very well. Before I begin, I want to thank President Niinisto of Finland for graciously hosting today's summit.

President Putin and I were saying how lovely it was and what a great job they did. I also want to congratulate Russia and President Putin for having done such an excellent job in hosting the World Cup. It was really one of the best ever and your team also did very well. It was a great job.

I'm here today to continue the proud tradition of bold American diplomacy. From the earliest days of our republic, American leaders have understood that diplomacy and engagement is preferable to conflict and hostility.

A productive dialogue is not only good for the United States and good for Russia but it is good for the world. The disagreements between our two countries are well-known and President Putin and I discussed them at length today.

But if we're going to solve many of the problems facing our world, then we are going to have to find ways to cooperate in pursuit of shared interests. Too often in both recent past and long ago, we have seen the consequences when diplomacy is left on the table.

We have also seen the benefits of cooperation. In the last century, our nations fought alongside one another in the Second World War. Even during the tensions of the Cold War, when the world looked much different than it does today, the United States and Russia were able to maintain a strong dialogue.

But our relationship has never been worse than it is now.

However, that changed, as of about four hours ago.

I really believe that. Nothing would be easier politically than to refuse to meet, to refuse to engage, but that would not accomplish anything.

As president, I cannot make decisions on foreign policy in a futile effort to appease partisan critics, or the media, or Democrats who want to do nothing but resist and obstruct.

Constructive dialogue between the United States and Russia affords the opportunity to open new pathways toward peace and stability in our world.

I would rather take a political risk in pursuit of peace than to risk peace in pursuit of politics.

As president, I will always put what is best for America and what is best for the American people.

During today's meeting, I addressed directly with President Putin the issue of Russian interference in our elections.

I felt this was a message best delivered in person. We spent a great deal of time talking about it and President Putin may very well want to address it and very strongly, because he feels very strongly about it and he has an interesting idea.

We also discussed one of the most critical challenges facing humanity: nuclear proliferation.

I provided an update on my meeting last month with Chairman Kim on the denuclearization of North Korea and after today, I am very sure that President Putin and Russia want very much to end that problem. Going to work with us and I appreciate that commitment.

The president and I also discussed the scourge of radical Islamic terrorism. Both Russia and the United States have suffered horrific terrorist attacks and we have agreed to maintain open communication between our security agencies to protect our citizens from this global menace.

Last year, we told Russia about a planned attack in St. Petersburg and they were able to stop it cold. They found them. They stopped them. There was no doubt about it.

I appreciated President Putin's phone call afterwards to thank me. I also emphasized the importance of placing pressure on Iran to halt its nuclear ambitions and to stop its campaign of violence throughout the area, throughout the Middle East.

As we discussed at length, the crisis in Syria is a complex one.

Cooperation between our two countries has the potential to save hundreds of thousands of lives.

I also made clear that the United States will not allow Iran to benefit from our successful campaign against ISIS. We have just about eradicated ISIS in the area.

We also agreed that representatives from our national security councils will meet to follow up on all of the issues we addressed today and to continue the progress we have started right here in Helsinki.

Today's meeting is only the beginning of a longer process but we have taken the first steps toward a brighter future and one with a strong dialogue and a lot of thought.

Our expectations are grounded in realism but our hopes are grounded in America's desire for friendship, cooperation and peace. And I think I can speak on behalf of Russia when I say that also.

President Putin, I want to thank you again for joining me for these important discussions and for advancing open dialogue between Russia and the United States.

Our meeting carries on a long tradition of diplomacy between Russia, the United States for the greater good of all and this was a very constructive day. This was a very constructive few hours that we spent together.

It's in the interest of both of our countries to continue our conversation and we have agreed to do so.

I'm sure we'll be meeting again in the future often and hopefully we will solve every one of the problems that we discussed today.

So again, President Putin, thank you very much.

**REPORTER:** Good afternoon. My name is Alexei Meshkov, Interfax Information Agency. I have a question to President Trump. During your recent European tour, you mentioned that the implementation of the Nord Stream 2 gas pipeline makes Europe a hostage of Russia. And you suggested that you could free Europe from this by supplying American LNG. But this cold winter, actually it showed that the current model, current mechanism, of supply of fuel to Europe is quite viable. At the same time, as far as I know, the U.S. had to buy even Russian gas for Boston. I have a question. The implementation of your idea has a political tinge to it or is this a practical one? Because there will be a gap formed in the supply and demand mechanism and first it's the consuming countries who will fall into this gap. And the second question, before the meeting with President Putin, you called him an adversary, a rival, and yet you expressed hope that you will be able to bring this relationship to a new level. Did you manage to do this?

**TRUMP:** No, actually I called him a competitor and a good competitor he is.

And I think the word competitor is a compliment. I think that we will be competing, when you talk about the pipeline. I'm not sure necessarily that it's in the best interest of Germany or not but that was a decision that they made.

We'll be competing. As you know the United States is now or soon will be, but I think it actually is right now, the largest in the oil and gas world.

So we're going to be selling LNG and we'll have to be competing with the pipeline and I think we'll compete successfully, although there is a little advantage locationally.

So I just wish them luck. I mean, I did. I discussed with Angela Merkel in pretty strong tones but I also know where they're all coming from and they have a very close source.

So we'll see how that all works out. But we have lots of sources now and the United States is much different than it was a number of years ago when we weren't able to extract what we can extract today. So today we're number one in the world at that. And I think we'll be out there competing very strongly. Thank you very much.

**PUTIN:** If I may, I'd throw in, I'd throw in some two cents. We talked to the president including this subject as well. We are aware of the stance of President Trump and I think that we, as a major oil and gas power and the United States as a major oil and gas power as well, we could work together on regulation of international markets because neither of us is actually interested in the plummeting of the prices and the consumers will suffer as well and the consumers in the United States will suffer as well.

And the shale gas production will suffer because beyond a certain price bracket it's no longer profitable to produce gas but nor we are interested in driving prices up because it will drain juices, life juices, from all other sectors of the economy from machinebuilding, etc. So we do have space for cooperation here, as the first thing. Then about the Nord Stream 2—Mr. President voiced his concerns about the possibility of disappearance of transit through Ukraine and I reassured Mr. President that Russia stands ready to maintain this transit.

Moreover, we stand ready to extend this transit contract that is about to expire next year. In case, if the dispute between the economic entities dispute will be settled in the Stockholm Arbitration Court.

**REPORTER, JEFF MASON,** *REUTERS*: Thank you. Mr. President, you tweeted this morning that it's U.S. foolishness, stupidity, and the Mueller probe that is responsible for the decline in U.S. relations with Russia. Do you hold Russia at all accountable or anything in particular? And if so, what would you what would you consider them that they are responsible for?

**TRUMP:** Yes I do. I hold both countries responsible. I think that the United States has been foolish. I think we've all been foolish. We should have had this dialogue a long time ago, a long time frankly before I got to office. And I think we're all to blame.

I think that the United States now has stepped forward, along with Russia, and we're getting together and we have a chance to do some great things, whether it's nuclear proliferation in terms of stopping, have to do it, ultimately that's probably the most important thing that we can be working on.

But I do feel that we have both made some mistakes. I think that the probe is a disaster for our country. I think it's kept us apart, it's kept us separated.

There was no collusion at all. Everybody knows it. People are being brought out to the fore. So far that I know virtually none of it related to the campaign.

And they're gonna have to try really hard to find somebody that did relate to the campaign. That was a clean campaign. I beat Hillary Clinton easily and frankly we beat her.

And I'm not even saying from the standpoint...we won that race. And it's a shame that there can even be a little bit of a cloud over it. People know that. People understand it. But the main thing and we discussed this also is zero collusion and it has had a negative impact upon the relationship of the two largest nuclear powers in the world.

We have 90 percent of nuclear power between the two countries. It's ridiculous. It's ridiculous what's going on with the probe.

**REPORTER:** For President Putin, if I could follow up as well. Why should Americans and why should President Trump believe your statement that Russia did not intervene in the 2016 election, given the evidence that U.S. intelligence agencies have provided? And will you consider extraditing the 12 Russian officials that were indicted last week by a U.S. grand jury?

**TRUMP:** Well, I'm going to let the president answer the second part of that question. But, as you know, the whole concept of that came up perhaps a little bit before but it came out as a reason why the Democrats lost an election, which frankly, they should have been able to win because the electoral college is much more advantageous for Democrats, as you know, than it is to Republicans. We won the Electoral College by a lot. 306 to 223, I believe.

And that was a well fought, that was a well fought battle. We did a great job. And frankly, I'm going to let the president speak to the second part of your question. But just to say it one time again and I say it all the time, there was no collusion. I didn't know the president.

There was nobody to collude with. There was no collusion with the campaign and every time you hear all of these you know 12 and 14—stuff that has nothing to do and frankly they admit—these are not people involved in the campaign.

But to the average reader out there, they're saying well maybe that does. It doesn't. And even the people involved, some perhaps told mis-stories or in one case the FBI said there was no lie. There was no lie. Somebody else said there was. We ran a brilliant campaign and that's why I'm president. Thank you.

**PUTIN:** As to who is to be believed and to who is not to be believed, you can trust no one—if you take this—where did you get this idea that President Trump trusts me or I trust him?

He defends the interests of the United States of America. And I do defend the interests of the Russian Federation. We do have interests that are common.

We are looking for points of contact. There are issues where our postures diverge and we are looking for ways to reconcile our differences, how to make our effort more meaningful.

We should not proceed from the immediate political interests that guide certain political powers in our countries.

We should be guided by facts. Could you name a single fact that would definitively prove the collusion? This is utter nonsense.

Just like the president recently mentioned. Yes, the public at large in the United States had a certain perceived opinion of the candidates during the campaign. But there's nothing particularly extraordinary about it. That's a usual thing.

President Trump, when he was a candidate, he mentioned the need to restore the Russia U.S. relationship and it's clear that a certain part of American society felt sympathetic about it and different people could express their sympathy in different ways.

But isn't that natural? Isn't it natural to be sympathetic towards a person who is willing to restore the relationship with our country, who wants to work with us? We heard the accusations about the Concorde country. Well, as far as I know, this company hired American lawyers and the accusations doesn't have a fighting chance in the American courts.

So there's no evidence when it comes to the actual facts. So we have to be guided by facts, not by rumors.

Now let's get back to the issue of these 12 alleged intelligence officers of Russia. I don't know the full extent of the situation, but President Trump mentioned this issue and I will look into it.

So far, I can say the following: the things that are off the top of my head. We have an acting, an existing agreement between the United States of America and the Russian Federation, an existing treaty, that dates back to 1999, the Mutual Assistance on Criminal Cases. This treaty is in full effect. It works quite efficiently.

On average, we initiate about 100-150 criminal cases upon the request from foreign states.

For instance, the last year, there was one extradition case on the request sent by the United States. So this treaty has specific legal procedures. We can offer that the appropriate commission headed by special attorney Mueller.

He can use this treaty as a solid foundation and send a formal and official request to us so that we would interrogate, we would hold the questioning of these individuals who he believes are privy to some crimes and our law enforcement are perfectly able to do this questioning and send the appropriate materials to the United States.

Moreover, we can meet you halfway. We can make another step. We can actually permit official representatives of the United States, including the members of this very commission headed by Mr. Mueller, we can lead them into the country and they will be present at this questioning.

But in this case, there's another condition. This kind of effort should be a mutual one. Then we would expect that the Americans would reciprocate and that they would question officials including the officers of law enforcement and intelligence services of the United States, whom we believe have something to do with illegal actions on the territory of Russia. And we have to request the presence of our law enforcement.

For instance, we can bring up Mr. Browder in this particular case. Business associates of Mr. Browder have earned over one and a half billion dollars in Russia. They never paid any taxes, neither in Russia nor in the United States and yet the money escaped the country, they were transferred to the United States.

They sent a huge amount of money—400 million—as a contribution to the campaign of Hillary Clinton.

Well, that's their personal case, it might have been legal, the contribution itself, but the way the money was earned was illegal.

So we have a solid reason to believe that some intelligence officers accompanied and guided these transactions. So we have an interest of questioning them. That could be a first step and we can also extend it. Options abound.

And they all can be found in an appropriate legal framework.

**REPORTER:** Did you want President Trump to win the election and did you direct any of your officials to help him do that?

**PUTIN:** Yes, I wanted him to win. Because he talked about bringing the U.S. Russia relationship back to normal.

I think there were three questions from the Russian pool. Russia Today, you have the floor.

**REPORTER:** Mr. President, would you please go into the details, if possible, any specific arrangements for the U.S. to work together with Russia in Syria, if any of these kind of arrangements were made today or discussed? My question to

President Putin in Russian: Since we brought up the issue of football several times, I use the football language: Mr. Pompeo mentioned that when we talk about the Syrian cooperation, the ball is in the Syrian court. Mr. Putin, in Russian court—is it true? And how would you use this fact—them having a ball?

**TRUMP:** Well, I guess I'll answer the first part of the question. We've worked with Israel long and hard for many years, many decades. I think we've never, never has anyone, any country been closer than we are.

President Putin also is helping Israel and we both spoke with Bibi Netanyahu and they would like to do certain things with respect to Syria, having to do with the safety of Israel.

So in that respect, we absolutely would like to work in order to help Israel and Israel will be working with us.

So both countries would work jointly.

And I think that when you look at all of the progress that's been made in certain sections with the eradication of ISIS, we're about 98 percent, 99 percent there, and other things that have taken place that we've done and that frankly Russia has helped us with in certain respects.

But I think that they're working with Israel is a great thing and creating safety for Israel is something that both President Putin and I would like to see very much.

One little thing I might add to that is the helping of people. Helping of people. Because you have such horrible, if you see and I've seen reports and I've seen pictures, I've seen just about everything. And if we can do something to help the people of Syria get back into some form of shelter and on a humanitarian basis, and that's what the word was really a humanitarian basis. I think that both of us would be very interested in doing that and we are. We will do that. Thank you very much.

**REPORTER:** Excuse me. But for now no specific agreements for instance between the militaries—

**TRUMP:** Well our militaries do get along.

In fact our military actually have gotten along probably better than our political leaders for years but our militaries do get along very well and they do coordinate in Syria and other places. Ok? Thank you.

**PUTIN:** Yes, we did mention this. We mentioned the humanitarian track of this issue. Yesterday, I discussed this with French president Mr. Macron and we reached an agreement that together with European countries, including France, will step up this effort.

On our behalf, we'll provide military cargo aircraft to deliver the humanitarian cargo and today I brought up this issue with President Trump. I think there is plenty of things to look into.

The crucial thing here is that huge amount of refugees are in Turkey, in Lebanon, in Jordan in the states that border, are adjacent to Syria. If we help them, the migratory pressure upon the European states will drop, will be decreased many fold.

And I believe it's crucial from any point of view, from humanitarian point of view, from the point of view of helping people, helping the refugees and in general

I agree, I concur with President Trump our military cooperate quite successfully together. They do get along and I hope they will be able to do so in future.

And we will keep working in the Astana format—I mean Russia Turkey and Iran which I informed President Trump about.

But we do stand ready to link these efforts to the so-called small group of states so that the process would be a broader one, it would be a multidimensional one.

And so that we will be able to maximize our fighting chance to get the ultimate success in the issue of Syria.

And speaking about having the ball in our court in Syria.

President Trump has just mentioned that we've successfully concluded the World Football Cup.

Speaking of the football, actually. Mr. President I'll give this ball to you. And now the ball is in your court.

All the more that the United States will host the World Cup in 2026.

**TRUMP:** That's right. Thank you very much. We do host it and we hope we do as good a job. That's very nice. That will go to my son Barron. We have no question. In fact, Melania, here you go.

**REPORTER, AP:** President Trump, you first. Just now, President Putin denied having anything to do with the election interference in 2016. Every U.S. intelligence agency has concluded that Russia did. My first question for you sir is, who do you believe? My second question is would you now, with the whole world watching, tell President Putin, would you denounce what happened in 2016 and would you warn him to never do it again?

**TRUMP:** So let me just say that we have two thoughts. You have groups that are wondering why the FBI never took the server. Why haven't they taken the server? Why was the FBI told to leave the office of the Democratic National Committee?

I've been wondering that. I've been asking that for months and months and I've been tweeting it out and calling it out on social media. Where is the server? I want to know where is the server and what is the server saying?

With that being said, all I can do is ask the question.

My people came to me, Dan Coates, came to me and some others they said they think it's Russia. I have President Putin. He just said it's not Russia.

I will say this: I don't see any reason why it would be. But I really do want to see the server but I have, I have confidence in both parties.

I really believe that this will probably go on for a while but I don't think it can go on without finding out what happened to the server. What happened to the servers of the Pakistani gentleman that worked on the DNC?

Where are those servers? They're missing. Where are they? What happened to Hillary Clinton's emails? 33,000 emails gone, just gone. I think in Russia they wouldn't be gone so easily.

I think it's a disgrace that we can't get Hillary Clinton's thirty three thousand e-mails.

I have great confidence in my intelligence people but I will tell you that President

Putin was extremely strong and powerful in his denial today and what he did is an incredible offer.

He offered to have the people working on the case come and work with their investigators, with respect to the 12 people. I think that's an incredible offer. Ok? Thank you.

**PUTIN:** I'd like to add something to this. After all, I was an intelligence officer myself and I do know how dossiers are made up. Just a second. That's the first thing. Now the second thing.

I believe that Russia is a democratic state and I hope you're not denying this right to your own country. You're not denying that United States is a democracy. Do you believe the United States is a democracy?

And if so, if it is a democratic state, then the final conclusion and this kind of dispute can only be delivered by a trial, by the court, not by the executive, by the law enforcement.

For instance, the Concord company that was brought up is being accused—it's been accused of interference. But this company does not constitute the Russian state.

It does not represent the Russian state. And I brought several examples before.

Well, you have a lot of individuals in the United States, take George Soros for instance, with multibillion capitals. But it doesn't make him, his position, the posture of the United States. No it does not. Well, it's the same case.

There is the issue of trying a case in the court and the final say is for the court to deliver.

We are now talking about the private individuals and not about the particular states. And as far as the most recent allegations is concerned about the Russian intelligence officers, we do have an intergovernmental treaty.

Please do send us the request. We will analyze it properly and we will send a formal response. And as I said we can extend this cooperation. But we should do it on a reciprocal basis because we would await our Russian counterparts to provide us access to the persons of interest for us, whom we believe can have something to do with intelligence services.

Let's discuss the specific issues and not use the Russia and the U.S. relationship as a loose change, for this internal political struggle.

**REPORTER:** A question for President Putin. Two questions for you, sir. Can you tell me what President Trump may have indicated to you about officially recognizing Crimea as part of Russia? And then secondly, sir, do you, does the Russian government have any compromising material on President Trump or his family?

**PUTIN:** (chuckles) President Trump and—well, the posture of President Trump on Crimea is well known and he stands firmly by it, he continue to maintain that it was illegal to annex it. We—our viewpoint is different. We held a referendum in strict compliance with the UN Charter and the international legislation. For us, this issue, we put *unintelligible* to this issue. And now to the compromising material.

Yeah, I did heard these rumors that we allegedly collected compromising material on Mr. Trump when he was visiting Moscow.

Now, our distinguished colleague, let me tell you this.

When President Trump was at Moscow back then I didn't even know that he was in Moscow. I treat President Trump with utmost respect. But back then, when he was a private individual, a businessman, nobody informed me that he was in Moscow.

Well, let's take St. Petersburg economic forum, for instance. There were over 500 American businessmen—high ranking, the high level ones, I don't even remember the last names of each and every one of them.

Do you think that we tried to collect compromising material on each and every single one of them? Well, it's difficult to imagine an utter nonsense of a bigger scale than this.

Well, please just disregard these issues and don't think about this anymore again

**TRUMP:** And I have to say if they had it, it would have been out long ago and if anybody watched Peter Strzok testify over the last couple of days and I was in Brussels watching it, it was a disgrace to the FBI, it was a disgrace to our country. And you would say that was a total witch hunt. Thank you very much everybody. Thank you.

### Print Citations

**CMS:** Trump, Donald, and Vladimir Putin. "Joint Press Conference at the Helsinki Summit." Speeches presented at the Presidential Palace, Helsinki, Finland, July 16, 2018. In *The Reference Shelf: Representative American Speeches 2017-2018*, edited by Micah L. Issit, 97-109. Ipswich, MA: H.W. Wilson, 2018.

**MLA:** Trump, Donald, and Vladimir Putin. "Joint Press Conference at the Helsinki Summit." Presidential Palace, 16 July 2018, Helsinki, Finland. Presentation. *The Reference Shelf: Representative American Speeches 2017-2018*, edited by Micah L. Issit, H.W. Wilson, 2018, pp. 97-109.

**APA:** Trump, D., & Putin, V. (2018, July 16). Joint press conference at the Helsinki summit. Presidential Palace, Helsinki, Finland. In M.L. Issit (Ed.), *The reference shelf: Representative American speeches 2017-2018* (pp. 97-109). Ipswich, MA: H.W. Wilson. (Original work published 2018)

# Proposal for the United States Space Force

## By Mike Pence

*Mike Pence is a former lawyer and US congressman for the state of Indiana. After serving as a conservative radio host in the 1990s, Pence was elected to the US House of Representatives in 2001, serving in that capacity until 2013. That year, Pence was elected governor of Indiana, a position he held until 2017 when he was invited to serve as vice president under Donald Trump. Pence has drawn criticism for his stance on LGBT rights and his position on abortion. In this White House briefing, Vice President Pence discusses national security and the controversial Donald Trump proposal for the creation of a "Space Force," envisioned as a sixth branch of the US military in charge of enhancing security for operations in space.*

Secretary Mattis, Deputy Secretary Shanahan, General Selva, General Goldfein, members of the Armed Forces of the United States of America, and all the men and women of the United States Department of Defense who each and every day oversee the greatest military in the history of the world: Thank you for all you do every day for the American people. (Applause.)

It is my great honor, Mr. Secretary, to join you here today at the Pentagon. And let me begin by bringing greetings from your Commander-in-Chief, who has from the very earliest days of this administration proved himself to be a great champion of the Armed Forces of the United States, committed to strengthening American security here on Earth and in space. I bring greetings from the 45th President of the United States of America, President Donald Trump. (Applause.)

In his Inaugural Address to the nation, President Trump proclaimed that the United States stands, in his words, "at the birth of a new millennium, ready to unlock the mysteries of space."

And since day one of our administration, this President has kept his promise to restore America's proud legacy of leadership in space, believing that space is essential to our nation's security, prosperity, and our very way of life.

Last year, after it had lain dormant for nearly a quarter-century, President Trump revived the National Space Council to reinvigorate and coordinate space activities across our government.

It is my great honor, as Vice President, to serve as the Chairman of the National Space Council. And I'm pleased to report that President Trump has already signed three new space policy directives to reorient our space program toward human

---

Delivered on August 9, 2018, at the Pentagon, Washington, DC.

exploration, unleash America's burgeoning commercial space companies, and safe-guard our vital space assets with new space traffic management policy.

But as Commander-in-Chief, President Trump's highest priority is the safety and security of the American people. And while, too often, previous administrations all but neglected the growing security threats emerging in space, President Trump stated clearly and forcefully that space is, in his words, "a warfighting domain, just like…land, [and] air, and sea."

And just as we've done in ages past, the United States of America, under his leadership, will meet the emerging threats on this new battlefield with American ingenuity and strength to defend our nation, protect our people, and carry the cause of liberty and peace into the next great American frontier.

In 1939, at the start of the Second World War, the U.S. Army Air Corps was still a fledgling organization. But as Nazi air forces bombed their way from Warsaw to London, our military commanders took decisive action then to meet that new threat head on.

By 1945, the American military had nearly 30 times the number of planes, and 85 times the number of pilots and support crews compared to just six years earlier.

America and our allies emerged victorious from World War II because of the strength of our armed forces, and because our armed forces adapted to meet the emerging threats of the day. We knew that airpower had forever changed the nature of war, so we marshaled the resources and the will to build the most powerful air force the world had ever seen.

And just two years after that terrible conflict, our nation created a new branch of service to secure American dominance in the skies for generations to come with the creation of the United States Air Force.

Now the time has come to write the next great chapter in the history of our armed forces, to prepare for the next battlefield where America's best and bravest will be called to deter and defeat a new generation of threats to our people and to our nation. The time has come to establish the United States Space Force.

And that's what brings us here today. Seven weeks ago, President Trump directed the Department of Defense "to immediately begin the process necessary to establish a Space Force as the sixth branch of the armed forces."

The President made it clear that our ultimate objective is to create a new branch of our military that is separate from, and equal to, five other branches.

Today, the Department of Defense will release a report outlining the first stages of our administration's plan to implement the President's guidance and turn his vision into a reality.

This report reviews the national security space activities within the Department of Defense, and it identifies concrete steps that our administration will take to lay the foundation for a new Department of the Space Force.

Now, to be clear, the Space Force will not be built from scratch because the men and the women who run and protect our nation's space programs today are already the best in the world. And since the dawn of the Space Age, America has remained the best in space. (Applause.)

Over the past 60 years, the United States has assembled the largest and most sophisticated constellation of military and intelligence satellites in the world.

We've pioneered the technology to leverage American power in space here on Earth, and give our warfighters the intelligence that they need, and give our intelligence community the information they need to maintain a strategic advantage wherever our warfighters are operating.

Across this Department and our intelligence agency, there are literally tens of thousands of military personnel, civilians, and contractors operating and supporting our space systems, and together they're the eyes and the ears of America's warfighters around the globe. And they do a remarkable job.

I've seen their work firsthand. I've traveled across the country to meet with the men and women who are fighting for America's future in space in my first year and a half on this job, from the airmen of the 50th Space Wing at Schriever Air Force Base, whose fleet of surveillance, navigation, and communication satellites increase the agility, precision, and effectiveness of our armed forces; to the engineers of the Missile Defense Agency at Redstone Arsenal in Alabama who are forging the next generation of rockets to strengthen our missile defense; to the many other bases and facilities across the country where our men and women in uniform work together with our intelligence community and our allies to protect our people, our nation, and our interests around the world.

And over the past 18 months, President Trump and our entire administration have taken decisive action to strengthen American power in space as well.

President Trump recently signed the largest investment in our national defense since the days of Ronald Reagan. (Applause.) And that new Defense budget included new resources for two cutting-edge military communications satellites and nearly $1 billion for our space defense programs. And today, we renew the President's call on the Congress of the United States to invest an additional $8 billion in our space security systems over the next five years.

The men and women of this Department have also taken historic steps to secure American leadership in space. At the direction of Secretary Mattis, the Department of Defense is fielding a new generation of jam-resistant GPS and communications satellites and new missile-warning satellites that are smaller, tougher, and more maneuverable than ever before.

And while these steps have been vital to our national defense, they're really only a beginning. They're only a beginning of meeting the rising security threats our nation faces in space today and in the future. As President Trump has said, in his words, "It is not enough to merely have an American presence in space; we must have American dominance in space." And so we will. (Applause.)

And that's precisely why we're beginning the process of establishing a Space Force as the sixth branch of our armed forces. Just as in the past, when we created the Air Force, establishing the Space Force is an idea whose time has come.

The space environment has fundamentally changed in the last generation. What was once peaceful and uncontested is now crowded and adversarial. Today, other nations are seeking to disrupt our space-based systems and challenge American supremacy in space as never before.

For many years, nations from Russia and China to North Korea and Iran have pursued weapons to jam, blind, and disable our navigation and communications satellites via electronic attacks from the ground.

But recently, our adversaries have been working to bring new weapons of war into space itself. In 2007, China launched a missile that tracked and destroyed one of its own satellites—a highly provocative demonstration of China's growing capability to militarize space.

Russia has been designing an airborne laser to disrupt our space-based system. And it claims to be developing missiles that can be launched from an aircraft mid-flight to destroy American satellites.

Both China and Russia have been conducting highly sophisticated on-orbit activities that could enable them to maneuver their satellites into close proximity of ours, posing unprecedented new dangers to our space systems.

Both nations are also investing heavily in what are known as hypersonic missiles designed to fly up to five miles per second at such low altitudes that they could potentially evade detection by our missile-defense radars. In fact, China claimed to have made its first successful test of a hypersonic vehicle just last week.

China and Russia are also aggressively working to incorporate anti-satellite attacks into their warfighting doctrines. In 2015, China created a separate military enterprise to oversee and prioritize its warfighting capabilities in space.

As their actions make clear, our adversaries have transformed space into a warfighting domain already. And the United States will not shrink from this challenge. (Applause.) Under President Trump's leadership, we will meet it head on to defend our nation and build a peaceful future here on Earth and in space.

America will always seek peace in space as on the Earth. But history proves that peace only comes through strength. And in the realm of outer space, the United States Space Force will be that strength in the years ahead. (Applause.)

Now, the report the Department of Defense will release today, that Secretary Mattis just referenced, represents a critical step toward establishing the Space Force as the sixth branch of our armed forces. It actually identifies four actions that we will take to evolve our space capabilities, and they are built on the lessons of the past.

We all remember the hard lesson learned in the early 1980s, as the tragic debacle of Desert One took place. Eight American patriots fell in the line of duty while trying to rescue their fellow Americans who were being held hostage in Iran.

In the wake of that failed mission, America resolved to ensure that our joint warfighters would always have the training, coordination, and leadership they needed to accomplish their missions. And the steps that our nation took in the years that followed paved the way for the creation of the United States Special Operations Command.

Since that time, this vital combatant command has directed our Special Operations Forces to become the most effective and lethal fighting force in the history of the world. (Applause.) Our Special Operations Forces, through this unified command, have been defending our security and advancing interests, as they do to this very hour, in every corner of the globe.

Along those same lines, today's report calls for the creation of a new unified combatant command for space: The United States Space Command.

This new command structure for the physical domain of space, led by a four-star flag officer, will establish unified command and control for our Space Force operations, ensure integration across the military, and develop the space warfighting doctrine, tactics, techniques, and procedures of the future.

The second step this report calls for is the creation of an elite group of joint warfighters specializing in the domain of space who will form the backbone of the nation's newest armed service: Space Operations Force.

Just like our Special Operations Forces, a Space Operations Force will draw men and women from across the military and will grow into their own unique and cohesive community. They'll support the combatant commands by providing space expertise in times of crisis and conflict.

Third, this report calls for the creation of a new joint organization, the Space Development Agency, that will ensure the men and women of the Space Force have the cutting-edge warfighting capabilities that they need and deserve.

While our adversaries have been busy weaponizing space, too often we have bureaucratized it. And over time, our ability to adapt to new and emerging threats has been stifled by needless layers of red tape.

The Space Development Agency will break free from ineffective and duplicative bureaucratic structures to focus on innovation, experimentation, and forging the technologies of the future.

The men and women of the Department of Defense have pioneered some of the most groundbreaking discoveries in our armed forces that literally have revolutionized our national defense in times of need, from General Schriever's creation of the intercontinental ballistic missile to Admiral Rickover's development of the Navy's nuclear enterprise.

And now we must do our part to make bold breakthroughs, strengthen America's industrial base, and deliver the cutting-edge warfighting capabilities faster than our adversaries could ever imagine. And that's exactly what Americans will do. (Applause.)

Finally, this report calls for clear lines of responsibility and accountability to manage the process of standing up and scaling up the United States Department of the Space Force.

Creating a new branch of the military is not a simple process. It will require collaboration, diligence, and above all, leadership. As challenges arise, deadlines approach, there must be someone in charge who can execute, hold others accountable, and be responsible for the results.

So we will create a single civilian position, reporting to the Secretary of Defense, to oversee the growth and expansion of this new branch of service. This position will be a new Assistant Secretary of Defense for Space. And this leader will be key to the critical transition to a fully independent Secretary of the Space Force in the years ahead.

President Trump and I are grateful—truly grateful to Secretary Mattis for this Department's diligence in preparing this report. And our administration will soon take action to implement these recommendations, with the objective of establishing the United States Department of the Space Force by the year 2020.

Ultimately, Congress must act to establish this new Department which will organize, train, and equip the United States Space Force.

Our administration is already working with leaders in the Congress to do just that. We're building bipartisan support for our plan, working closely with committee counterparts like Congressman Mac Thornberry, and Congressman Adam Smith, and Congressman Mike Rogers, and Congressman Jim Cooper.

Next February, in the President's budget, we will call on the Congress to marshal the resources we need to stand up the Space Force.

And before the end of next year, our administration will work with the Congress to enact the statutory authority for the Space Force in the National Defense Authorization Act.

Our nation's armed forces have always been the vanguard of advancing American leadership here on Earth and beyond. And the Space Force is the next and the natural evolution of American military strength.

The first American rockets in space were launched by our military. The first American satellites to orbit the Earth were on reconnaissance missions, peering behind the Iron Curtain. The first Americans to step forward to venture into the unknown were the world's greatest aviators and test pilots from the Navy, the Air Force, and the Marine Corps.

And the next generation of Americans to confront the emerging threats in the boundless expanse of space will be wearing the uniform of the United States of America as well. (Applause.)

And I'll promise you, your Commander-in-Chief is going to continue to work tirelessly toward this goal, and we expect you all to do the same.

And to all the men and women of this Department: This is the moment. Now is the time to act quickly, using all the tools at your disposal to lead our nation forward with President Trump's vision to meet the challenges that lie ahead.

There is much work to do. Success will demand the very best of each of you. So be bold, be creative, unencumbered by the past or the status quo. And remember, when it comes to defending our nation and protecting our way of life, the only thing we can't afford is inaction. The American people deserve our very best, and they will have it.

As the President will discuss in further detail in the days ahead, the United States Space Force will strengthen our security, it will ensure our prosperity, and it will also carry American ideals into the boundless expanse of space.

While other nations increasingly possess the capability to operate in space, not all of them share our commitment to freedom, to private property, and the rule of law. So as we continue to carry American leadership in space, so also will we carry America's commitment to freedom into this new frontier. (Applause.)

So this is the moment. Now is the time to do as Americans have always done in ages past, to lead with strength and a pioneering spirit into the future. And under the leadership of President Trump, our Commander-in-Chief, we will take the first bold steps to ensure our security on Earth and in outer space with renewed American strength.

And as we embark, we do so with faith. Faith in all of you who have answered the call to serve in the uniform of the United States of America at such a time as this in the life of our nation. Faith to all the incredible civilian personnel who serve here in the Department of Defense with equal devotion to our nation.

And we do so with that other kind of faith as well. And just as generations of Americans have carried those who have taken to the skies in the defense of freedom borne upon their prayers, I want to assure all of you, who will be called to this enterprise, that you can be confident. You can be confident that you will go with the prayers of millions of Americans who will claim on your behalf, as generations have claimed before, those ancient words, that if you "rise on the wings of the dawn, if [you] settle on the far side of the sea," even if you go up to the heavens, "even there His hand will guide [you], His right hand will hold [you] fast." And He will hold fast this great nation in the great beyond.

So thank you for your service to the country for all of you who have been called to serve in our armed forces. With your unwavering commitment, with the courage of our men and women in uniform, with the continued support of the American people, with the vision and leadership of our Commander-in-Chief, and with God's help, I know we will give America the defense she needs here on Earth and in the outer reaches of space.

Thank you. And God bless you. And God bless the United States of America. (Applause.)

### Print Citations

**CMS:** Pence, Mike. "Proposal for the United States Space Force." Speech presented at the Pentagon, Washington, DC, August 9, 2018. In *The Reference Shelf: Representative American Speeches 2017-2018*, edited by Micah L. Issit, 110-116. Ipswich, MA: H.W. Wilson, 2018.

**MLA:** Pence, Mike. "Proposal for the United States Space Force." Pentagon, 9 August 2018, Washington, DC. Presentation. *The Reference Shelf: Representative American Speeches 2017-2018*, edited by Micah L. Issit, H.W. Wilson, 2018, pp. 110-116.

**APA:** Pence, M. (2018, August 9). Proposal for the United States Space Force. Pentagon, Washington, DC. In M.L. Issit (Ed.), *The reference shelf: Representative American speeches 2017-2018* (pp. 110-116). Ipswich, MA: H.W. Wilson. (Original work published 2018)

# 3

# Political Responses to the Establishment

Bernie Sanders via Wikimedia

An outspoken critic of the Trump administration, Senator Bernie Sanders responded to the first State of the Union address by pointing out inaccuracies in the president's claims and by speaking out about the financial issues still affecting many Americans.

# Response to Donald Trump's 2018 State of the Union Address

## By Bernie Sanders

Bernie Sanders is a US senator for the state of Vermont, and he previously spent six-teen years in the House of Representatives. Sanders was catapulted into the national spotlight during his 2016 bid for the Democratic Party nomination for the presidency against Hillary Clinton. Though Sanders lost the nomination to Clinton, he demon-strated the ability to generate a strong, grassroots support base. A 2018 report from Morning Consult indicated that Sanders was the most popular of all US congressmen, with a 72 percent approval rating overall. Sanders has become well-known as an out-spoken political activist and critic of the Trump administration. In this 2018 speech, Sanders points out potentially inaccurate statements made by Trump in promotion of his presidency and discusses the financial burdens faced by American citizens.

Good evening. Thanks for joining us.

Tonight, I want to take a few minutes of your time to respond to President Trump's State of the Union speech. But I want to do more than just that. I want to talk to you about the major crises facing our country that, regrettably, President Trump chose not to discuss. I want to talk to you about the lies that he told during his campaign and the promises he made to working people which he did not keep.

Finally, I want to offer a vision of where we should go as a nation which is far different than the divisiveness, dishonesty, and racism coming from the Trump Ad-ministration over the past year.

President Trump talked tonight about the strength of our economy. Well, he's right. Official unemployment today is 4.1 percent which is the lowest it has been in years and the stock market in recent months has soared. That's the good news.

But what President Trump failed to mention is that his first year in office marked the lowest level of job creation since 2010. In fact, according to the Bureau of Labor Statistics, 254,000 fewer jobs were created in Trump's first 11 months in office than were created in the 11 months before he entered office.

Further, when we talk about the economy, what's most important is to under-stand what is happening to the average worker. And here's the story that Trump failed to mention tonight.

Over the last year, after adjusting for inflation, the average worker in America saw a wage increase of, are you ready for this, 4 cents an hour, or 0.17%. Or, to put

Delivered on January 30, 2018, Facebook.

it in a different way, that worker received a raise of a little more than $1.60 a week. And, as is often the case, that tiny wage increase disappeared as a result of soaring health care costs.

Meanwhile, at a time of massive wealth and income inequality, the rich continue to get much richer while millions of American workers are working two or three jobs just to keep their heads above water. Since March of last year, the three richest people in America saw their wealth increase by more than $68 billion. Three people. A $68 billion increase in wealth. Meanwhile, the average worker saw an increase of 4 cents an hour.

Tonight, Donald Trump touted the bonuses he claims workers received because of his so-called "tax reform" bill. What he forgot to mention is that only 2% of Americans report receiving a raise or a bonus because of this tax bill.

What he also failed to mention is that some of the corporations that have given out bonuses, such as Walmart, AT&T, General Electric, and Pfizer, are also laying off tens of thousands of their employees. Kimberly-Clark, the maker of Kleenex and Huggies, recently said they were using money from the tax cut to restructure—laying off more than 5,000 workers and closing 10 plants.

What Trump also forgot to tell you is that while the Walton family of Walmart, the wealthiest family in America, and Jeff Bezos of Amazon, the wealthiest person in this country, have never had it so good, many thousands of their employees are forced onto Medicaid, food stamps, and public housing because of the obscenely low wages they are paid. In my view, that's wrong. The taxpayers of this country should not be providing corporate welfare to the wealthiest families in this country.

## Trump's Broken Promises

Now, let me say a few words about some of the issues that Donald Trump failed to mention tonight, and that is the difference between what he promised the American people as a candidate and what he has delivered as president.

Many of you will recall, that during his campaign, Donald Trump told the American people how he was going to provide "health insurance for everybody," with "much lower deductibles."

That is what he promised working families all across this country during his campaign. But as president he did exactly the opposite. Last year, he supported legislation that would have thrown up to 32 million people off of the health care they had while, at the same time, substantially raising premiums for older Americans.

The reality is that although we were able to beat back Trump's effort to repeal the Affordable Care Act, 3 million fewer Americans have health insurance today than before Trump took office and that number will be going even higher in the coming months.

During his campaign, Trump promised not to cut Social Security, Medicare or Medicaid.

As president, however, he supported a Republican Budget Resolution that proposed slashing Medicaid by $1 trillion and cutting Medicare by $500 billion.

Further, President Trump's own budget called for cutting Social Security Disability Insurance by $64 billion.

During Trump's campaign for president, he talked about how he was going to lower prescription drug prices and take on the greed of the pharmaceutical industry which he said was "getting away with murder." Tonight he said "one of my greatest priorities is to reduce the price of prescription drugs."

But, as president, Trump nominated Alex Azar, a former executive of the Eli Lilly Company—one of the largest drug companies in this country—to head up the Department of Health and Human Services.

Trump spoke about how other countries "drugs cost far less," yet he has done nothing to allow Americans to purchase less expensive prescription drugs from abroad or to require Medicare to negotiate drug prices—which he promised he would do when he ran for president.

During the campaign, Donald Trump told us that: "The rich will not be gaining at all" under his tax reform plan.

Well, that was quite a whopper. As president, the tax reform legislation Trump signed into law a few weeks ago provides 83 percent of the benefits to the top one percent, drives up the deficit by $1.7 trillion, and raises taxes on 92 million middle class families by the end of the decade.

During his campaign for president, Trump talked about how he was going to take on the greed of Wall Street which he said "has caused tremendous problems for us."

As president, not only has Trump not taken on Wall Street, he has appointed more Wall Street billionaires to his administration than any president in history. And now, on behalf of Wall Street, he is trying to repeal the modest provisions of the Dodd-Frank legislation which provide consumer protections against Wall Street thievery.

## What Trump Didn't Say

But what is also important to note is not just Trump's dishonesty. It is that tonight he avoided some of the most important issues facing our country and the world.

How can a president of the United States give a State of the Union speech and not mention climate change? No, Mr. Trump, climate change is not a "hoax." It is a reality which is causing devastating harm all over our country and all over the world and you are dead wrong when you appoint administrators at the EPA and other agencies who are trying to decimate environmental protection rules, and slow down the transition to sustainable energy.

How can a president of the United States not discuss the disastrous Citizens United Supreme Court decision which allows billionaires like the Koch brothers to undermine American democracy by spending hundreds of millions of dollars to elect candidates who will represent the rich and the powerful?

How can he not talk about Republican governors efforts all across this country to undermine democracy, suppress the vote and make it harder for poor people or people of color to vote?

How can he not talk about the fact that in a highly competitive global economy, hundreds of thousands of bright young people are unable to afford to go to college, while millions of others have come out of school deeply in debt?

How can he not talk about the inadequate funding and staffing at the Social Security Administration which has resulted in thousands of people with disabilities dying because they did not get their claims processed in time?

How can he not talk about the retirement crisis facing the working people of this country and the fact that over half of older workers have no retirement savings? We need to strengthen pensions in this country, not take them away from millions of workers.

How can he not talk about the reality that Russia, through cyberwarfare, interfered in our election in 2016, is interfering in democratic elections all over the world, and according to his own CIA director will likely interfere in the 2018 midterm elections that we will be holding. How do you not talk about that unless you have a very special relationship with Mr. Putin?

## What Trump Did Talk About

Now, let me say a few words about what Trump did talk about.

Trump talked about DACA and immigration, but what he did not tell the American people is that he precipitated this crisis in September by repealing President Obama's executive order protecting Dreamers.

We need to seriously address the issue of immigration but that does not mean dividing families and reducing legal immigration by 25-50 percent. It sure doesn't mean forcing taxpayers to spend $25 billion on a wall that candidate Trump promised Mexico would pay for. And it definitely doesn't mean a racist immigration policy that excludes people of color from around the world.

To my mind, this is one of the great moral issues facing our country. It would be unspeakable and a moral stain on our nation if we turned our backs on these 800,000 young people who were born and raised in this country and who know no other home but the United States.

And that's not just Bernie Sanders talking. Poll after poll shows that over 80 percent of the American people believe that we should protect the legal status of these young people and provide them with a path toward citizenship.

We need to pass the bi-partisan DREAM Act, and we need to pass it now.

President Trump also talked about the need to rebuild our country's infrastructure. And he is absolutely right. But the proposal he is bringing forth is dead wrong.

Instead of spending $1.5 trillion over ten years rebuilding our crumbling infrastructure, Trump would encourage states to sell our nation's highways, bridges, and other vital infrastructure to Wall Street, wealthy campaign contributors, even foreign governments.

And how would Wall Street and these corporations recoup their investments? By imposing massive new tolls and fees paid for by American commuters and homeowners.

The reality is that Trump's plan to privatize our nation's infrastructure is an old idea that has never worked and never will work.

Tonight, Donald Trump correctly talked about the need to address the opioid crisis. Well, I say to Donald Trump, you don't help people suffering from opioid addiction by cutting Medicaid by $1 trillion. If you are serious about dealing with this crisis, we need to expand, not cut Medicaid.

## Conclusion/A Progressive Agenda

My fellow Americans. The simple truth is that, according to virtually every poll, Donald Trump is the least popular president after one year in office of any president in modern American history. And the reason for that is pretty clear. The American people do not want a president who is compulsively dishonest, who is a bully, who actively represents the interests of the billionaire class, who is anti-science, and who is trying to divide us up based on the color of our skin, our nation of origin, our religion, our gender, or our sexual orientation.

That is not what the American people want. And that reality is the bad news that we have to deal with.

But the truth is that there is a lot of good news out there as well. It's not just that so many of our people disagree with Trump's policies, temperament, and behavior. It is that the vast majority of our people have a very different vision for the future of our country than what Trump and the Republican leadership are giving us.

In an unprecedented way, we are witnessing a revitalization of American democracy with more and more people standing up and fighting back. A little more than a year ago we saw millions of people take to the streets for the women's marches and a few weeks ago, in hundreds of cities and towns around the world, people once again took to the streets in the fight for social, economic, racial and environmental justice.

Further, we are seeing the growth of grassroots organizations and people from every conceivable background starting to run for office—for school board, city council, state legislature, the U.S. House and the U.S. Senate.

In fact, we are starting to see the beginning of a political revolution, something long overdue.

And these candidates, from coast to coast, are standing tall for a progressive agenda, an agenda that works for the working families of our country and not just the billionaire class. These candidates understand that the United States has got to join the rest of the industrialized world and guarantee health care to all as a right, not a privilege, through a Medicare for All, single-payer program.

They understand that at a time of massive income and wealth inequality, when the top one-tenth of one percent now owns almost as much wealth as the bottom 90 percent, we should not be giving tax breaks for billionaires but demanding that they start paying their fair share of taxes.

They know that we need trade policies that benefit working people, not large multi-national corporations.

They know that we have got to take on the fossil fuel industry, transform our energy system and move to sustainable energies like wind, solar and geothermal.

They know that we need a $15 an hour federal minimum wage, free tuition at public colleges and universities, and universal childcare.

They understand that it is a woman who has the right to control their own bodies, not state and federal governments, and that woman has the right to receive equal pay for equal work and work in a safe environment free from harassment.

They also know that if we are going to move forward successfully as a democracy we need real criminal justice reform and we need to finally address comprehensive immigration reform.

Yes. I understand that the Koch brothers and their billionaire friends are planning to spend hundreds of millions of dollars in the 2018 mid-term elections supporting the Trump agenda and right-wing Republicans. They have the money, an unlimited amount of money. But we have the people, and when ordinary people stand up and fight for justice there is nothing that we cannot accomplish. That has been the history of America, and that is our future.

Thank you all and good night.

## Print Citations

**CMS:** Sanders, Bernie. "Response to President Trump's 2018 State of the Union Speech." Speech presented on Facebook, January 30, 2018. In *The Reference Shelf: Representative American Speeches 2017-2018*, edited by Micah L. Issit, 119-124. Ipswich, MA: H.W. Wilson, 2018.

**MLA:** Sanders, Bernie. "Response to President Trump's 2018 State of the Union Speech." Facebook, 30 January 2018. Presentation. *The Reference Shelf: Representative American Speeches 2017-2018,* edited by Micah L. Issit, H.W. Wilson, 2018, pp. 119-124.

**APA:** Sanders, B. (2018, January 30). Response to President Trump's 2018 State of the Union speech. Facebook. In M.L. Issit (Ed.), *The reference shelf: Representative American speeches 2017-2018* (pp. 119-124). Ipswich, MA: H.W. Wilson. (Original work published 2018)

# The State of American Democracy

## By Barack Obama

*Former president Barack Obama was in office from 2008 to 2016 and made history as America's first African-American president. The son of an immigrant father from Kenya, Obama attended Harvard Law School and was the first African American to head the* Harvard Law Review, *before entering politics in Chicago, Illinois. Obama was elected to the Illinois State Senate in 1996 and was elected to the US Senate in 2004. Obama's historic presidential campaign in 2007-2008 drew international attention and resulted in the highest voter participation ratings in the last half century when he defeated Republican Challenger John McCain to win the presidency. In this speech from September of 2018, former president Obama discusses President Donald Trump and the increasingly vitriolic political environment that has developed in the United States.*

**OBAMA:** Hey! Hello, Illinois! I-L-L!

**AUDIENCE:** I-L-L!

**OBAMA:** I-L-L!

**AUDIENCE:** I-L-L!

**OBAMA:** I-L-L!

**AUDIENCE:** I-L-L!

**OBAMA:** Okay, okay. Just checking to see if you're awake. Please have a seat, everybody. It is good to be home. It's good to see corn.

**OBAMA:** Beans. I was trying to explain to somebody as we were flying in, that's corn. That's beans. And they were very impressed at my agricultural knowledge. Please give it up for Amaury once again for that outstanding introduction. I have a bunch of good friends here today, including somebody who I served with, who is one of the finest senators in the country, and we're lucky to have him, your Senator, Dick Durbin is here. I also noticed, by the way, former Governor Edgar here, who I haven't seen in a long time, and somehow he has not aged and I have. And it's great to see you, Governor. I want to thank President Killeen and everybody at the U of I System for making it possible for me to be here today. And I am deeply honored at the Paul Douglas Award that is being given to me. He is somebody who set the path for so much outstanding public service here in Illinois.

Delivered on September 7, 2018, at the University of Illinois Champaign-Urbana, Champaign, IL.

Now, I want to start by addressing the elephant in the room. I know people are still wondering why I didn't speak at the commencement.

The student body president sent a very thoughtful invitation. The students made a spiffy video. And when I declined, I hear there was speculation that I was boycotting campus until Antonio's Pizza reopened.

So I want to be clear. I did not take sides in that late-night food debate. The truth is, after eight years in the White House, I needed to spend some time one-on-one with Michelle if I wanted to stay married.

And she says hello, by the way. I also wanted to spend some quality time with my daughters, who were suddenly young women on their way out the door. And I should add, by the way, now that I have a daughter in college, I can tell all the students here, your parents suffer.

They cry privately. It is brutal. So please call.

Send a text.

We need to hear from you, just a little something. And truth was, I was also intent on following a wise American tradition. Of ex-presidents gracefully exiting the political stage, making room for new voices and new ideas. And we have our first president, George Washington, to thank for setting that example. After he led the colonies to victory as General Washington, there were no constraints on him really, he was practically a god to those who had followed him into battle.

There was no Constitution, there were no democratic norms that guided what he should or could do. And he could have made himself all-powerful, he could have made himself potentially President for life. And instead he resigned as Commander-in-Chief and moved back to his country estate. Six years later, he was elected President. But after two terms, he resigned again, and rode off into the sunset. The point Washington made, the point that is essential to American democracy, is that in a government of and by and for the people, there should be no permanent ruling class. There are only citizens, who through their elected and temporary representatives, determine our course and determine our character.

I'm here today because this is one of those pivotal moments when every one of us, as citizens of the United States, need to determine just who it is that we are, just what it is that we stand for. And as a fellow citizen, not as an ex-president, but as a fellow citizen, I am here to deliver a simple message, and that is that you need to vote because our democracy depends on it.

Now, some of you may think I'm exaggerating when I say this November's elections are more important than any I can remember in my lifetime. I know politicians say that all the time. I have been guilty of saying it a few times, particularly when I was on the ballot.

But just a glance at recent headlines should tell you that this moment really is different. The stakes really are higher. The consequences of any of us sitting on the sidelines are more dire. And it's not as if we haven't had big elections before or big choices to make in our history. The fact is, democracy has never been easy, and our founding fathers argued about everything. We waged a civil war. We overcame depression. We've lurched from eras of great progressive change to periods of retrenchment. Still, most Americans alive today, certainly the students who are here, have operated under some common assumptions about who we are and what we stand for.

Out of the turmoil of the industrial revolution and the Great Depression, America adapted a new economy, a 20th century economy—guiding our free market with regulations to protect health and safety and fair competition, empowering workers with union movements; investing in science and infrastructure and educational institutions like U of I; strengthening our system of primary and secondary education, and stitching together a social safety net. And all of this led to unrivaled prosperity and the rise of a broad and deep middle class in the sense that if you worked hard, you could climb the ladder of success.

And not everyone was included in this prosperity. There was a lot more work to do. And so in response to the stain of slavery and segregation and the reality of racial discrimination, the civil rights movement not only opened new doors for African-Americans, it also opened up the floodgates of opportunity for women and Americans with disabilities and LGBT Americans and others to make their own claims to full and equal citizenship. And although discrimination remained a pernicious force in our society and continues to this day, and although there are controversies about how to best ensure genuine equality of opportunity, there's been at least rough agreement among the overwhelming majority of Americans that our country is strongest when everybody's treated fairly, when people are judged on the merits and the content of their character, and not the color of their skin or the way in which they worship God or their last names. And that consensus then extended beyond our borders. And from the wreckage of World War II, we built a postwar web, architecture, system of alliances and institutions to underwrite freedom and oppose Soviet totalitarianism and to help poorer countries develop.

This American leadership across the globe wasn't perfect. We made mistakes. At times we lost sight of our ideals. We had fierce arguments about Vietnam, and we had fierce arguments about Iraq. But thanks to our leadership, a bipartisan leadership, and the efforts of diplomats and Peace Corps volunteers, and most of all thanks to the constant sacrifices of our men and women in uniform, we not only reduced the prospects of war between the world's great powers, we not only won the Cold War, we helped spread a commitment to certain values and principles, like the rule of law and human rights and democracy and the notion of the inherent dignity and worth of every individual. And even those countries that didn't abide by those principles were still subject to shame and still had to at least give lip service for the idea. And that provided a lever to continually improve the prospects for people around the world.

That's the story of America, a story of progress. Fitful progress, incomplete progress, but progress. And that progress wasn't achieved by just a handful of famous leaders making speeches. It was won because of countless quiet acts of heroism and dedication by citizens, by ordinary people, many of them not much older than you. It was won because rather than be bystanders to history, ordinary people fought and marched and mobilized and built and, yes, voted to make history.

Of course, there's always been another darker aspect to America's story. Progress doesn't just move in a straight line. There's a reason why progress hasn't been easy and why throughout our history every two steps forward seems to sometimes produce one step back. Each time we painstakingly pull ourselves closer to our founding ideals, that all of us are created equal, endowed by our Creator with certain inalienable rights; the ideals that say every child should have opportunity and every man and woman in this country who's willing to work hard should be able to find a job and support a family and pursue their small piece of the American Dream; our ideals that say we have a collective responsibility to care for the sick and the infirm, and we have a responsibility to conserve the amazing bounty, the natural resources of this country and of this planet for future generations, each time we've gotten closer to those ideals, somebody somewhere has pushed back. The status quo pushes back. Sometimes the backlash comes from people who are genuinely, if wrongly, fearful of change. More often it's manufactured by the powerful and the privileged who want to keep us divided and keep us angry and keep us cynical because that helps them maintain the status quo and keep their power and keep their privilege. And you happen to be coming of age during one of those moments. It did not start with Donald Trump. He is a symptom, not the cause.

He's just capitalizing on resentments that politicians have been fanning for years. A fear and anger that's rooted in our past, but it's also born out of the enormous upheavals that have taken place in your brief lifetimes.

And, by the way, it is brief. When I heard Amaury was eleven when I got elected, and now Amaury's starting a company, that was yesterday. But think about it. You've come of age in a smaller, more connected world, where demographic shifts and the winds of change have scrambled not only traditional economic arrangements, but our social arrangements and our religious commitments and our civic institutions. Most of you don't remember a time before 9/11, when you didn't have to take off your shoes at an airport. Most of you don't remember a time when America wasn't at war, or when money and images and information could travel instantly around the globe, or when the climate wasn't changing faster than our efforts to address it. This change has happened fast, faster than any time in human history. And it created a new economy that has unleashed incredible prosperity.

But it's also upended people's lives in profound ways. For those with unique skills or access to technology and capital, a global market has meant unprecedented wealth. For those not so lucky, for the factory worker, for the office worker, or even middle managers, those same forces may have wiped out your job, or at least put you in no position to ask for a raise. As wages slowed and inequality accelerated, those at the top of the economic pyramid have been able to influence government to skew things even more in their direction: cutting taxes on the wealthiest Americans, unwinding regulations and weakening worker protections, shrinking the safety net. So you have come of age during a time of growing inequality, of fracturing of economic opportunity. And that growing economic divide compounded other divisions in our country: regional, racial, religious, cultural. It made it harder to build consensus on issues. It made politicians less willing to compromise, which increased gridlock, which made people even more cynical about politics.

And then the reckless behavior of financial elites triggered a massive financial crisis, ten years ago this week, a crisis that resulted in the worst recession in any of our lifetimes and caused years of hardship for the American people, for many of your parents, for many of your families. Most of you weren't old enough to fully focus on what was going on at the time, but when I came into office in 2009, we were losing 800,000 jobs a month. 800,000. Millions of people were losing their homes. Many were worried we were entering into a second Great Depression. So we worked hard to end that crisis, but also to break some of these longer term trends. And the actions we took during that crisis returned the economy to healthy growth and initiated the longest streak of job creation on record. And we covered another 20 million Americans with health insurance and we cut our deficits by more than half, partly by making sure that people like me, who have been given such amazing opportunities by this country, pay our fair share of taxes to help folks coming up behind me.

And by the time I left office, household income was near its all-time high and the uninsured rate had hit an all-time low and wages were rising and poverty rates were falling. I mention all this just so when you hear how great the economy's doing right now, let's just remember when this recovery started.

I mean, I'm glad it's continued, but when you hear about this economic miracle that's been going on, when the job numbers come out, monthly job numbers, suddenly Republicans are saying it's a miracle. I have to kind of remind them, actually, those job numbers are the same as they were in 2015 and 2016.

Anyway, I digress. So we made progress, but—and this is the truth—my administration couldn't reverse forty-year trends in only eight years, especially once Republicans took over the House of Representatives in and decided to block everything we did, even things they used to support.

So we pulled the economy out of crisis, but to this day, too many people who once felt solidly middle-class still feel very real and very personal economic insecurity. Even though we took out bin Laden and wound down the wars in Iraq and our combat role in Afghanistan, and got Iran to halt its nuclear program, the world's still full of threats and disorder. That comes streaming through people's televisions every single day. And these challenges get people worried. And it frays our civic trust. And it makes a lot of people feel like the fix is in and the game is rigged, and nobody's looking out for them. Especially those communities outside our big urban centers.

And even though your generation is the most diverse in history, with a greater acceptance and celebration of our differences than ever before, those are the kinds of conditions that are ripe for exploitation by politicians who have no compunction and no shame about tapping into America's dark history of racial and ethnic and religious division

Appealing to tribe, appealing to fear, pitting one group against another, telling people that order and security will be restored if it weren't for those who don't look like us or don't sound like us or don't pray like we do, that's an old playbook. It's as old as time. And in a healthy democracy it doesn't work. Our antibodies kick in, and people of goodwill from across the political spectrum callout the bigots and the fearmongers, and work to compromise and get things done and promote the better angels of our nature. But when there's a vacuum in our democracy, when we don't vote, when we take our basic rights and freedoms for granted, when we turn away and stop paying attention and stop engaging and stop believing and look for the newest diversion, the electronic versions of bread and circuses, then other voices fill the void. A politics of fear and resentment and retrenchment takes hold. And demagogues promise simple fixes to complex problems. They promise to fight for the little guy even as they cater to the wealthiest and the most powerful. They promise to clean up corruption and then plunder away. They start undermining norms that ensure accountability, try to change the rules to entrench their power further. And they appeal to racial nationalism that's barely veiled, if veiled at all.

Sound familiar? Now, understand, this is not just a matter of Democrats versus Republicans or liberals versus conservatives. At various times in our history, this kind of politics has infected both parties. Southern Democrats were the bigger defenders of slavery. It took a Republican President, Abraham Lincoln, to end it. Dixiecrats filibustered anti-lynching legislation, opposed the idea of expanding civil rights, and although it was a Democratic President and a majority Democratic Congress, spurred on by young marchers and protestors, that got the Civil Rights Act and the Voting Rights Act over the finish line, those historic laws also got passed because of the leadership of Republicans like Illinois' own Everett Dirksen.

So neither party has had a monopoly on wisdom, neither party has been exclusively responsible for us going backwards instead of forwards. But I have to say this because sometimes we hear, oh, a plague on both your houses. Over the past few decades, it wasn't true when Jim Edgar was governor here in Illinois or Jim Thompson was governor. I've got a lot of good Republican friends here in Illinois. But over the past few decades, the politics of division, of resentment and paranoia has unfortunately found a home in the Republican Party.

This Congress has championed the unwinding of campaign finance laws to give billionaires outsized influence over our politics; systemically attacked voting rights to make it harder for the young people, the minorities, and the poor to vote.

Handed out tax cuts without regard to deficits. Slashed the safety net wherever it could. Cast dozens of votes to take away health insurance from ordinary Americans. Embraced wild conspiracy theories, like those surrounding Benghazi, or my birth certificate.

Rejected science, rejected facts on things like climate change. Embraced a rising absolutism from a willingness to default on America's debt by not paying our bills, to a refusal to even meet, much less consider, a qualified nominee for the Supreme Court because he happened to be nominated by a Democratic President. None of this is conservative. I don't mean to pretend I'm channeling Abraham Lincoln now, but that's not what he had in mind, I think, when he helped form the Republican Party.

It's not conservative. It sure isn't normal. It's radical. It's a vision that says the protection of our power and those who back us is all that matters, even when it hurts the country. It's a vision that says the few who can afford a high-priced lob-byist and unlimited campaign contributions set the agenda. And over the past two years, this vision is now nearing its logical conclusion.

So that with Republicans in control of Congress and the White House, without any checks or balances whatsoever, they've provided another $. trillion in tax cuts to people like me who, I promise, don't need it, and don't even pretend to pay for them. It's supposed to be the party, supposedly, of fiscal conservatism. Suddenly deficits do not matter, even though, just two years ago, when the deficit was lower, they said, I couldn't afford to help working families or seniors on Medicare because the deficit was an existential crisis. What changed? What changed? They're subsidizing corporate polluters with taxpayer dollars, allowing dishonest lenders to take advan-tage of veterans and students and consumers again. They've made it so that the only nation on earth to pull out of the global climate agreement, it's not North Korea, it's not Syria, it's not Russia or Saudi Arabia. It's us. The only country. There are a lot of countries in the world.

We're the only ones.

They're undermining our alliances, cozying up to Russia. What happened to the Republican Party? Its central organizing principle in foreign policy was the fight against Communism, and now they're cozying up to the former head of the KGB, actively blocking legislation that would defend our elections from Russian attack. What happened? Their sabotage of the Affordable Care Act has already cost more than three million Americans their health insurance. And if they're still in pow-er next fall, you'd better believe they're coming at it again. They've said so. In a healthy democracy, there's some checks and balances on this kind of behavior, this kind of inconsistency, but right now there's none. Republicans who know better in Congress—and they're there, they're quoted saying, Yeah, we know this is kind of crazy—are still bending over backwards to shield this behavior from scrutiny or accountability or consequence. Seem utterly unwilling to find the backbone to safe-guard the institutions that make our democracy work.

And, by the way, the claim that everything will turn out okay because there are people inside the White House who secretly aren't following the President's orders, that is not a check—I'm being serious here—that's not how our democracy is sup-posed to work.

These people aren't elected. They're not accountable. They're not doing us a service by actively promoting 90 percent of the crazy stuff that's coming out of this White House and then saying, Don't worry, we're preventing the other 10 percent. That's not how things are supposed to work. This is not normal.

These are extraordinary times. And they're dangerous times. But here's the good news. In two months we have the chance, not the certainty but the chance, to re-store some semblance of sanity to our politics.

Because there is actually only on real check on bad policy and abuses of power, and that's you. You and your vote. Look, Americans will always have disagreements on policy. This is a big country, it is a raucous country. People have different points of view. I happen to be a Democrat. I support Democratic candidates. I believe our policies are better and that we have a bigger, bolder vision of opportunity and equality and justice and inclusive democracy. We know there are a lot of jobs young people aren't getting a chance to occupy or aren't getting paid enough or aren't getting benefits like insurance. It's harder for young people to save for a rainy day, let alone retirement. So Democrats aren't just running on good old ideas like a higher minimum wage, they're running on good new ideas like Medicare for all, giving workers seats on corporate boards, reversing the most egregious corporate tax cuts to make sure college students graduate debt-free.

We know that people are tired of toxic corruption, and that democracy depends on transparency and accountability. So Democrats aren't just running on good old ideas like requiring presidential candidates to release their tax returns, and barring lobbyists from making campaign contributions, but on good new ideas like barring lobbyists from getting paid by foreign governments. We know that climate change isn't just coming. It is here. So Democrats aren't just running on good old ideas like increasing gas mileage in our cars—which I did and which Republicans are trying to reverse—but on good new ideas like putting a price on carbon pollution. We know that in a smaller, more connected world, we can't just put technology back in a box, we can't just put walls up all around America. Walls don't keep out threats like terrorism or disease—and that's why we propose leading our alliances and helping other countries develop, and pushing back against tyrants. And Democrats talk about reforming our immigration so, yes, it is orderly and it is fair and it is legal, but it continues to welcome strivers and dreamers from all around the world. That's why I'm a Democrat, that's the set of ideas that I believe in. Oh, I am here to tell you that even if you don't agree with me or Democrats on policy, even if you believe in more Libertarian economic theories, even if you are an evangelical and our position on certain social issues is a bridge too far, even if you think my assessment of immigration is mistaken and that Democrats aren't serious enough about immigration enforcement, I'm here to tell you that you should still be concerned with our current course and should still want to see a restoration of honesty and decency and lawfulness in our government.

It should not be Democratic or Republican, it should not be a partisan issue to say that we do not pressure the Attorney General or the FBI to use the criminal justice system as a cudgel to punish our political opponents.

Or to explicitly call on the Attorney General to protect members of our own party from prosecution because an election happens to be coming up. I'm not making that up. That's not hypothetical. It shouldn't be Democratic or Republican to say that we don't threaten the freedom of the press because—they say things or publish stories we don't like.

I complained plenty about Fox News—but you never heard me threaten to shut them down, or call them enemies of the people. It shouldn't be Democratic or Republican to say we don't target certain groups of people based on what they look like or how they pray. We are Americans. We're supposed to standup to bullies.

Not follow them.

We're supposed to stand up to discrimination. And we're sure as heck supposed to stand up, clearly and unequivocally, to Nazi sympathizers.

How hard can that be? Saying that Nazis are bad. I'll be honest, sometimes I get into arguments with progressive friends about what the current political movement requires. There are well-meaning folks passionate about social justice, who think things have gotten so bad, the lines have been so starkly drawn, that we have to fight fire with fire, we have to do the same things to the Republicans that they do to us, adopt their tactics, say whatever works, make up stuff about the other side. I don't agree with that. It's not because I'm soft. It's not because I'm interested in promoting an empty bipartisanship. I don't agree with it because eroding our civic institutions and our civic trust and making people angrier and yelling at each other and making people cynical about government, that always works better for those who don't believe in the power of collective action.

You don't need an effective government or a robust press or reasoned debate to work when all you're concerned about is maintaining power. In fact, the more cynical people are about government and the angrier and more dispirited they are about the prospects for change, the more likely the powerful are able to maintain their power. But we believe that in order to move this country forward, to actually solve problems and make people's lives better, we need a well-functioning government, we need our civic institutions to work. We need cooperation among people of different political persuasions. And to make that work, we have to restore our faith in democracy. We have to bring people together, not tear them apart. We need majorities in Congress and state legislatures who are serious about governing and want to bring about real change and improvements in people's lives.

And we won't win people over by calling them names, or dismissing entire chunks of the country as racist, or sexist, or homophobic. When I say bring people together, I mean all of our people. You know, this whole notion that has sprung up recently about Democrats need to choose between trying to appeal to the white working class voters, or voters of color, and women and LGBT Americans, that's nonsense. I don't buy that. I got votes from every demographic. We won by reaching out to everybody and competing everywhere and by fighting for every vote.

And that's what we've got to do in this election and every election after that.

And we can't do that if we immediately disregard what others have to say from the start because they're not like us, because they're not—because they're white or they're black or they're men or women, or they're gay or they're straight; if we think that somehow there's no way they can understand how I'm feeling, and therefore don't have any standing to speak on certain matters because we're only defined by certain characteristics.

That doesn't work if you want a healthy democracy. We can't do that if we traffic in absolutes when it comes to policy. You know, to make democracy work we have to be able to get inside the reality of people who are different, have different experiences, come from different backgrounds. We have to engage them even when it is frustrating; we have to listen to them even when we don't like what they have to say; we have to hope that we can change their minds and we have to remain open to them changing ours.

And that doesn't mean, by the way, abandoning our principles or caving to bad policy in the interests of maintaining some phony version of "civility." That seems to be, by the way, the definition of civility offered by too many Republicans: We will be polite as long as we get a hundred percent of what we want and you don't callus out on the various ways that we're sticking it to people. And we'll click our tongues and issue vague statements of disappointment when the President does something outrageous, but we won't actually do anything about it. That's not civility. That's abdicating your responsibilities.

But again I digress. Making democracy work means holding on to our principles, having clarity about our principles, and then having the confidence to get in the arena and have a serious debate. And it also means appreciating that progress does not happen all at once, but when you put your shoulder to the wheel, if you're willing to fight for it, things do get better. And let me tell you something, particularly young people here. Better is good. I used to have to tell my young staff this all the time in the White House. Better is good. That's the history of progress in this country. Not perfect. Better. The Civil Rights Act didn't end racism, but it made things better. Social Security didn't eliminate all poverty for seniors, but it made things better for millions of people.

Do not let people tell you the fight's not worth it because you won't get everything that you want. The idea that, well, you know there's racism in America so I'm not going to bother voting. No point. That makes no sense. You can make it better. Better's always worth fighting for. That's how our founders expected this system of self-government to work; that through the testing of ideas and the application of reason and evidence and proof, we could sort through our differences and nobody would get exactly what they wanted, but it would be possible to find a basis for common ground.

And that common ground exists. Maybe it's not fashionable to say that right now. It's hard to see it with all the nonsense in Washington, it's hard to hear it with all the noise. But common ground exists. I have seen it. I have lived it. I know there are white people who care deeply about black people being treated unfairly. I have talked to them and loved them. And I know there are black people who care deeply about the struggles of white rural America. I'm one of them and I have a track record to prove it

I know there are evangelicals who are deeply committed to doing something about climate change. I've seen them do the work. I know there are conservatives who think there's nothing compassionate about separating immigrant children from their mothers. I know there are Republicans who believe government should only perform a few minimal functions but that one of those functions should be making sure nearly 3,000 Americans don't die in a hurricane and its aftermath.

Common ground's out there. I see it every day. Just how people interact, how people treat each other. You see it on the ball field. You see it at work. You see it in places of worship. But to say that a common ground exists doesn't mean it will inevitably win out. History shows the power of fear. And the closer that we get to Election Day, the more those invested in the politics of fear and division will work, will do anything to hang on to their recent gains.

Fortunately I am hopeful because out of this political darkness I am seeing a great awakening of citizenship all across the country. I cannot tell you how encouraged I've been by watching so many people get involved for the first time, or the first time in a long time. They're marching and they're organizing and they're registering people to vote, and they're running for office themselves. Look at this crop of Democratic candidates running for Congress and running for governor, running for the state legislature, running for district attorney, running for school board. It is a movement of citizens who happen to be younger and more diverse and more female than ever before, and that's really useful.

We need more women in charge. But we've got first-time candidates, we've got veterans of Iraq and Afghanistan, record numbers of women—Americans who previously maybe didn't have an interest in politics as a career, but laced up their shoes and rolled up their sleeves and grabbed a clipboard because they too believe, this time's different; this moment's too important to sit out. And if you listen to what these candidates are talking about, in individual races across the country, you'll find they're not just running against something, they are running for something. They're running to expand opportunity and they're running to restore the honor and compassion that should be the essence of public service.

And speaking as a Democrat, that's when the Democratic Party has always made the biggest difference in the lives of the American people, when we led with conviction and principle and bold new ideas. The antidote to a government controlled by a powerful fear, a government that divides, is a government by the organized, energized, inclusive many. That's what this moment's about. That has to be the answer. You cannot sit back and wait for a savior. You can't opt out because you don't feel sufficiently inspired by this or that particular candidate. This is not a rock concert, this is not Coachella. You don't need a messiah. All we need are decent, honest, hardworking people who are accountable—and who have America's best interests at heart.

And they'll step up and they'll join our government and they will make things better if they have support. One election will not fix everything that needs to be fixed, but it will be a start. And you have to start it. What's going to fix our democracy is you.

People ask me, what are you going to do for the election? No, the question is: What are you going to do? You're the antidote. Your participation and your spirit and your determination, not just in this election but in every subsequent election, and in the days between elections.

Because in the end, the threat to our democracy doesn't just come from Donald Trump or the current batch of Republicans in Congress or the Koch Brothers and their lobbyists, or too much compromise from Democrats, or Russian hacking. The biggest threat to our democracy is indifference. The biggest threat to our democracy is cynicism—a cynicism that's led too many people to turn away from politics and stay home on Election Day. To all the young people who are here today, there are now more eligible voters in your generation than in any other, which means your generation now has more power than anybody to change things. If you want it, you can make sure America gets out of its current funk. If you actually care about it, you have the power to make sure we seize a brighter future. But to exercise that clout, to exercise that power, you have to show up.

In the last midterms election, in, fewer than one in five young people voted. One in five. Not two in five, or three in five. One in five. Is it any wonder this Congress doesn't reflect your values and your priorities? Are you surprised by that?

This whole project of self-government only works if everybody's doing their part. Don't tell me your vote doesn't matter. I've won states in the presidential election because of five, ten, twenty votes per precinct. And if you thought elections don't matter, I hope these last two years have corrected that impression.

So if you don't like what's going on right now—and you shouldn't—do not complain. Don't hashtag. Don't get anxious. Don't retreat. Don't binge on whatever it is you're bingeing on. Don't lose yourself in ironic detachment. Don't put your head in the sand. Don't boo. Vote.

Vote. If you are really concerned about how the criminal justice system treats African-Americans, the best way to protest is to vote—not just for Senators and Representatives, but for mayors and sheriffs and state legislators. Do what they just did in Philadelphia and Boston, and elect state's attorneys and district attorneys who are looking at issues in a new light, who realize that the vast majority of law enforcement do the right thing in a really hard job, and we just need to make sure that all of them do. If you're tired of politicians who offer nothing but "thoughts and prayers" after a mass shooting, you've got to do what the Parkland kids are doing. Some of them aren't even eligible to vote, yet they're out there working to change minds and registering people, and they're not giving up until we have a Congress that sees your lives as more important than a campaign check from the NRA.

You've got to vote. If you support the #MeToo movement, you're outraged by stories of sexual harassment and assault inspired by the women who shared them, you've got to do more than retweet a hashtag. You've got to vote.

Part of the reason women are more vulnerable in the workplace is because not enough women are bosses in the workplace—which is why we need to strengthen and enforce laws that protect women in the workplace not just from harassment but from discrimination in hiring and promotion, and not getting paid the same amount for doing the same work. That requires laws. Laws get passed by legislators.

You've got to vote. When you vote, you've got the power to make it easier to afford college, and harder to shoot up a school. When you vote, you've got the power to make sure a family keeps its health insurance; you could save somebody's life. When you vote, you've got the power to make sure white nationalists don't feel emboldened to march with their hoods off or their hoods on in Charlottesville in the middle of the day.

Thirty minutes. Thirty minutes of your time. Is democracy worth that? We have been through much darker times than these, and somehow each generation of

Americans carried us through to the other side. Not by sitting around and waiting for something to happen, not by leaving it to others to do something, but by leading that movement for change themselves. And if you do that, if you get involved, and you get engaged, and you knock on some doors, and you talk with your friends, and you argue with your family members, and you change some minds, and you vote, something powerful happens.

Change happens. Hope happens. Not perfection. Not every bit of cruelty and sadness and poverty and disease suddenly stricken from the earth. There will still be problems. But with each new candidate that surprises you with a victory that you supported, a spark of hope happens. With each new law that helps a kid read or helps a homeless family find shelter or helps a veteran get the support he or she has earned, each time that happens, hope happens. With each new step we take in the direction of fairness and justice and equality and opportunity, hope spreads.

And that can be the legacy of your generation. You can be the generation that at a critical moment stood up and reminded us just how precious this experiment in democracy really is, just how powerful it can be when we fight for it, when we believe in it. I believe in you. I believe you will help lead us in the right direction. And I will be right there with you every step of the way. Thank you, Illinois. God bless. God bless this country we love. Thank you.

## Print Citations

**CMS:** Obama, Barack. "The State of American Democracy." Speech presented at the University of Illinois Champaign-Urbana, Champaign, IL, September 7, 2018. In *The Reference Shelf: Representative American Speeches 2017-2018*, edited by Micah L. Issit, 125-137. Ipswich, MA: H.W. Wilson, 2018.

**MLA:** Obama, Barack. "The State of American Democracy." University of Illinois Champaign-Urbana, 7 September 2018, Champaign, IL. Presentation. *The Reference Shelf: Representative American Speeches 2017-2018,* edited by Micah L. Issit, H.W. Wilson, 2018, pp. 125-137.

**APA:** Obama, B. (2018, September 7). The state of American democracy. University of Illinois Champaign-Urbana, Champaign, IL. In M.L. Issit (Ed.), *The reference shelf: Representative American speeches 2017-2018* (pp. 125-137). Ipswich, MA: H.W. Wilson. (Original work published 2018)

# Remarks on Corruption in Washington

## By Elizabeth Warren

*Senator Elizabeth Warren is one of the most popular Democratic senators and has been frequently cited as a potential candidate for a future presidential election. After graduating with a degree in law from Rutgers University, Warren became a professor of law at Harvard University and elsewhere and became a leading expert on middle-class finance and bankruptcy law. Warren served under President Barack Obama and helped to create the Consumer Financial Protection Bureau and, in 2013, won election to the US Senate for the state of Massachusetts. In this speech from 2018 to the National Press Club, Warren discusses corruption in the government and in the Trump White House and discusses future strategies to increase political transparency.*

I want to begin with two numbers. 73. 18.

For more than half a century, the National Election Survey has been asking Americans a simple question: Do you trust the federal government to do the right thing all of the time, or at least most of the time?

In 1958, the first year this survey was conducted, the number was 73—that is, 73% of Americans polled said, yes, they trusted their government to do the right thing at least most of the time.

For a long time, the number remained high.

1968 was a year of historic convulsions. Martin Luther King, Jr. was assassinated, Bobby Kennedy was killed, North Korea captured a US surveillance ship, and North Vietnam launched the Tet offensive. Faith in government went down, but overall, it held firm. 62% still trusted government.

After Watergate, the number took a big hit, dropping to 36%.

But today?

Eighteen.

From 73 to 18. Not even one in five Americans today trust their government to do the right thing.

I'd love to stand here and tell you that this was some sudden drop after Donald Trump was elected, but that wouldn't be true.

This problem is far bigger than Trump.

The way I see it, a loss of faith this broad, and this profound, is more than a problem—it is a crisis. A crisis of faith.

This is the kind of crisis that leads people to turn away from democracy. The kind of crisis that forces people to stop believing in what we can do together. The

Delivered on August 21, 2018, at the National Press Club, Washington, DC.

kind of crisis that creates fertile ground for cynicism and discouragement. The kind of crisis that gives rise to authoritarians.

Why have so many people lost faith? Thoughtful people give different answers. Some say it's the result of politicians making government the enemy. And that's true.

Since Watergate, generation after generation of American politicians have attacked the very idea that our government can do anything right. Recall Ronald Reagan's famous line: What are the nine most terrifying words in the English language? I'm from the government and I'm here to help.

Really? Government help is terrifying? Give me a break. Do you know what's actually terrifying? Hurricanes like Katrina and Maria are terrifying, which is why victims of natural disasters ask for government help. After a lifetime of hard work, growing old and going broke is terrifying, which is why the American people strongly support Social Security. Choosing between food and medicine is terrifying, and that's why the American people rise up and take to the streets when Republicans try to cut back Medicare and Medicaid.

And there's so much more that we want to work on together. Americans want roads and bridges. They want power and water systems. They want a top-notch economic system. They want real cybersecurity and a military that defends our nation. And they want a government that can deliver those things.

Government can be a powerful force for good—but only when it works for the people. And the American people understand that today, it doesn't.

Our national crisis of faith in government boils down to this simple fact: people don't trust their government to do the right thing because they think government works for the rich, the powerful and the well-connected and not for the American people.

And here's the kicker: They're right.

At a time when this country faces enormous challenges, our government actively serves the richest and most powerful and turns its back on everyone else.

At a time of skyrocketing inequality and stagnant wages for the middle class, our government is giving gargantuan handouts to the wealthiest Americans.

At a time when mass incarceration grinds down human beings and destroys communities of color, our government is putting more cash into the for-profit prison industry.

At a time when sea levels are rising and the health threats posed by climate change are accelerating by the day, our government is handing over both taxpayer money and federally protected lands to the fossil fuel industry.

At a time of staggering drug prices and soaring out of pocket costs, our government tucks tail and runs away from any serious challenge to big Pharma and greedy insurance companies.

At a time of crippling student loan debt, our government is bending over backwards to help bogus for-profit colleges and student loan companies get richer by cheating students.

Across the board, our government—*our* government—is failing to fix the problems that face *our* working families. Instead, it's making the problems worse by giving more money, more power, and more advantages to those who already have all three.

And so often—whether it leads to poisoned water or toxic bank loans—communities of color are hit first and hit hardest.

Our government systematically favors the rich over the poor, the donor class over the working class, the well-connected over the disconnected.

This is deliberate, and we need to call this what it is—corruption, plain and simple.

Corruption has seeped into the fabric of our government, tilting thousands of decisions away from the public good and toward the desires of those at the top. And, over time, bit by bit, like a cancer eating away at our democracy, corruption has eroded Americans' faith in our government.

I know that's a stark assessment. But I'm not here to describe the death of democracy. I'm here to talk about fighting back. I'm here because I believe that change is hard, but change is possible.

Change can start with reforming how our largest companies operate. Last week, I introduced the Accountable Capitalism Act, which would restore the once-common idea that giant American corporations should look out for a broad range of American stakeholders. By requiring our largest companies to seat workers on their boards, limiting the ability of executives to get rich quick off short-term stock price bumps, and giving shareholders and Directors a real say in corporate political spending, this bill could go a long way toward restoring real economic democracy in America. And in the process, it would ensure that when American businesses engage with our government, they are speaking on behalf of their entire communities—and not simply as megaphones for the wealthy and the powerful.

Getting American corporations to start acting like responsible American citizens is an important first step toward limiting corruption. But broader changes are needed.

Today, I'm introducing the most ambitious anti-corruption legislation proposed in Congress since Watergate. This is an aggressive set of reforms that would fundamentally change the way Washington does business. These reforms have one simple aim: to take power in Washington away from the wealthy, the powerful, and the well-connected who have corrupted our government and put power back in the hands of the American people.

We can do this. We must do this. And when we do, we will restore the faith of the American people—not just in our government, but faith in democracy itself.

The recent explosion of big political spending has delivered a gut-punch to our democracy. I do what I can by not taking any PAC money or any money from federal lobbyists. There's a lot of work to do on campaign finance, starting with overturning *Citizens United*. But that's not **nearly** enough. The corrupting influence of big money in Washington reaches much further than political campaigns.

Big money eats away at the heart of our democracy. Over the last few decades, it has created a pervasive culture of soft corruption that colors virtually every important decision in Washington.

Consider a couple of examples:

First, the rich and powerful buy their way into Congressional offices. Exhibit A: Mick Mulvaney. After he left Congress, Mulvaney told a roomful of bankers that he had a rule in his office: if a lobbyist didn't give him money, the lobbyist didn't get a meeting—he met only with those lobbyists who ponied up for his campaign war chest. Today, Mulvaney is President Trump's head of the Office of Management and Budget and the person running the Consumer Financial Protection Bureau. And when he made these comments right out in public with the press listening in, Trump and pretty much every Republican in Washington just shrugged.

The rich and powerful also offer up some pretty nice gifts for public servants to do their bidding. In the early 2000s, Congressman Billy Tauzin started pushing an idea: expand Medicare to cover prescription drugs. Good for seniors—in fact, life saving for some. But also very good for Big Pharma—more prescriptions filled, more money coming in.

And it might all have landed there, with seniors getting drug coverage and drug companies selling more drugs—but Big Pharma wanted more. Number one on their list was a flat prohibition on the worrisome possibility that the government might actually negotiate for lower drug prices. And Billy delivered—which I'm sure had nothing to do with the more than $200,000 in campaign contributions the Congressman received from the drug industry.

Today, Big Pharma rakes in billions from seniors on Medicare while charging sky-high prices for the drugs they need—and no one in government can negotiate those prices. And what happened to Billy?

In December of 2003, the very same month the bill was signed into law, PhRMA—the drug companies' biggest lobbying group—dangled the possibility that Billy could be their next CEO.[3]

In February of 2004, Congressman Tauzin announced that he wouldn't seek re-election. Ten months later, he became CEO of PhRMA—at an annual salary of $2 million. Big Pharma certainly knows how to say "thank you for your service."

Sometimes the payoff comes upfront. Goldman Sachs handed Gary Cohn over a quarter of a billion dollars on his way out the door to become the head of President Trump's National Economic Council.[4] A quarter of a billion dollars to help quarter-back a tax package that included giveaways worth just over a quarter of a billion to Goldman—in the first quarter of 2018 alone.[5] That's quite the return on investment for Goldman Sachs. For the taxpayers who paid Mr. Cohn's salary and were under the mistaken impression that Mr. Cohn was working for them, the return was not so good.

The examples are everywhere these days. A Commerce Secretary who acts like a cartoon version of a Wall Street fat cat, awash in financial conflicts, intertwined with Russian financial interests, suspected of swindling millions from his business partners and using his official position to pump up his fortune through shady stock trading.[6] An EPA Administrator who resigns in disgrace over corruption, only to be replaced with another EPA Administrator who belongs in the coal baron's hall of fame.[7] A Congressman facing indictment for insider trading.[8]

Let's face it: there's no real question that the Trump era has given us the most nakedly corrupt leadership this nation has seen in our lifetimes. But they are not the *cause* of the rot—they're just the biggest, stinkiest example of it.

Corruption is a form of public cancer, and Washington's got it bad. It's time for treatment, time to isolate and quarantine the ability of big money to infect the decisions made every day by every branch of our government.

This problem is enormous—but we've dealt with enormous problems before. We just need some big reform ideas and a willingness to fight for real change. So here's the **First Big Change—Padlock the revolving door between big business and government.**

Ban elected and appointed officials from becoming lobbyists after they leave office. Not for *one* year. Not for *two* years. For the rest of their *lives*. Sorry, Billy. No more Congressman Pharma.

And no more pre-bribes like the Gary Cohn giveaway. No special deals for millions and millions of dollars to the policymakers who will be in a position to pay back their old employers.

We can also lock the revolving door for people who have led a company that got caught breaking the law or anyone who worked as a lobbyist for *any* corporation. A six-year time-out before that lobbyist or outlaw CEO can take a job in government. And we can limit the ability of America's biggest and most powerful companies to gain unfair market advantages from vacuuming up every former regulator on the market.

Sure, there's lots of expertise in the private sector, and government should be able to tap that expertise. And, yes, public servants should be able to use their expertise when they leave government. But we've gone way past expertise and are headed directly into graft. Padlock the revolving door.

Here's my **Second Big Change: Stop self-dealing by public officials**. If a person works for the government, then that work should serve the public. No making policy decisions to help yourself instead of taxpayers.

Right now, that problem begins with a President who may be vulnerable to financial blackmail from a hostile foreign power and God knows who else—a President and his family who may be personally profiting off hundreds of policy decisions every day—but we don't know, because he won't show us his tax returns and won't get rid of his personal business interests.

The truth is, it's *insane* that we have to *beg* the President of the United States to put the American people ahead of his own business interests. Insane.

Presidents should not be able to own companies on the side. And we shouldn't have to beg candidates to let the American people to see their financial interests. That should be the *law*—not just for presidential candidates, but for *every* candidate for *every* federal office.

While we're at it, enough of the spectacle of HHS Secretaries and herds of congressmen caught up in insider trading schemes. It's time to ban elected officials and senior agency officials from owning or trading any company stocks while in office.

They can put their savings in conflict-free investments like mutual funds or they can pick a different line of work.

**Third Big Change—End lobbying as we know it.** The term "lobbying" has been around for nearly two hundred years. And our Constitution protects "the right of the people...to petition the Government for a redress of grievances." But as recently as the 1970s there was no real corporate lobbying industry. There were lobbyists here and there, but there were not enough to fill a school bus.[9]

Today, the national Chamber of Commerce spends tens of millions of dollars to block policies that threaten the profits of a handful of America's richest corporations.[10] They currently occupy an enormous building facing the White House, a sort of visual alternative to the government elected by the people. But back in the 1970s, the Chamber had no presence in DC to speak of. That started to change in 1972, when a hotshot corporate lawyer named Lewis Powell wrote a secret memo for the Chamber.

The Powell Memo declared that the free enterprise system was under assault and urged the Chamber to mobilize America's biggest businesses and establish themselves as a political force to be reckoned with.

It was a declaration of war on democracy. Powell called on corporations to raise armies of lobbyists and descend on Washington. And, boy, did they respond.

Today, lobbying is a multi-billion-dollar industry—more than $3.3 billion in 2017 alone. More than eleven thousand registered lobbyists are deployed to work day and night to influence our government, largely on behalf of wealthy clients.[11] And, by the way, that memo worked out pretty well for Lewis Powell too—a few months later, he was named to the Supreme Court.[12]

Nobody would argue that companies have nothing to contribute to our democratic process. Of course they do. But today, lobbyists working for the wealthy and well-connected crowd the halls of government like it's happy hour every hour. And particularly in Congress, where staff budgets and in-house expertise continue to shrink,[13] it's easier than ever for them to simply overwhelm our democracy so that the lobbyists—or the lobbyists' paying clients—are the only ones whose stories get heard.

That's not how a government of the people—all the people—is supposed to work. So let's fix it.

Start by fixing the Swiss cheese definition of a "lobbyist." Require everyone who gets paid to influence government to register.

And bring lobbying out into the sunlight. Make every single *meeting* between a lobbyist and a public official a matter of public record. Require public disclosure of any documents that lobbyists provide to government officials. Put it all online. And if that seems overwhelming—too many meetings, too many company-drafted bills, too many love notes—think about what that means is going on in the dark recesses of our government right now.

Put a windfall tax on excessive lobbying, to ensure that when companies spend millions trying to stop the government from protecting the public, the cops on the beat get more resources to fight back.

And while we're at it, let's strengthen the government's independence from lobbyists. Raising Congressional salaries to track other federal officials would mean that low-paid staffers don't feel compelled to audition for jobs with influence peddlers when they should be standing up to them.

Finally, let's just plain get rid of some of the most corrosive and dangerous lobbying practices. The trial of Donald Trump's campaign manager has exposed how foreign governments hide their efforts to influence the American government through lobbying.[14] We should ban Americans from getting paid to lobby for foreign governments—period. If foreign governments want to express their views, they can use their diplomats.

One more piece: End legalized lobbyist bribery by prohibiting lobbyists from writing campaign checks or giving personal gifts to anyone running for or holding federal office.

Reining in corporate lobbyists will make a big difference. But there's more.

Too often, decisions in the federal agencies charged with implementing our laws end up captured by the very same corporate giants that they're supposed to be keeping in check. It's time for that to stop. Corporations should have a seat at the table, but they shouldn't take over the whole restaurant.

And that's my **Fourth Big Change—End corporate capture of rulemaking.** Start by empowering beleaguered agencies to stand up to well-heeled corporate giants that don't want to follow any rules.

When someone lies to a court, we call it "perjury." But, too often, when companies lie to regulatory agencies during the rulemaking process, they just call it "analysis"—and no one bats an eye. Meanwhile, Donald Trump's EPA has the gall to try to block objective, high quality science from being considered in the rulemaking[15] process.

Enough of this garbage. Prosecute companies that knowingly mislead government agencies. And stop the practice of companies paying for sham "studies" designed to derail the rulemaking process. Instead, let's force anyone who submits a study to a regulatory agency to disclose who's paying for it and who's editing it. If studies with financial and editorial conflicts don't meet minimal methodological standards, throw them out before they disrupt the process.

**Fifth Big Change—Restore faith that ordinary people can get a fair shake in our courts.** For starters, strengthen the code of conduct for all federal judges—no stock trading, no payments from corporations for attending events, no honoraria for giving speeches, no lavish getaways and fancy hunting trips funded by billionaires.

And I mean **all** federal judges, including Supreme Court justices. I've heard Supreme Court justices say we should just trust that they'll be ethical all on their own. Yeah, right. I watched as Justice Gorsuch trotted over to Trump International Hotel to give a speech sponsored by a political organization that has worked for decades to break the backs of unions.[16] A few months later, Justice Gorsuch delivered the deciding vote to crush public sector unions.[17] What union member believed that her side actually had a fair hearing? There's a reason judges should be required to avoid even the appearance of favoritism.

The courts should also be more open. Individuals and small businesses should be able to have their day in court. Americans should be able to see easily what's happening in the judicial process. Public filings should be easier to access online and free to the public. And it's ten years' past time for us to start audio livestreaming federal appellate and Supreme Court proceedings.

**Finally, Big Change Number Six—Hire a new independent sheriff to police corruption.** There are dedicated public servants that enforce our ethics laws, but they have less authority than security guards at the mall. Build a new anticorruption agency to make sure that all key federal officials—even powerful Senators and Presidents—file disclosures and get rid of conflicts. Close up the loopholes in federal open records laws. This agency can shine floodlights on government actions and empower the public and press with new tools to help safeguard our democracy.

And we can do our best to insulate the sheriff's office from partisan politics and give it the tools it needs to seriously investigate violations and punish offenders.

Washington corruption is not a small problem, and it will not be rooted out with small solutions. In addition to the big changes I talked about today, my legislation contains dozens more ideas to promote clean government, from giant reforms to small tweaks and everything in between.

These changes will require everyone who runs for or who holds office to change at least some of their practices—including me. Many of these ideas challenge the most fundamental assumptions about how business is currently done in our nation's capital. Inside Washington, some of these proposals will be very unpopular, even with some of my friends. Outside Washington, I expect that most people will see these ideas as no-brainers and be shocked they're not already the law.

I'm sure the people who make big money off the current system will yell and scream and spend millions of dollars trying to stop these changes. And the all-day-long pundits and Washington insiders who live in the same neighborhoods and eat at the same sushi bars and go to the same book parties will say "this will never pass" and try to color me naïve for even trying. But it's that kind of self-serving group-think that's allowed corruption to spread through this town for decades.

Besides, such nay-saying ignores our history: Our country has responded to deep corruption with bold action before.

I won't pretend to be sure I've gotten everything exactly right. I'm willing and eager to discuss the details. My bill proposes a year-long transition for people to adapt to the new system before these changes would go into effect. But here is my promise: I plan to fight to pass as many of these reforms as possible. I believe we can break the stranglehold that the wealthy and well-connected hold over our government. I believe we can get our democracy working again.

There are millions of good people working in government. People who show up to do a hard day's work in federal, state and local government, determined to deliver essential services and their best judgments on behalf of the public.

Men and women who are uniquely aware that they owe their jobs—and their salaries—to you, the people of the United States.

They are Members of Congress on both sides of the aisle, their staffs, interns and volunteers.

They are career public servants, serving here at home and in remote corners of the world.

They are unified by a belief in the greater good of government. It's that belief, that shared vision of what it means to live and work and fight for a future in *our* democracy that gives me hope.

We owe everyone fighting for that greater good a debt of gratitude.

But we also owe them rules that promote an unwavering determination to serve the public—and only the public.

This is not about big government versus small government. It's about whether government works for the wealthy and well-connected or government works for the people.

Only 18% of Americans believe our government is doing right most of the time. But I'm not throwing my hands up and walking away. I'm not giving in to the cynicism. I still believe that in our darkest hours, at our lowest points, government can be a force for good to bring us back together.

And here's the good news: deep down, still Americans believe it, too.

You see it in the fight to make government affirm healthcare as a basic human right.

You see it in the fight to make government stand for people and against giant corporations.

You see it the fight to insulate government from the influence of corporate contributions.

You see it in the fight to make government a force for healing our racial and cultural divides.

Americans know that they have a government that isn't working for them. But instead of giving up, more and more people are demanding a government that is run *by* the people *for* the people.

A country where everyone—everyone—has a fighting chance to get ahead. A country that stands for truth, honesty, compassion and service to one another. A country and a government that's worth believing in and worth fighting for.

That's the country I believe in. That's the government I will fight for. I believe we can save our government, and together we can make it work for the people.

## Notes

1. Pew Research Center, "Public Trust in Government: 1958–2017," http://www.peoplepress.org/2017/12/14/public-trust-in-government-1958-2017/
2. https://www.americanprogress.org/issues/race/news/2016/04/25/136361/5-things-to-know-about-communities-ofcolor-and-environmental-justice/
3. *NBC News*, "Tauzin Aided Drug Firms, Then They Hired Him," Mike Stuckey,

March 22, 2006, http://www.nbcnews.com/id/11714763/t/tauzin-aided-drug-firms-then-they-hired-him/#.W3RIQs5KhhE

4.  *New York Times*, "Goldman's $285 Million Package for Gary Cohn Is Questioned," Kate Kelly, January 25, 2017, https://www.nytimes.com/2017/01/25/business/dealbook/goldman-sachs-gary-cohn-285-million-departurepackage.html

5.  *Wall Street Journal*, "The Biggest U.S. Banks Made $2.5 Billion from Tax Law—in One Quarter," Michael Rapaport, April 17, 2018, https://www.wsj.com/articles/the-four-biggest-u-s-banks-made-2-3-billion-from-taxlawin-one-quarter-1523984836

6.  *Forbes*, "Lies, China and Putin: Solving the Mystery of Wilbur Ross' Missing Fortune," Dan Alexander, June 18, 2018, https://www.forbes.com/sites/danalexander/2018/06/18/lies-china-and-putin-solving-the-mystery-of-wilburross-missing-fortune-trump-commerce-secretary-cabinet-conflicts-of-interest/#68ee049b7e87

7.  *Vox*, "Scott Pruitt Is Leaving behind a Toxic Mess at the EPA," Umair Irfan, July 9, 2018, https://www.vox.com/2018/7/6/17539834/scott-pruitt-resigns-andrew-wheeler-epa-legacy

8.  *Washington Post*, "New York Congressman Facing Insider Trading Charges Suspends Relection Bid," Michael Scherer, August 11, 2018, https://www.washingtonpost.com/powerpost/new-york-congressman-facing-insidertrading-charges-suspends-bid/2018/08/11/92c818ba-9d72-11e8-b60b1c897f17e185_story.html?utm_term=.810c8775a29f

9.  Moyers, "The Powell Memo: A Call-to-Arms for Corporations," September 14, 2012, https://billmoyers.com/content/the-powell-memo-a-call-to-arms-for-corporations/.

10.  Centre for Responsive Politics, "US Chamber of Commerce," https://www.opensecrets.org/lobby/clientsum.php?id=D000019798

11.  Center for Responsive Politics, "Lobbying Database," https://www.opensecrets.org/lobby/index.php

12.  "Supreme Court nominations," https://www.senate.gov/pagelayout/reference/nominations/reverseNominations.shtml

13.  Brookings, "Vital States: Congress Has a Staffing Problem, Too," May 24, 2017, https://www.brookings.edu/blog/fixgov/2017/05/24/vital-stats-congress-has-a-staffing-problem-too/

14.  *New York Times*, "Mueller's Digging Exposes Culture of Foreign Lobbying and Its Big Paydays," Mark Mazzetti and Katie Benner, August 1, 2018, https://www.nytimes.com/2018/08/01/us/politics/fara-foreign-agentsmueller.html

15.  *Forbes*, "EPA Chief Scott Pruitt: Delete Decades of Science in the Name of 'Transparency'," Trevor Nance, April 24, 2018, https://www.forbes.com/sites/trevornace/2018/04/24/epa-chief-scott-pruitt-delete-decades-ofscience-in-the-name-of-transparency/

16.  *Politico*, "Gorsuch Speech at Trump Hotel Attracts Protests," Josh Gerstein,

September 28, 2017, https://www.politico.com/story/2017/09/28/neil-gorsuch-trump-hotel-speech-243251

17. *New York Times*, "Supreme Court Ruling Delivers a Sharp Blow to Labor Unions," Adam Liptak, June 27, 2017, https://www.nytimes.com/2018/06/27/us/politics/supreme-court-unions-organized-labor.htm.

## Print Citations

**CMS:** Warren, Elizabeth. "Remarks on the Corruption in Washington." Speech presented at the National Press Club, Washington, DC, August 21, 2018. In *The Reference Shelf: Representative American Speeches 2017-2018*, edited by Micah L. Issit, 138-148. Ipswich, MA: H.W. Wilson, 2018.

**MLA:** Warren, Elizabeth. "Remarks on the Corruption in Washington." National Press Club, 21 August 2018, Washington, DC. Presentation. *The Reference Shelf: Representative American Speeches 2017-2018,* edited by Micah L. Issit, H.W. Wilson, 2018, pp. 138-148.

**APA:** Warren, E. (2018, August 21). Remarks on the corruption in Washington. National Press Club, Washington, DC. In M.L. Issit (Ed.), *The reference shelf: Representative American speeches 2017-2018* (pp. 138-148). Ipswich, MA: H.W. Wilson. (Original work published 2018)

# Propaganda and the Political Manipulation of the Media

## By Jeff Flake

*Congressman Jeff Flake is a six-term United States senator representing the state of Arizona having served on the Judiciary Committee, the Energy and Natural Resources Committee, and the Foreign Relations Committee. In 2017, Flake drew international headlines when he announced his retirement from the Senate after the completion of his ongoing term and used his speech to question Donald Trump's fitness to serve as president of the United States. Flake's feud with Trump proceeded over the course of the ensuing year. In 2018, Flake called for an FBI investigation regarding sexual assault claims made against Supreme Court nominee Brett Kavanaugh, becoming one of the few congressional Republicans to voice concern about Kavanaugh's fitness for the office. In this speech from January of 2018, Flake speaks about Trump's criticisms and use of national media to mislead and manipulate the American public.*

Mr. President, near the beginning of the document that made us free, our Declaration of Independence, Thomas Jefferson wrote: "We hold these truths to be self-evident..." So, from our very beginnings, our freedom has been predicated on truth. The founders were visionary in this regard, understanding well that good faith and shared facts between the governed and the government would be the very basis of this ongoing idea of America.

As the distinguished former member of this body, Daniel Patrick Moynihan of New York, famously said: "Everyone is entitled to his own opinion, but not to his own facts." During the past year, I am alarmed to say that Senator Moynihan's proposition has likely been tested more severely than at any time in our history.

It is for that reason that I rise today, to talk about the truth, and its relationship to democracy. For without truth, and a principled fidelity to truth and to shared facts, Mr. President, our democracy will not last.

2017 was a year which saw the truth—objective, empirical, evidence-based truth—more battered and abused than any other in the history of our country, at the hands of the most powerful figure in our government. It was a year which saw the White House enshrine "alternative facts" into the American lexicon, as justification for what used to be known simply as good old-fashioned falsehoods. It was the year in which an unrelenting daily assault on the constitutionally-protected free press was launched by that same White House, an assault that is as unprecedented as it

---

Delivered on January 17, 2018, at the US Senate, Washington, DC.

is unwarranted. "The enemy of the people," was what the president of the United States called the free press in 2017.

Mr. President, it is a testament to the condition of our democracy that our own president uses words infamously spoken by Josef Stalin to describe his enemies. It bears noting that so fraught with malice was the phrase "enemy of the people," that even Nikita Khrushchev forbade its use, telling the Soviet Communist Party that the phrase had been introduced by Stalin for the purpose of "annihilating such individuals" who disagreed with the supreme leader.

This alone should be a source of great shame for us in this body, especially for those of us in the president's party. For they are shameful, repulsive statements. And, of course, the president has it precisely backward—despotism is the enemy of the people. The free press is the despot's enemy, which makes the free press the guardian of democracy. When a figure in power reflexively calls any press that doesn't suit him "fake news," it is that person who should be the figure of suspicion, not the press.

I dare say that anyone who has the privilege and awesome responsibility to serve in this chamber knows that these reflexive slurs of "fake news" are dubious, at best. Those of us who travel overseas, especially to war zones and other troubled areas around the globe, encounter members of U.S. based media who risk their lives, and sometimes lose their lives, reporting on the truth. To dismiss their work as fake news is an affront to their commitment and their sacrifice.

According to the International Federation of Journalists, 80 journalists were killed in 2017, and a new report from the Committee to Protect Journalists documents that the number of journalists imprisoned around the world has reached 262, which is a new record. This total includes 21 reporters who are being held on "false news" charges.

Mr. President, so powerful is the presidency that the damage done by the sustained attack on the truth will not be confined to the president's time in office. Here in America, we do not pay obeisance to the powerful—in fact, we question the powerful most ardently—to do so is our birthright and a requirement of our citizenship—and so, we know well that no matter how powerful, no president will ever have dominion over objective reality.

No politician will ever get to tell us what the truth is and is not. And anyone who presumes to try to attack or manipulate the truth to his own purposes should be made to realize the mistake and be held to account. That is our job here. And that is just as Madison, Hamilton, and Jay would have it.

Of course, a major difference between politicians and the free press is that the press usually corrects itself when it gets something wrong. Politicians don't.

No longer can we compound attacks on truth with our silent acquiescence. No longer can we turn a blind eye or a deaf ear to these assaults on our institutions. And Mr. President, an American president who cannot take criticism—who must constantly deflect and distort and distract—who must find someone else to blame—is charting a very dangerous path. And a Congress that fails to act as a check on the president adds to the danger.

Now, we are told via twitter that today the president intends to announce his choice for the "most corrupt and dishonest" media awards. It beggars the belief that an American president would engage in such a spectacle. But here we are.

And so, 2018 must be the year in which the truth takes a stand against power that would weaken it. In this effort, the choice is quite simple. And in this effort, the truth needs as many allies as possible. Together, my colleagues, we are powerful. Together, we have it within us to turn back these attacks, right these wrongs, repair this damage, restore reverence for our institutions, and prevent further moral vandalism.

Together, united in the purpose to do our jobs under the Constitution, without regard to party or party loyalty, let us resolve to be allies of the truth—and not partners in its destruction.

It is not my purpose here to inventory all of the official untruths of the past year. But a brief survey is in order. Some untruths are trivial—such as the bizarre contention regarding the crowd size at last year's inaugural.

But many untruths are not at all trivial—such as the seminal untruth of the president's political career—the oft-repeated conspiracy about the birthplace of President Obama. Also not trivial are the equally pernicious fantasies about rigged elections and massive voter fraud, which are as destructive as they are inaccurate—to the effort to undermine confidence in the federal courts, federal law enforcement, the intelligence community and the free press, to perhaps the most vexing untruth of all—the supposed "hoax" at the heart of special counsel Robert Mueller's Russia investigation.

To be very clear, to call the Russia matter a "hoax"—as the president has many times—is a falsehood. We know that the attacks orchestrated by the Russian government during the election were real and constitute a grave threat to both American sovereignty and to our national security. It is in the interest of every American to get to the bottom of this matter, wherever the investigation leads.

Ignoring or denying the truth about hostile Russian intentions toward the United States leaves us vulnerable to further attacks. We are told by our intelligence agencies that those attacks are ongoing, yet it has recently been reported that there has not been a single cabinet-level meeting regarding Russian interference and how to defend America against these attacks. Not one. What might seem like a casual and routine untruth—so casual and routine that it has by now become the white noise of Washington—is in fact a serious lapse in the defense of our country.

Mr. President, let us be clear. The impulses underlying the dissemination of such untruths are not benign. They have the effect of eroding trust in our vital institutions and conditioning the public to no longer trust them. The destructive effect of this kind of behavior on our democracy cannot be overstated.

Mr. President, every word that a president utters projects American values around the world. The values of free expression and a reverence for the free press have been our global hallmark, for it is our ability to freely air the truth that keeps our government honest and keeps a people free. Between the mighty and the modest, truth is the great leveler. And so, respect for freedom of the press has always been one of our most important exports.

But a recent report published in our free press should raise an alarm. Reading from the story:

"In February...Syrian President Bashar Assad brushed off an Amnesty International report that some 13,000 people had been killed at one of his military prisons by saying, "You can forge anything these days, we are living in a fake news era."

In the Philippines, President Rodrigo Duterte has complained of being "demonized" by "fake news." Last month, the report continues, with our President, quote "laughing by his side" Duterte called reporters "spies."

In July, Venezuelan President Nicolas Maduro complained to the Russian propaganda outlet, that the world media had "spread lots of false versions, lots of lies" about his country, adding, "This is what we call 'fake news' today, isn't it?"

There are more:

"A state official in Myanmar recently said, "There is no such thing as Rohingya. It is fake news," referring to the persecuted ethnic group.

Leaders in Singapore, a country known for restricting free speech, have promised "fake news" legislation in the new year."

And on and on. This feedback loop is disgraceful, Mr. President. Not only has the past year seen an American president borrow despotic language to refer to the free press, but it seems he has in turn inspired dictators and authoritarians with his own language. This is reprehensible.

We are not in a "fake news" era, as Bashar Assad says. We are, rather, in an era in which the authoritarian impulse is reasserting itself, to challenge free people and free societies, everywhere.

In our own country, from the trivial to the truly dangerous, it is the range and regularity of the untruths we see that should be cause for profound alarm, and spur to action. Add to that the by-now predictable habit of calling true things false, and false things true, and we have a recipe for disaster. As George Orwell warned, "The further a society drifts from the truth, the more it will hate those who speak it."

Any of us who have spent time in public life have endured news coverage we felt was jaded or unfair. But in our positions, to employ even idle threats to use laws or regulations to stifle criticism is corrosive to our democratic institutions. Simply put: it is the press's obligation to uncover the truth about power. It is the people's right to criticize their government. And it is our job to take it.

What is the goal of laying siege to the truth? President John F. Kennedy, in a stirring speech on the 20th anniversary of the Voice of America, was eloquent in answer to that question:

"We are not afraid to entrust the American people with unpleasant facts, foreign ideas, alien philosophies, and competitive values. For a nation that is afraid to let its people judge the truth and falsehood in an open market is a nation that is afraid of its people."

Mr. President, the question of why the truth is now under such assault may well be for historians to determine. But for those who cherish American constitutional democracy, what matters is the effect on America and her people and her standing in an increasingly unstable world—made all the more unstable by these very fabrications. What matters is the daily disassembling of our democratic institutions.

We are a mature democracy—it is well past time that we stop excusing or ignoring—or worse, endorsing—these attacks on the truth. For if we compromise the truth for the sake of our politics, we are lost.

I sincerely thank my colleagues for their indulgence today. I will close by borrowing the words of an early adherent to my faith that I find has special resonance at this moment. His name was John Jacques, and as a young missionary in England he contemplated the question: "What is truth?" His search was expressed in poetry and ultimately in a hymn that I grew up with, titled "Oh Say, What is Truth." It ends as follows:

"Then say, what is truth? 'Tis the last and the first,

For the limits of time it steps o'er.

Tho the heavens depart and the earth's fountains burst.

Truth, the sum of existence, will weather the worst,

Eternal… unchanged… evermore."

Thank you, Mr. President. I yield the floor.

## Print Citations

**CMS:** Flake, Jeff. "Propaganda and the Political Manipulation of the Media." Speech presented at the US Senate, Washington, DC, January 17, 2018. In *The Reference Shelf: Representative American Speeches 2017-2018*, edited by Micah L. Issit, 149-153. Ipswich, MA: H.W. Wilson, 2018.

**MLA:** Flake, Jeff. "Propaganda and the Political Manipulation of the Media." US Senate, 17 January 2018, Washington, DC. Presentation. *The Reference Shelf: Representative American Speeches 2017-2018*, edited by Micah L. Issit, H.W. Wilson, 2018, pp. 149-153.

**APA:** Flake, J. (2018, January 17). Propaganda and the political manipulation of the media. US Senate, Washington, DC. In M.L. Issit (Ed.), *The reference shelf: Representative American speeches 2017-2018* (pp. 149-153). Ipswich, MA: H.W. Wilson. (Original work published 2018)

# 4

# Outsiders and Activists

Photo by Robb Wilson, via Wikimedia

A survivor of the school shooting at Marjory Stoneman Douglas high school, activist Emma Gonzalez has had a powerful effect in the fight for tougher gun control laws, and in protesting the government's failure to address gun violence.

# We Call BS

## By Emma Gonzalez

*Emma Gonzalez is an American high school student who attended Marjory Stoneman Douglas high school and was in the school on February 14th when a mass shooting claimed the lives of seventeen students and staff members. In the wake of the shooting, Gonzalez and a collection of fellow classmates became nationally famous for their advocacy of gun control legislation and their criticism of the NRA and other gun rights groups. In this speech from February 2018, Gonzalez and a group of students and activists talk about governmental failures to address gun violence.*

We haven't already had a moment of silence in the House of Representatives, so I would like to have another one. Thank you.

Every single person up here today, all these people should be home grieving. But instead we are up here standing together because if all our government and President can do is send thoughts and prayers, then it's time for victims to be the change that we need to see. Since the time of the Founding Fathers and since they added the Second Amendment to the Constitution, our guns have developed at a rate that leaves me dizzy. The guns have changed but our laws have not.

We certainly do not understand why it should be harder to make plans with friends on weekends than to buy an automatic or semi-automatic weapon. In Florida, to buy a gun you do not need a permit, you do not need a gun license, and once you buy it you do not need to register it. You do not need a permit to carry a concealed rifle or shotgun. You can buy as many guns as you want at one time.

I read something very powerful to me today. It was from the point of view of a teacher. And I quote: When adults tell me I have the right to own a gun, all I can hear is my right to own a gun outweighs your student's right to live. All I hear is mine, mine, mine, mine.

Instead of worrying about our AP Gov chapter 16 test, we have to be studying our notes to make sure that our arguments based on politics and political history are watertight. The students at this school have been having debates on guns for what feels like our entire lives. AP Gov had about three debates this year. Some discussions on the subject even occurred during the shooting while students were hiding in the closets. The people involved right now, those who were there, those posting, those tweeting, those doing interviews and talking to people, are being listened to for what feels like the very first time on this topic that has come up over 1,000 times in the past four years alone.

---

Delivered on February 17, 2018, at a gun control rally, Broward County Federal Courthouse, Fort Lauderdale, FL.

I found out today there's a website shootingtracker.com. Nothing in the title suggests that it is exclusively tracking the USA's shootings and yet does it need to address that? Because Australia had one mass shooting in 1999 in Port Arthur (and after the) massacre introduced gun safety, and it hasn't had one since. Japan has never had a mass shooting. Canada has had three and the UK had one and they both introduced gun control and yet here we are, with websites dedicated to reporting these tragedies so that they can be formulated into statistics for your convenience.

I watched an interview this morning and noticed that one of the questions was, do you think your children will have to go through other school shooter drills? And our response is that our neighbors will not have to go through other school shooter drills. When we've had our say with the government—and maybe the adults have gotten used to saying "it is what it is," but if us students have learned anything, it's that if you don't study, you will fail. And in this case if you actively do nothing, people continually end up dead, so it's time to start doing something.

We are going to be the kids you read about in textbooks. Not because we're going to be another statistic about mass shooting in America, but because, just as David said, we are going to be the last mass shooting. Just like *Tinker v. Des Moines*, we are going to change the law. That's going to be Marjory Stoneman Douglas in that textbook and it's going to be due to the tireless effort of the school board, the faculty members, the family members and most of all the students. The students who are dead, the students still in the hospital, the student now suffering PTSD, the students who had panic attacks during the vigil because the helicopters would not leave us alone, hovering over the school for 24 hours a day.

There is one tweet I would like to call attention to. So many signs that the Florida shooter was mentally disturbed, even expelled for bad and erratic behavior. Neighbors and classmates knew he was a big problem. Must always report such instances to authorities again and again. We did, time and time again. Since he was in middle school, it was no surprise to anyone who knew him to hear that he was the shooter. Those talking about how we should have not ostracized him, you didn't know this kid. OK, we did. We know that they are claiming mental health issues, and I am not a psychologist, but we need to pay attention to the fact that this was not just a mental health issue. He would not have harmed that many students with a knife.

And how about we stop blaming the victims for something that was the student's fault, the fault of the people who let him buy the guns in the first place, those at the gun shows, the people who encouraged him to buy accessories for his guns to make them fully automatic, the people who didn't take them away from him when they knew he expressed homicidal tendencies, and I am not talking about the FBI. I'm talking about the people he lived with. I'm talking about the neighbors who saw him outside holding guns.

If the President wants to come up to me and tell me to my face that it was a terrible tragedy and how it should never have happened and maintain telling us how nothing is going to be done about it, I'm going to happily ask him how much money he received from the National Rifle Association.

You want to know something? It doesn't matter, because I already know. Thirty million dollars. And divided by the number of gunshot victims in the United States in the one and one-half months in 2018 alone, that comes out to being $5,800. Is that how much these people are worth to you, Trump? If you don't do anything to prevent this from continuing to occur, that number of gunshot victims will go up and the number that they are worth will go down. And we will be worthless to you.

To every politician who is taking donations from the NRA, shame on you.

(Crowd chants) Shame on you.

If your money was as threatened as us, would your first thought be, how is this going to reflect on my campaign? Which should I choose? Or would you choose us, and if you answered us, will you act like it for once? You know what would be a good way to act like it? I have an example of how to not act like it. In February of 2017, one year ago, President Trump repealed an Obama-era regulation that would have made it easier to block the sale of firearms to people with certain mental illnesses.

From the interactions that I had with the shooter before the shooting and from the information that I currently know about him, I don't really know if he was mentally ill. I wrote this before I heard what Delaney said. Delaney said he was diagnosed. I don't need a psychologist and I don't need to be a psychologist to know that repealing that regulation was a really dumb idea.

Republican Senator Chuck Grassley of Iowa was the sole sponsor on this bill that stops the FBI from performing background checks on people adjudicated to be mentally ill and now he's stating for the record, "Well, it's a shame the FBI isn't doing background checks on these mentally ill people." Well, duh. You took that opportunity away last year.

The people in the government who were voted into power are lying to us. And us kids seem to be the only ones who notice and our parents to call BS. Companies trying to make caricatures of the teenagers these days, saying that all we are self-involved and trend-obsessed and they hush us into submission when our message doesn't reach the ears of the nation, we are prepared to call BS. Politicians who sit in their gilded House and Senate seats funded by the NRA telling us nothing could have been done to prevent this, we call BS. They say tougher guns laws do not decrease gun violence. We call BS. They say a good guy with a gun stops a bad guy with a gun. We call BS. They say guns are just tools like knives and are as dangerous as cars. We call BS. They say no laws could have prevented the hundreds of senseless tragedies that have occurred. We call BS. That us kids don't know what we're talking about, that we're too young to understand how the government works. We call BS.

If you agree, register to vote. Contact your local congresspeople. Give them a piece of your mind.

(Crowd chants) Throw them out.

**Print Citations**

**CMS:** Gonzalez, Emma. "We Call BS." Speech presented at the gun control rally, Broward County Federal Courthouse, Fort Lauderdale, FL, February 17, 2018. In *The Reference Shelf: Representative American Speeches 2017-2018*, edited by Micah L. Issit, 157-160. Ipswich, MA: H.W. Wilson, 2018.

**MLA:** Gonzalez, Emma. "We Call BS." Gun control rally, Broward County Federal Courthouse, 17 February 2018, Fort Lauderdale, FL. Presentation. *The Reference Shelf: Representative American Speeches 2017-2018,* edited by Micah L. Issit, H.W. Wilson, 2018, pp. 157-160.

**APA:** Gonzalez, E. (2018, February 17). We call BS. Gun control rally, Broward County Federal Courthouse, Fort Lauderdale, FL. In M.L. Issit (Ed.), *The reference shelf: Representative American speeches 2017-2018* (pp. 157-160). Ipswich, MA: H.W. Wilson. (Original work published 2018)

# At the 2018 Women's March

## By Viola Davis

*Actor Viola Davis is an international celebrity known for her roles in films and television. Born in South Carolina and raised in Rhode Island, Davis attended the Juilliard School of Performing Arts before beginning to work as a professional actor. She is the only African-American actress to win Tony, Oscar, and Emmy Awards during the course of her career, after winning a Best Supporting Actress Oscar for her role in the 2017 adaptation of the play* Fences *alongside Denzel Washington. In this speech from 2018, Davis addresses the crowds gathered at the national Women's March, an activist movement started in 2017 in response to the election of Donald Trump that generated the largest single-day protest in American history. In her speech, Davis speaks about the history of racism and sexism and discusses the importance of the #MeToo movement in addressing sexism and injustice.*

In the word of my fellow American, Malcolm X: I'm gonna make it plain. In 1877, America, the greatest country on this planet, put in place laws called the Jim Crow laws. And the Jim Crow laws restricted the rights of quadroons, octoroons, blacks, Hispanics, Indians, Malays. Restricted medical, restricted relationships, restricted education, restricted life. It told us we were less than, and it came on the heels of the 13th Amendment. It came on the heels of 55 individuals, great Americans, writing the greatest document, called the Constitution of the United States, saying, "We the people."

Now, the reason why those destructive laws came into place I think can be greatly described by Martin Luther King [Jr.]. And what he said about time is, he said, I'm not ready to wait 100 to 200 years for things to change. That I think actually time is neutral. That it can either be used constructively or destructively. That human progress rarely rolls on inevitability. It is through human dedication and effort that we move forward. And that when we don't work, what happens is that time actually becomes an ally to the primitive forces of social stagnation, and the guardians of the status quo are in their oxygen tanks keeping the old order alive.

And so that time needs to be helped, by every single moment, doing right. The reason why Jim Crow laws were in place, that stifled my rights and your rights, is because we fell asleep. We fall asleep when we're moving ahead and we don't look to the left and right and see we're not including people in this move ahead. Because really, at the end of the day, we only move forward when it doesn't cost us anything.

---

Delivered on January 20, 2018, at the Women's March, Washington, DC.

But I'm here today saying that no one and nothing can be great unless it costs you something.

One out of every five women will be sexually assaulted and raped before she reaches the age of 18. One out of six boys. If you are a woman of color and you are raped before you reach the age of 18, then you are 66 percent more likely to be sexually assaulted again. Seventy percent of girls who are sex-trafficked are girls of color. They are coming out of the foster-care system, they are coming out of poverty. It is a billion-dollar industry. When they go into the sex-trafficking business—and they call it a business, trust me—more than likely, they are gang raped.

I am speaking today not just for the "Me Too's" because, I was a "Me Too," but when I raise my hand, I am aware of all the women who are still in silence. The women who are faceless. The women who don't have the money and don't have the constitution and who don't have the confidence and who don't have the images in our media that gives them a sense of self-worth enough to break their silence that's rooted in the shame of assault. That's rooted in the stigma of assault.

Written on the Statute of Liberty is: Come. Come you tireless, poor, yearning to breathe free. To breathe free. Every single day, your job as an American citizen is not just to fight for your rights. It's to fight for the right of every individual that is taking a breath, whose heart is pumping and breathing on this earth. And like the originators of the "Me Too's," the Fannie Lou Hamers, the Recy Taylors, who in 1944 was gang-raped by six white men and she spoke up. Rosa Parks fought for her rights. She was silenced. To the Tarana Burkes, to the originators, to the first women to speak up. It cost them something. Nothing and no one can be great without a cost.

Listen, I am always introduced as an award-winning actor. But my testimony is one of poverty. My testimony is one of being sexually assaulted and very much seeing a childhood that was robbed from me. And I know that every single day, when I think of that, I know that the trauma of those events are still with me today. And that's what drives me to the voting booth. That's what allows me to listen to the women who are still in silence. That's what allows me to even become a citizen on this planet, is the fact that we are here to connect. That we are as 324 million people living on this earth, to know that every day, we breathe and we live. That we got to bring up everyone with us.

I stand in solidarity of all women who raise their hands because I know that it was not easy. And my hope for the future—my hope, I do hope—is that we never go back. That it's not just about clapping your hands and screaming and shouting every time someone says something that sounds good. It's about keeping it rolling once you go home.

## Print Citations

**CMS:** Davis, Viola. "Speech at the 2018 Women's March." Speech presented at the Women's March, Washington, DC, January 20, 2018. In *The Reference Shelf: Representative American Speeches 2017-2018*, edited by Micah L. Issit, 161-163. Ipswich, MA: H.W. Wilson, 2018.

**MLA:** Davis, Viola. "Speech at the 2018 Women's March." Women's March, 20 January 2018, Washington, DC. Presentation. *The Reference Shelf: Representative American Speeches 2017-2018,* edited by Micah L. Issit, H.W. Wilson, 2018, pp. 161-163.

**APA:** Davis, V. (2018, January 20). Speech at the 2018 Women's March. Women's March, Washington, DC. In M.L. Issit (Ed.), *The reference shelf: Representative American speeches 2017-2018* (pp. 161-163). Ipswich, MA: H.W. Wilson. (Original work published 2018)

# Identity, Gender, and Politics

## By Oprah Winfrey

*Actress and entrepreneur Oprah Winfrey is one of the best-known media personalities in the world. After starting her career as a television host in Baltimore, Maryland, Winfrey appeared in several hit movies, receiving an Academy Award nomination for her role in* The Color Purple *in 1985. Returning to television, Winfrey launched the* Oprah Winfrey Show *in 1986 and, building on the success of the program, expanded her media company to include* O Magazine *and a media production company, Harpo Productions. Winfrey is the first African American woman to win the Cecil B. DeMille Award for lifetime achievement from the Golden Globes. Winfrey's acceptance speech made international news as she utilized the platform to address the #MeToo movement and the critical problem of sexual abuse in America. After the speech, fans speculated about a future presidential run for Winfrey, who denied the rumors that she was considering a campaign.*

In 1964, I was a little girl sitting on the linoleum floor of my mother's house in Milwaukee watching Anne Bancroft present the Oscar for best actor at the 36th Academy Awards. She opened the envelope and said five words that literally made history: "The winner is Sidney Poitier." Up to the stage came the most elegant man I ever remembered. His tie was white, his skin was black—and he was being celebrated. I'd never seen a black man being celebrated like that. I tried many, many times to explain what a moment like that means to a little girl, a kid watching from the cheap seats as my mom came through the door bone tired from cleaning other people's houses. But all I can do is quote and say that the explanation in Sidney's performance in *Lilies of the Field*: "Amen, amen, amen, amen."

In 1982, Sidney received the Cecil B. DeMille award right here at the Golden Globes and it is not lost on me that at this moment, there are some little girls watching as I become the first black woman to be given this same award. It is an honor—it is an honor and it is a privilege to share the evening with all of them and also with the incredible men and women who have inspired me, who challenged me, who sustained me and made my journey to this stage possible. Dennis Swanson who took a chance on me for *A.M. Chicago*. Saw me on the show and said to Steven Spielberg, she's Sophia in *The Color Purple*. Gayle who's been a friend and Stedman who's been my rock.

I want to thank the Hollywood Foreign Press Association. We know the press is under siege these days. We also know it's the insatiable dedication to uncovering the

Delivered on January 7, 2018, at the 75th Golden Globe Awards, Beverly Hills, CA.

absolute truth that keeps us from turning a blind eye to corruption and to injustice. To—to tyrants and victims, and secrets and lies. I want to say that I value the press more than ever before as we try to navigate these complicated times, which brings me to this: what I know for sure is that speaking your truth is the most powerful tool we all have. And I'm especially proud and inspired by all the women who have felt strong enough and empowered enough to speak up and share their personal stories. Each of us in this room are celebrated because of the stories that we tell, and this year we became the story.

But it's not just a story affecting the entertainment industry. It's one that transcends any culture, geography, race, religion, politics, or workplace. So I want tonight to express gratitude to all the women who have endured years of abuse and assault because they, like my mother, had children to feed and bills to pay and dreams to pursue. They're the women whose names we'll never know. They are domestic workers and farm workers. They are working in factories and they work in restaurants and they're in academia, engineering, medicine, and science. They're part of the world of tech and politics and business. They're our athletes in the Olympics and they're our soldiers in the military.

And there's someone else, Recy Taylor, a name I know and I think you should know, too. In 1944, Recy Taylor was a young wife and mother walking home from a church service she'd attended in Abbeville, Alabama, when she was abducted by six armed white men, raped, and left blindfolded by the side of the road coming home from church. They threatened to kill her if she ever told anyone, but her story was reported to the NAACP where a young worker by the name of Rosa Parks became the lead investigator on her case and together they sought justice. But justice wasn't an option in the era of Jim Crow. The men who tried to destroy her were never persecuted. Recy Taylor died ten days ago, just shy of her 98th birthday. She lived as we all have lived, too many years in a culture broken by brutally powerful men. For too long, women have not been heard or believed if they dare speak the truth to the power of those men. But their time is up. Their time is up.

Their time is up. And I just hope—I just hope that Recy Taylor died knowing that her truth, like the truth of so many other women who were tormented in those years, and even now tormented, goes marching on. It was somewhere in Rosa Parks' heart almost 11 years later, when she made the decision to stay seated on that bus in Montgomery, and it's here with every woman who chooses to say, "Me too." And every man—every man who chooses to listen.

In my career, what I've always tried my best to do, whether on television or through film, is to say something about how men and women really behave. To say how we experience shame, how we love and how we rage, how we fail, how we retreat, persevere, and how we overcome. I've interviewed and portrayed people who've withstood some of the ugliest things life can throw at you, but the one quality all of them seem to share is an ability to maintain hope for a brighter morning, even during our darkest nights. So I want all the girls watching here, now, to know that a new day is on the horizon. And when that new day finally dawns, it will be because of a lot of magnificent women, many of whom are right here in this room tonight, and some pretty phenomenal men, fighting hard to make sure that they become the leaders who take us to the time when nobody ever has to say "me too" again."

## Print Citations

**CMS:** Winfrey, Oprah. "Identity, Gender, and Politics." Speech presented at the 75th Golden Globe Awards, Beverly Hills, CA, January 7, 2018. In *The Reference Shelf: Representative American Speeches 2017-2018*, edited by Micah L. Issit, 164-166. Ipswich, MA: H.W. Wilson, 2018.

**MLA:** Winfrey, Oprah. "Identity, Gender, and Politics." 75th Golden Globe Awards, 7 January 2018, Beverly Hills, CA. Presentation. *The Reference Shelf: Representative American Speeches 2017-2018*, edited by Micah L. Issit, H.W. Wilson, 2018, pp. 164-166.

**APA:** Winfrey, O. (2018, January 7). Identity, gender, and politics. 75th Golden Globe Awards, Beverly Hills, CA. In M.L. Issit (Ed.), *The reference shelf: Representative American speeches 2017-2018* (pp. 164-166). Ipswich, MA: H.W. Wilson. (Original work published 2018)

# Separating Children from Their Parents

## By Leah Cayasso

*12-year-old Leah Cayasso, the daughter of an undocumented migrant, gave this speech at the Washington, DC, "Families Belong Together" protest event. Though young, Cayasso captivated the audience with her personal, heartfelt protests against the Trump administration's immigration policies, and her speech was later carried by the national press and shared through social media, reaching millions of viewers. The Families Belong Together movement is a grassroots social justice movement that held protests in Washington, DC, New York, and 700 associated protests worldwide. The gathering in Washington, DC, where Cayasso spoke, attracted a crowd of between 30,000 and 50,000.*

Dear community,

My name is Leah. I am 12 years old and I am from Miami, Florida.

I am the proud daughter of a domestic worker who loves me very much. My mom's job is very important, unlike other government stuff. She takes care of children as a nanny and makes sure they are healthy and safe. Our government instead harms children and deports parents every day.

I am here today because the government is separating and detaining refugee parents and children at the border who are looking for safety. Our government also continues to separate US citizen children like me from their parents every day. This is evil. It needs to stop.

It makes me sad to know that children can't be with their parents. I don't understand why they are being so mean to us children. Don't they know how much we love our families?

Don't they have a family, too? Why don't they care about us children?

Why do they hurt us like this? It is unfair that they got to spend time with their families today while there are children in detention centers and in cages all alone missing their parents who are thrown in jail.

I live with the constant fear of losing my mom to deportation. My mom is strong, beautiful and brave. She is also a person who taught me how to speak up when I see things that aren't fair.

ICE wants to take away my mom from me. I don't like to live with this fear. It's scary. I can't sleep, I can't study, I am stressed. I am afraid that they will take my mom away while she is at work, out driving or at home. I don't understand why this

Delivered on June 30, 2018, at the Families Belong Together event, Washington, DC.

administration won't support mothers who just want a better life for their children. This needs to change!

We cannot allow them to keep hurting families, communities and children. I know that together we can make things better for families and kids.

I want to be an example to other kids who are going through the same problems as me. I want to tell kids at the border and all over the country not to give up, and fight for their families. We are all human, and deserve to be loved and cared for. We are children!

Our government has to do the right thing and stop separating us from our parents and stop locking us up. I won't give up fighting for the right to stay with my mom. I am not asking for a favor. It is my right to stay as a child to live in peace with my mother and the rest of my family.

Leah finished with a message to her mother, delivered in Spanish: "Mom, I love you very much and I will always fight for you!"

## Print Citations

**CMS:** Cayasso, Leah. "Separating Children from Their Parents." Speech presented at the Families Belong Together event, Washington, DC, June 30, 2018. In *The Reference Shelf: Representative American Speeches 2017-2018*, edited by Micah L. Issit, 167-168. Ipswich, MA: H.W. Wilson, 2018.

**MLA:** Cayasso, Leah. "Separating Children from Their Parents." Families Belong Together event, 30 June 2018, Washington, DC. Presentation. *The Reference Shelf: Representative American Speeches 2017-2018,* edited by Micah L. Issit, H.W. Wilson, 2018, pp. 167-168.

**APA:** Cayasso, L. (2018, June 30). Separating children from their parents. Families Belong Together event, Washington, DC. In M.L. Issit (Ed.), *The reference shelf: Representative American speeches 2017-2018* (pp. 167-168). Ipswich, MA: H.W. Wilson. (Original work published 2018)

# Comments on the NFL Anthem Protests

## By Beto O'Rourke

*Beto O'Rourke is a US Representative for Texas's 16th district and a nominee for the US Senate in 2018, running against incumbent Republican Ted Cruz. O'Rourke is a Texas native and attended Columbia University. O'Rourke was first elected to public office as a member of the El Paso City Council, where he served from 2005 until 2011. O'Rourke, a moderate Democrat, ran a heavily grass-roots campaign and did not accept PAC contributions. He became known for his alternative campaigning approaches, such as meeting supporters for running sessions with speeches delivered at stops along the course. O'Rourke and Cruz disagree on a number of issues, including marijuana legalization, immigration, healthcare reform, and the anthem protests. At a campaign event in August of 2018, O'Rourke responded to an audience question about the NFL Anthem protests with a short answer that went viral and a video of the event was shared over social media.*

AUDIENCE MEMBER: I kind of wanted to know how you personally felt about how disrespectful it is, like you have the NFL players kneeling during the national anthems. I wanted to know if you found that disrespectful to our country, to our veterans, and anybody related to that? I find it incredibly frustrating that people seem to be ok with that. And I would just like to hear your input.

BETO O'ROURKE: Thank you. Thanks for a great question, again, on a really tough issue that if we don't talk about, is not going to get batter. And the question is how do you feel about NFL players who take a knee during the national anthem? And is it disrespectful to this country, to the flag, to service members who are right there tonight, where it is tonight in Afghanistan, and those former service members, retirees, and veterans who are here with us today? Thank you each for your service.

My short answer is no, I don't think it's disrespectful. Here's my longer answer, but I'm gonna try to make sure that I get this right, because I think it's a really important question. And reasonable people can disagree on this issue, let's begin there, and it makes them no less American to come down on a different conclusion on this issue, right? You can feel as the young man does, you can feel as I do, you're every bit as American, all the same.

But I'm reminded—somebody mentioned reading the Taylor Branch book. You did. *Parting the Waters in the King Years,* and when you read that book and found out what Dr. King and this non-violent, peaceful movement to get better—cause they didn't get full civil rights for their fellow Americans—the challenges that they

---

Delivered on August 16, 2018, at a town hall meeting, Quail Point Lodge, Horseshoe Bay, TX.

face—those who died in Philadelphia, Mississippi for the crime of trying to be a man, trying to be a woman, in this country. The young girls who died in the church bombing, those who were beaten within an inch of their life crossing the Edmund Pettus bridge in Selma, Alabama, with John Lewis, those who were punched in the face, spat upon, dragged out by their collar at the Woolworth lunch counter, for sitting with white people at that same lunch counter, in the same country where their fathers may have bled the same blood on the battlefields of Omaha Beach, or Okinawa, or anywhere that anyone ever served in this country.

The freedoms that we have were purchased not just by those in uniform, and they definitely were. But also by those who took their lives in their hands riding those Greyhound Busses, the Freedom Riders in the deep south in the 1960s who knew full well that they would be arrested, and they were, serving time in the Mississippi State Penitentiary. Rosa Parks getting from the back of the bus to the front of the bus. Peaceful, non-violent protests, including taking a knee at a football game to point out that black men, unarmed, Black teenagers, unarmed, are being killed at a frightening level right now, including by members of law enforcement without accountability and without justice.

And this problem—as grave as it is—is not gonna fix itself and they're frustrated, frankly, and those in position of public trust and power who have been unable to resolve this, or bring justice for what has been done, and stop it from continuing to happen in this country.

And so non-violently, peacefully, while the eyes of this country are watching these games, they take a knee to bring our attention and our focus to this problem to ensure that we fix it. That is why they're doing it and I can think of nothing more American than to peacefully stand up, or take a knee, for your rights anytime, anywhere, any place. So, thank you very much for asking the question.

## Print Citations

**CMS:** O'Rourke, Beto. "Comments on the NFL Anthem Protests." Speech presented at a town hall meeting, Quail Point Lodge, Horseshoe Bay, TX, August 22, 2018. In *The Reference Shelf: Representative American Speeches 2017-2018*, edited by Micah L. Issit, 169-170. Ipswich, MA: H.W. Wilson, 2018.

**MLA:** O'Rourke, Beto. "Comments on the NFL Anthem Protests." Town hall meeting, Quail Point Lodge, 22 August 2018, Horseshoe Bay, TX. Presentation. *The Reference Shelf: Representative American Speeches 2017-2018,* edited by Micah L. Issit, H.W. Wilson, 2018, pp. 169-170.

**APA:** O'Rourke, B. (2018, August 16). Comments on the NFL anthem protests. Town hall meeting, Quail Point Lodge, Horseshoe Bay, TX. In M.L. Issit (Ed.), *The reference shelf: Representative American speeches 2017-2018* (pp. 169-170). Ipswich, MA: H.W. Wilson. (Original work published 2018)

# Ambassador of Conscience Speech

## By Colin Kaepernick

*Colin Kaepernick is a former professional football player and quarterback for the San Francisco 49ers from 2011 to 2016. In 2016, Kaepernick became a national figure when he took a knee during the performance of the US national anthem in order to protest racial and police violence against black men. Kaepernick's protest inspired a number of other players to engage in similar protests during the national anthem performance, some kneeling like Kaepernick, others standing with their fists raised. Donald Trump became a famous critic of Kaepernick and the anthem protests, insinuating that protestors lacked patriotism. In 2018, Kaepernick was selected by the nonprofit humanitarian organization Amnesty International to receive the year's Ambassador of Conscience award. In his acceptance speech, Kaepernick speaks about violence against African Americans and the anthem protests.*

It is only fitting that I have the honor of Eric Reid introducing me for this award. In many ways, my recognition would not be possible without our brotherhood. I truly consider him to be more than a friend—Eric, his wife, his children…they are all a part of my family.

Not only did he kneel by my side during the national anthem throughout the entire 2016 NFL season, but Eric continued to use his platform as a professional football player to protest systemic oppression, specifically police brutality against Black and brown people.

Eric introducing me for this prestigious award brings me great joy.

But I am also pained by the fact that his taking a knee, and demonstrating courage to protect the rights of Black and brown people in America, has also led to his ostracization from the NFL when he is widely recognized as one of the best competitors in the game and in the prime of his career.

People sometimes forget that love is at the root of our resistance.

My love for Eric has continually grown over the course of our ongoing journey. His brotherhood, resilience, and faith have shined brightly in moments of darkness. My love for my people serves as the fuel that fortifies my mission. And it is the people's unbroken love for themselves that motivates me, even when faced with the dehumanizing norms of a system that can lead to the loss of one's life over simply being Black.

History has proven that there has never been a period in the history of America where anti-Blackness has not been an ever-present terror. Racialized oppression and

Delivered on April 21, 2018, at Amnesty International, Amsterdam, Netherlands.

dehumanization is woven into the very fabric of our nation—the effects of which can be seen in the lawful lynching of Black and brown people by the police, and the mass incarceration of Black and brown lives in the prison industrial complex. While America bills itself as the land of the free, the receipts show that the U.S. has incarcerated approximately 2.2 million people, the largest prison population in the history of humankind.

As police officers continue to terrorize Black and brown communities, abusing their power, and then hiding behind their blue wall of silence, and laws that allow for them to kill us with virtual impunity, I have realized that our love, that sometimes manifests as Black-rage, is a beautiful form of defiance against a system that seeks to suppress our humanity—A system that wants us to hate ourselves.

I remind you that love is at the root of our resistance.

It is our love for 12-year-old Tamir Rice, who was gunned down by the police in less than two seconds that will not allow us to bury our anger. It is our love for Philando Castille, who was executed in front of his partner and his daughter, that keeps the people fighting back. It is our love for Stephon Clark, who was lynched in his grandma's backyard that will not allow us to stop until we achieve liberation for our people.

Our love is not an individualized love—it is a collective love. A collective love that is constantly combating collective forms of racialized hate. Chattel slavery, Jim Crow, New Jim Crow, massive plantations, mass incarcerations, slave patrols, police patrols, we as a collective, since the colonization of the Americas have been combating collective forms of systemic racialized hate and oppression.

But I am hopeful. I am inspired.

This is why we have to protest. This is why we are so passionate. We protest because we love ourselves, and our people.

It was James Baldwin who said, to be Black in America, "and to be relatively conscious is to be in a rage almost all the time." My question is, why aren't all people? How can you stand for the national anthem of a nation that preaches and propagates, "freedom and justice for all," that is so unjust to so many of the people living there? How can you not be in rage when you know that you are always at risk of death in the streets or enslavement in the prison system? How can you willingly be blind to the truth of systemic racialized injustice? When Malcolm X said, "I'm for truth, no matter who tells it. I'm for justice, no matter who it is for or against. I'm a human being, first and foremost, and as such I'm for whoever and whatever benefits humanity as a whole." I took that to heart.

While taking a knee is a physical display that challenges the merits of who is excluded from the notion of freedom, liberty, and justice for all, the protest is also rooted in a convergence of my moralistic beliefs, and my love for the people.

Seeking the truth, finding the truth, telling the truth and living the truth has been, and always will be what guides my actions. For as long as I have a beating heart, I will continue on this path, working on behalf of the people.

Again...Love is at the root of our resistance.

Last but certainly not least; I would like to thank Amnesty International for The Ambassador of Conscience Award. But in truth, this is an award that I share with all of the countless people throughout the world combating the human rights violations of police officers, and their uses of oppressive and excessive force. To again quote Malcolm X, when he said that he, "will join in with anyone—I don't care what color you are—as long as you want to change this miserable condition that exists on this earth," I am here to join with you all in this battle against police violence.

## Print Citations

**CMS:** Kaepernick, Colin. "Ambassador of Conscience Speech." Speech presented at Amnesty International, Amsterdam, Netherlands, April 21, 2018. In *The Reference Shelf: Representative American Speeches 2017-2018*, edited by Micah L. Issit, 171-173. Ipswich, MA: H.W. Wilson, 2018.

**MLA:** Kaepernick, Colin. "Ambassador of Conscience Speech." Amnesty International, 21 April 2018, Amsterdam, Netherlands. Presentation. *The Reference Shelf: Representative American Speeches 2017-2018,* edited by Micah L. Issit, H.W. Wilson, 2018, pp. 171-173.

**APA:** Kaepernick, C. (2018, April 21). Ambassador of conscience speech. Amnestry International, Amsterdam, Netherlands. In M.L. Issit (Ed.), *The reference shelf: Representative American speeches 2017-2018* (pp. 171-173). Ipswich, MA: H.W. Wilson. (Original work published 2018)

# Standing Up and Speaking Out

## By Ximena Cid

*Ximena Cid is a professor of physics at Cal State Dominguez Hills University and a member of the Yaqui people, a native Mexican ethnolinguistic group from the Rio Yaqui region in the state of Sonora. Cid was one of numerous speakers who appeared at the 2018 March for Science celebration in Los Angeles, and spoke about the involvement of minorities in science and the importance of diversity in helping to provide different perspectives and ideas.*

Good afternoon everyone. Before I talk to you about my journey through physics and issues surround diversity and equity I want to acknowledge the Tongva peoples and the traditional lands we are standing on.

My name is Ximena Cid. I'm a Chicana Yaqui Physics Professor at Cal State Dominguez Hills.

I was that annoying kid that was always asking why and never satisfied with the answers. Parents and caregivers in the audience, y'all know who I'm talking about. That was me. Truth be told I'm still not always satisfied with simple answers so I continue to ask why. And that's what it means to be a scientist. To be someone who continues to seek answers supported by data.

I started my academic journey in astrophysics at UC Berkeley. To this day I never have more wonder and excitement than when I'm look up at a clear dark sky filled with stars (its kind of hard here in LA). While I was at Cal, I was the only woman and the only person of color in some of my classes. Though I loved my time at Cal, it was there that I first realized the additional challenges women and people of color endure in this field.

Not only is the physics population very white and very male, it is also primarily cis, able bodied, academically well prepared, and affluent. Currently in the US women earn about 60% of all bachelors' degrees and yet the number of women earning physics bachelors' degrees has remained constant at about 20% for the past 20 years. If we look at people of color, of any gender, earning physics degrees, that number is about 18%.

If we look at graduate degrees and higher the numbers are even smaller. The year I got my PhD, it was a pretty big year for indigenous physics PhDs. There were two of us. In the entire country. Two!

In grad school, I had some of the best and some of the worst times of my life.

Delivered on April 14, 2018, at the March for Science, Los Angeles, CA.

The sexual harassment and discrimination from some of my professors and some of my peers nearly broke me.

I would go through these cycles of defiance where I was demanding to have my presence acknowledge to just wanting to blend in. I changed the way I dressed to be either more feminine or less feminine. I could never figure out what was more threatening: being viewed as a woman, or being seen as one of the guys. Change that to woman of color and it becomes even more complex. This invisible/hypervisible yo-yo is exhausting and continues to be exhausting and I've asked myself many times: do I belong here?

There is a problem in this country. The memories of communities of color are filled with genocide. Slavery. Internment. Poverty. Violence. And our histories are systematically erased from textbooks and formal education. Our communities need to remember that our ancestors were Mathematicians and Engineers and Architects and Scientists. This knowledge runs in our blood and is part of our DNA. By deleting our history, not only do WE forget that these spaces are not new to us but the dominant populations can maintain that our presence and our voices are not valuable.

December 2015 after hearing opening remarks for the case *Fisher vs. University of Texas*, Supreme Court Justice Scalia, asked and I quote: "What unique perspective does a minority student bring to a physics class?" He further commented: that it does not benefit African-Americans to attend top tier schools. Rather they should attend less-advanced schools where they would do better. This is coming from the highest court in our country. So not only do law enforcement officers continue to kill unarmed black men for doing things like wearing hoodies or holding cellphones while sitting in their grandmother's backyard, but the highest court in our country, the court that decides on educational policies and equity, specifically are questioning whether or not people of color are valuable in spaces like physics.

Physicists study the interactions between energy and matter. If we can value antimatter and dark matter, surely we can recognize that black lives also matter.

These are the challenges we are facing. We need change.

So what can YOU do?

Students and science enthusiasts in the crowd: Your presence in physics and other STEM fields is extremely valuable. Researchers like Scott Page and others found that not only do diverse groups come up with more unique solutions for complex STEM problems, but they are more efficient. This means that diversity and diverse perspectives are a benefit to STEM. Take action to support yourselves and your peers.

Students, you have power because you are tuition paying bodies. As a collective, you have the power to demand that your administration hire diverse faculty that better reflect each of you. I know that it can be hard to advocate for yourself and find balance in hostile environments.

One way I have found support is connecting with like-minded friends and colleagues. Get involved with local and national organizations and societies. I am a life member with the Society for the Advancement of Chicanos and Native Americans in Science or SACNAS for short. And I am here today because of SACNAS. At a time when I felt completely isolated and alone SACNAS provided a space to create a connection between my Chicana Indigena identity and my physics identity.

Find mentors that will continue to support you on this academic journey and find many of them. Find a mentor that you feel comfortable with to get life advice, to get help organizing your educational and career goals, to vent to when you need release but also find a mentor that will keep it real and pull you back in when you are spiraling out.

Recognize that someone who looks like you might not be on your side and someone who is the complete opposite of you, might be your biggest advocate. So be open!

Then give back. Take leadership roles so you can provide opportunities for those following behind you. Physics is an intellectually challenging topic that few can master, yet our modern civilization depends on technology made possible by the discoveries of physicists. Leaders in our country recognize that there is a national need to nurture talent and produce more STEM professionals that are trained AND retained in this country.

That is why, as a board member with the National Society of Hispanic Physicists, I along with the rest of the board, have advocated and petitioned congress to support DACA recipients and DREAMERs.

Professionals in the crowd, push for your departments and colleagues to get training on implicit bias and other forms of micro and macro aggressions. Even if you see yourself as an advocate and ally, the more training you have, the more you can recognize and step in to stop damaging behavior. Do self-evaluations for hiring and admission practices that might negatively impact diverse communities.

And lastly, vote! Vote for representatives that believe in the reality of climate change, that are dedicated to equitable policies, that believe that immigrants and DACA recipients are vital for the growth of this country. And Vote for representatives that believe that quality public education is a right not privilege.

In the words of Nelson Mandela: Education is the most powerful weapon which you can use to change the world. My name is Ximena Cid. I am uniquely me but I'm not a unicorn. There are more of us out there that just need oportunity. Find us. Support us.

Si se puede!

### Print Citations

**CMS:** Cid, Ximena. "Standing Up and Speaking Out." Speech presented at the 2018 March for Science, Los Angeles, CA, April 14, 2018. In *The Reference Shelf: Representative American Speeches 2017-2018*, edited by Micah L. Issit, 174-177. Ipswich, MA: H.W. Wilson, 2018.

**MLA:** Cid, Ximena. "Standing Up and Speaking Out." 2018 March for Science, 14 April 2018, Los Angeles, CA. Presentation. *The Reference Shelf: Representative American Speeches 2017-2018,* edited by Micah L. Issit, H.W. Wilson, 2018, pp. 174-177.

**APA:** Cid, X. (2018, April 14). Standing up and speaking out. 2018 March for Science, Los Angeles, CA. In M.L. Issit (Ed.), *The reference shelf: Representative American speeches 2017-2018* (pp. 174-177). Ipswich, MA: H.W. Wilson. (Original work published 2018)

# Index